Hermeneutics as a
Theory of Understanding

Hermeneutics as a Theory of Understanding

Petr Pokorný

Translated from Czech by
Anna Bryson-Gustová

WILLIAM B. EERDMANS PUBLISHING COMPANY
GRAND RAPIDS, MICHIGAN / CAMBRIDGE, U.K.

This is a translation from the first part of the Czech original edition, "Hermeneutika jako teorie porozumění," by Petr Pokorný. (Twelve other scholars participated in the second and third parts of this publication, dealing with specific problems and demonstrating exegesis on individual samples.) Published in Prague by Vyšehrad Publishing House in 2005. The publication was the output document of the Czech research project MSM 112 700 001.

This English edition © 2011 William B. Eerdmans Publishing Company
All rights reserved

Published 2011 by
Wm. B. Eerdmans Publishing Co.
2140 Oak Industrial Drive N.E., Grand Rapids, Michigan 49505 /
P.O. Box 163, Cambridge CB3 9PU U.K.
www.eerdmans.com

Library of Congress Cataloging-in-Publication Data

Pokorný, Petr, 1933-
    Hermeneutics as a theory of understanding / Petr Pokorný; translated from Czech by Anna Bryson-Gustová.
    p.   cm.
    "This is a translation from the first part of the Czech original edition, 'Hermeneutika jako teorie porozumení,' by Petr Pokorný. Twelve other scholars participated in the second and third parts of this publication . . . published in Prague by Vyšehrad Publishing House in 2005."
    Includes bibliographical references and indexes.
    ISBN 978-0-8028-2721-0 (pbk.: alk. paper)
    1. Bible — Hermeneutics.   2. Hermeneutics — Religious aspects — Christianity.
    I. Hermeneutika jako teorie porozumění.   II. Title.

BS476.P6513   2011
220.601 — dc22

2011008123

Bible quotations in English: New Revised Standard Version — copyright © 1989. Abbreviations, when used, are according to S. M. Schwertner, *International Glossary of Abbreviations for Theology and Related Subjects*, Berlin–New York: de Gruyter, 1992 (2nd print.).

*Dedicated to James H. Charlesworth,
my colleague in research and longtime friend*

Contents

Foreword: Hermeneutics: Hearing God's Word Today,
by James Hamilton Charlesworth   xi

Preface   xv

1. **What Is Hermeneutics?**   1

    (Excursus on Theology and Philosophy)   3

2. **The World of Language**   7

    2.1. Language as an Encoding System   9

         2.1.1. Vocabulary   10

         (Excursus on Semiology)   11

         (Excursus on Experience)   12

         (Excursus on Phenomenology and Hermeneutics)   15

         2.1.2. Grammar (Syntax)   17

         (Excursus: Augustine's Reflections on Memory)   25

    2.2. The Question of the World of Language
    (or, From Syntax to Pragmatics)   28

         2.2.1. From Speech to Language, from Narration
    to Structure   28

         (Excursus: Structures and the Human World)   31

         2.2.2. Pragmatics   33

Contents

- 2.3. Hermeneutics, Transformational Grammar, and the "Future" of the Text — 36
- 2.4. Symbol and Metaphor — 37
  - 2.4.1. The Cognitive Function of Metaphor — 42
  - 2.4.2. Metaphor and Myth — 54
  - 2.4.3. The Double Face of Metaphor — 61
  - *(Excursus: Inside Metaphor)* — 64

3. Text — 67

- 3.1. The Graphic Character of the Written Text — 67
- 3.2. The Silence of the Text — 68
- 3.3. The Possibility of Misusing the Text — 70
- 3.4. The Fixed Character of the Text — 71
- 3.5. The Reduction of Redundancy — 73
- 3.6. The Successive Surface of the Written Text — 74
- 3.7. The Text between Tradition and the Future — 80
  - 3.7.1. Tradition as Our Bedrock — 81
  - *(Excursus on Intertextuality)* — 83
  - 3.7.2. Historical Criticism (1) — 85
  - *(Excursus on the Relationship between Author and Text)* — 88
  - 3.7.3. The Reader and the Text — 88
  - *(Excursus on the Hermeneutic Circle)* — 90
  - 3.7.4. Tradition and New Experiences — 94
  - 3.7.5. Tradition and Story — 98
  - *(Excursus on the Hermeneutic Quadrilateral)* — 101
- 3.8. The Effect of the Text — 103
  - 3.8.1. Canonization and Biblical Theology — 104
  - 3.8.2. The Aesthetic Impact of the Text — 108
- 3.9. Genre — 116
  - 3.9.1. The Bible as Inspiration for Modern Literary Scholarship — 119
  - *(Excursus on the Style of Commentary)* — 121

4. Methods of Interpretation — 123

    4.1. The Historical Background of Exegetical Methods and Hermeneutic Theories — 124

    4.2. Philology — 132

        4.2.1. Translation — 133

    4.3. Synchronic Interpretation and Projects Based on It — 138

        4.3.1. Rhetorical Criticism — 141

        4.3.2. The Synchronic Dimension of the Text in Initial Exegetical Operations — 154

    4.4. Historical Methods — 157

        4.4.1. Reconstruction of the Text — 158

        4.4.2. Paraphrase, Remythologization, Pragmatics — 161

        4.4.3. Historical Criticism (2) — 167

        4.4.4. "Cross-Cutting" Methods — 171

5. Interpretation — 177

    5.1. The Otherness and Attraction of Ancient Texts — 177

    5.2. The Meeting of Worlds — 178

    5.3. Understanding the Text as Part of Self-Understanding — 185

    5.4. Historicity and Revelation — 188

    5.5. Revelation and Witness — 189

        5.5.1. Revelation — 189

        5.5.2. Witness — 194

Index of Names — 201

Index of Biblical and Other Ancient References — 205

Foreword
Hermeneutics: Hearing God's Word Today

Approximately 1,000 ancient biblical manuscripts have been recovered from numerous caves along the western shores of the Dead Sea, near the lowest part of our fragile globe. Tiny silver amulets containing the Priestly (or Aaronic) Blessing (Num 6:23-27 [Birkat Kohanim]) were found in the Hinnom Valley of Jerusalem; they date from about 600 B.C.E. Along with these amulets, the Dead Sea Scrolls preserve our most ancient manuscript sources for what Jews and Christians judge to be God's Word. Thus, while these scrolls are ancient, they are not antiquarian. Homer's *Odyssey* is full of interesting insights for a safe navigation through life, but those who wrote and compiled the books in our Bible claim to have the way to please the Creator, who is cosmic judge. What makes a book inspired and important for hermeneutical reflection?

What does that mean? It means that the ancient biblical documents written by hand over 2,000 years ago are full of information that is deemed by Jews and Christians to be fundamentally important for understanding God's message to us today and helping us answer, or approximate an answer, to all the eternally fundamental questions of human existence. That is, the biblical Scriptures provide insights for contemplating, and sometimes answering, these deeply spiritual issues:

> Who am I, and how should I think and act?
> Who is God, and what is God's will?
> What is meant by "salvation" and "justification"?
> What does it mean to "hear" God's call?
> Why am I valuable, and how do I obtain this evaluation?
> How do I perceive God's mighty acts in history and the present?

Foreword

> What should one faithful to God do in the present?
> What is the meaning of time and eternity?
> How should I love God and other humans?
> What should be believed about a life after my own death?
> In life and death, how can I be faithful to the Creator?

Jews and Christians concur that these questions constitute the most important ones we confront in our brief life.

How do we move from these eternal questions to valid answers that are efficacious to us today? That is the task of hermeneutics.

I fully agree with Petr Pokorný's reflections on human experience. Since the Enlightenment, philosophers and theologians have disparaged and misunderstood the dimension of human existence we label "experience." Without experiencing the power of faith, one will never move from believing in the power of Moses' life or Jesus' message to inculcating it and making it personal. The psalmists knew the paradigmatic importance of experience. They could cry out, for example: "My God, my God, why have You abandoned me?" The poet who composed Psalm 22 was experiencing abandonment. Finally, the selfsame poet exclaims: "Because of You I offer praise in the great congregation." Why has the author changed his exclamations? It is because of experiencing God's presence: "He listened."

What is "hermeneutics," and what are the best methods for discerning the eternal in the ephemeral or God's Word in scriptural words? To supply answers, Pokorný has crafted this wonderful and deeply inspiring book. *Inter alia*, he illustrates that hermeneutics cannot be reduced to any single comprehensive methodology, since interpretation demands a combination of numerous methods. He also invites us to contemplate that Luther's *scriptura sui ipsius interpres* means that the Bible, because it is Scripture, should be allowed the power to interpret the interpreter's life.

Why should I read the methods discussed by Petr Pokorný? What credentials does he have that attract us to his reflections? Many answers appear as I reflect on the decades I have known him, both here in the United States and abroad in over a dozen countries, and especially in Israel and in the Czech Republic.

First, he is a dedicated and brilliant scholar; he is fluent in Hebrew, Greek, Coptic, and Latin and has mastered English, German, and Czech (his native speech). He refused to be manipulated by the Russian Communists, who too frequently controlled his destiny and that of his family. He also did not sell out to the established church. Like the reformer and martyr Jan Hus

Hermeneutics: Hearing God's Word Today

(c. 1370-1415), Pokorný has sought to be equally true to God's call and to honest inquiry. His mind is scintillating; for example, he points out that grammar is concerned with "transforming phenomena into a structure that is tailored to fit human needs (p. 20)." He astutely indicates how a text (from Latin *textum*, which means a "web" or "fabric") transcends times and places and can be interpreted in other times and locales while live speech continues only in fleeting memories (p. 73).

Pokorný has chosen a title from his life's voyages: *Hermeneutics as a Theory of Understanding*. I like the title; hermeneutics is a series of means, not one isolated end. As the Greek verb *hermēneuō* denotes "to imitate Hermes," so Hermes is the messenger who brought messages to humans from the gods. Jews and Christians believe in a Creator God; he spoke and continues to speak. Hermeneutics is the science of how to hear — and thus to obey — God's words and will; recall Deut 6:4: שְׁמַע יִשְׂרָאֵל יְהוָה אֱלֹהֵינוּ יְהוָה אֶחָד.

Second, Pokorný knows hermeneutics, as all attempts to understand, begins with words and language. Thus, he blends together disciplines — philosophy, philology, phenomenology, and theology — that tend to shed each other like oil and water. As is clear in the preparation of the *Oxford English Dictionary*, which took 70 years to complete, and pellucidly presented in Simon Winchester's *The Professor and the Madman*, and as M. Merleau-Ponty demonstrated in *Phenomenology of Perception*, words are our means of knowing our world and ourselves within it. Words and language should be comprehended before we seek to understand a text and then its interpretation. Texts, like words, often do not display; they point toward something. Thus, the words of the inspired prophets point us toward another world and the only One who should be acknowledged as King, Lord, and God.

Third, Pokorný focuses on the world of symbols and metaphors. No human culture was as advanced symbolically as the world that produced our Scriptures. Thus, in our search for the origin and meaning of the symbols and metaphors that define our culture, we must seek to indwell the world that produced them. As Michelangelo's painting of the mutilated Jew, preserved in the Hermitage, has little meaning until we perceive that the man is the crucified Jesus, whom the artist hailed as Savior and Lord, so words obtain their original power when we more adequately perceive the symbolic world that nurtured them.

Fourth, ancient texts are aesthetically pleasing because of the rhetoric they embody and the "otherness" in them. Too often hermeneutical moves drain the text and its sphere of meaning of mystery and wonder. The Scriptures were created by this Awe and are sustained by it. Thus, Pokorný shows

Foreword

how two worlds, our own and the authors' world, merge in ways that transcend finite methodologies.

Fifth, Pokorný helps us find paths that reveal how in understanding ancient Scriptures we begin to understand ourselves. The hermeneutic circle allows us to gain a deeper knowledge of ourselves as we progressively proceed deeper into the text by reexamining it (p. 91). In meeting the words (and to a certain extent the world) of Isaiah, Jeremiah, Jesus, and Paul, we often come face to face with ourselves.

If the Lord is our mirror, as the author of the 13th *Ode of Solomon* claimed, then we see ourselves in Him. Following inspirations from Matthias Flacius Illyricus, Friedrich Schleiermacher, Ferdinand de Saussure, and Paul Ricoeur, Pokorný wisely points out that hermeneutics, a theory of understanding, is not only a science but fundamentally an art, "in which inspiration, empathy, and personal decision (the intuitive side) form a bridge between knowledge of the general and encounter with the unique" (pp. 2-3). As archaeological reconstructions of the past demand virtually all scientific disciplines and rely ultimately on the genius of the interpreter who knows how to imagine the past, so hermeneutics, the art of interpreting Scripture, demands not only wisdom but also personal commitment and belief. Thus, Michael Polanyi rightly indicated all knowledge is personal knowledge; yet within a community of faith we can transcend the Narcissus of a mirror that reflected only one aging face, one time, and one world.

As Pokorný urges, as devout and faithful creatures we should seek "to return to the roots of the experience from which" Scriptures and dogmas "have sprung." Hermeneutics thus helps us to understand texts and traditions and the origins of our beliefs. Thus, we may obtain a better understanding of our own context and self-understanding. For the *homo religiosus,* that experience (which has hermeneutical value) includes spirituality. Hermeneutics helps us comprehend and communicate the Word again on target as it was in antiquity and moved from Jerusalem to Malta and from highlands to islands.

JAMES HAMILTON CHARLESWORTH
Princeton
Easter 2011

Preface

This is a textbook and at the same time a monograph that seeks to suggest new paths in hermeneutical discussion. It deals with most of the problems of hermeneutics, their role in society, and their impact in history, as well as with various methods used in communication and especially in exegesis. Its main aim is not, however, to introduce new methodologies or to investigate the character of human understanding by new, deep probes into material or literary documents. The principal intention is to define the philosophical and theological premises of individual projects of understanding — their interrelation, meaning, and function in interpretation, especially interpretation of an ancient text such as the Bible.

In my critical endeavors I have been greatly influenced by the work of Paul Ricoeur and his way of reflecting on the problems of literature. Indeed, I discussed this project with him during his visits in Prague. I would nonetheless discourage anyone from using this text as an introduction to his theory of literature. He has inspired me, but my reflections relate to a different area of research and go their own way.[1]

I have received valuable inspiration and criticism from many colleagues. I would like to thank them all, and especially Jiří Pechar and Jakub Čapek.

---

1. Ricoeur's contribution to hermeneutics is presented by David Klemm in his monograph *The Hermeneutical Theory of Paul Ricoeur* (Lewisburg, Pa.: Bucknell University Press, 1983) and by L. S. Mudge in his introduction to Ricoeur's studies from his Chicago period, "Paul Ricoeur on Biblical Interpretation," introduction to *Essays on Biblical Interpretation*, by P. Ricoeur (London: SPCK, 1981), 3-45 (including reaction by Ricoeur).

1. What Is Hermeneutics?

BIBLIOGRAPHY

Frye, Northrop. *The Great Code: The Bible and Literature*. New York: Harcourt Brace Jovanovich, 1982.

Grondin, Jean. *Einführung in die philosophische Hermeneutik*. Darmstadt: Wissenschaftliche Buchgesellschaft, 1991.

Jasper, David. *A Short Introduction to Hermeneutics*. Louisville, Ky.: Westminster John Knox Press, 2004.

Jeanrond, Werner G. *Text und Interpretation als Kategorien theologischen Denkens*. Tübingen: Mohr, 1986.

Jensen, Alexander S.. *Theological Hermeneutics*. London: SCM Press, 2007.

Lessing, Hans-Ulrich, ed. *Philosophische Hermeneutik*. Freiburg: Alber, 1999.

Morgan, Robert, with John Barton. *Biblical Interpretation*. Oxford: Oxford University Press, 1988.

Oeming, Manfred. *Biblische Hermeneutik*. Darmstadt: Wissenschaftliche Buchgesellschaft, 1998. ET *Contemporary Biblical Hermeneutics* (Hampshire, Eng.: Ashgate, 2006).

Palmer, Richard E. *Hermeneutics: Interpretation Theory in Schleiermacher, Dilthey, Heidegger, and Gadamer*. Evanston, Ill.: Northwestern University Press, 1969.

Pokorný, Petr, and Jan Roskovec, eds. *Philosophical Hermeneutics and Biblical Exegesis*. Tübingen: Mohr Siebeck, 2002.

Porter, Stanley E., and D. A. Carson, eds. *Linguistics and the New Testament: Critical Junctures*. Sheffield, Eng.: Sheffield Academic Press, 1999.

Ressequil, James L. *Narrative Criticism of the New Testament*. Grand Rapids: Baker Academic, 2005.

Ricoeur, Paul. *Du texte à l'action*. Paris: du Seuil, 1986. ET *From Text to Action* (Evanston, Ill.: Northwestern University Press, 1991).

Soulen, Richard N., and R. Kendall Soulen. *Handbook of Biblical Criticism*. 3d ed., rev. and expanded. Louisville, Ky.: Westminster John Knox Press, 2001.

Hermeneutics as a Theory of Understanding

Szondi, Peter. *Einführung in die literarische Hermeneutik.* Frankfurt: Suhrkamp, 1975. ET *Introduction to Literary Hermeneutics* (Cambridge: Cambridge University Press, 1995).
Tate, W. Randolph. *Biblical Interpretation: An Integrated Approach.* Peabody, Mass.: Hendrickson, 1991.
Weder, Hans. *Neutestamentliche Hermeneutik.* Zurich: Theologischer Verlag, 1986. 2d ed., 1989.
Wischmeyer, Oda. *Hermeneutik des Neuen Testaments. Ein Lehrbuch.* Tübingen: Francke, 2004.

Hermeneutics as a theory of interpretation has, as conceived of today, become a theory of understanding in general. It began to take shape in this modern form from the time of the Reformation, initially as an interpretation of individual biblical concepts (Matthias Flacius Illyricus, 1520-75). From the mid-eighteenth century onward, it is possible to speak of the modern tradition of hermeneutics, as described by the Hungarian-German literary theorist Peter Szondi (1929-71) in his groundbreaking studies. The leading representatives of this phase were Martin Chladenius (1710-59), Georg F. Meier (1718-77), and Friedrich Ast (1778-1841), whose influence came in the first quarter of the nineteenth century. This important phase culminated in the work of Friedrich D. E. Schleiermacher (1768-1834),[1] which likewise constituted a turning point. Schleiermacher placed a far more fundamental emphasis than Chladenius on the cognitive role of the human subject in formulating the overall meaning of the text or speech that was being interpreted, and he positioned hermeneutics on the boundary between science and art.[2] In so doing, he wanted to imply that it was not an exact science but one that was connected with history and with human subjects. This role was stressed more than half a century later by Wilhelm Dilthey (1833-1911) in his study "Die Entstehung der Hermeneutik" ("The Origins of Hermeneutics"), written in 1900.[3]

According to Schleiermacher, one of the main functions of hermeneutics is the interpretation of old texts, which requires a whole range of scientific approaches taken from the fields of history, philology, and linguistics (the historical side of hermeneutics). In the final analysis, however, it is after all probably more of an art, in which inspiration, empathy, and personal de-

---

1. See the contribution by Alice Kliková in the second volume of this hermeneutics.
2. F. D. E. Schleiermacher, "Hermeneutik," in *Werke in Auswahl,* ed. F. Lücke, vol. 4 (1927-28, repr. Aalen, 1967), 135-206, 137ff.
3. On the importance of Dilthey, see Ricoeur, *Du texte à l'action,* opening passage.

cision (the intuitive side) form a bridge between knowledge of the general and encounter with the unique.

Hermeneutics, which today has become a discipline bringing together all fields of science and the arts, has its roots far back in Greek philosophy and rhetoric, and even its modern history is more varied than might be supposed from what we have said about its German tradition. This is because this tradition first began to work systematically with the term "hermeneutics," whereas in the tradition of modern philosophy (esp. phenomenological philosophy) and linguistics, hermeneutic issues (such as the cognitive role of the subject, the definition of meaning, the function of signs, and self-understanding) were dealt with in various contexts and using different types of terminology. A good overview of these antecedents of contemporary hermeneutics is provided in an introduction by the Canadian literary theorist Jean Grondin, who has worked partly in Germany. I have therefore decided to refer readers to Grondin's work and to examine only certain selected issues relating to the history of hermeneutics.

The term "hermeneutics" is derived from the Greek word *hermēneuō*, which seems to have meant "imitating Hermes," who in Greek mythology was the messenger of the gods. Hermeneutics among other things thus indicated expressing divine matters in human speech. In the subchapters on metaphor we will consider the functions of language, which can in some ways be compared to this. The second meaning of this verb — namely, translating from one language to another — will be considered in chapter 4; it is only one aspect of the overall subject of hermeneutics, albeit a particularly instructive one. We devote most attention to the third meaning that *hermēneuō* had in antiquity — the interpretation of written texts.

Excursus on Theology and Philosophy

In what we have to say, we will be speaking of philosophy and of theology, sometimes even as though they were twin concepts. From the historical point of view, this is not altogether accurate, as theology and philosophy have frequently found themselves on opposite sides of issues. It is therefore necessary to clarify our terminology right at the start. Here we shall understand *philosophy* in its elementary meaning as reflection on a specific existence or state, with all the implications for orientation in the "life-world" (*Lebenswelt*, or world of lived experience), especially in history and society. And we shall refer to *theology* in the sense that primarily interests us in connection with hermeneutics —

that is, as a way of thinking that evaluates the basic Christian testimonies, plus the texts and implications related to those testimonies, and examines to what extent and in what form it is possible, using them as a basis, to arrive at an understanding of the world that is congruent and, under certain circumstances (the acceptance of the Christian testimony), philosophically relevant for people in today's world. From a purely methodological viewpoint, theology is a certain type of philosophy. The fact that it has so far been virtually the exclusive domain of Christians and Jews, for whom theology is at the same time a reflection on their own faith, does not mean that others could not devote themselves to it as well.

To a considerable extent indeed, theology is marked by its historical forms and the tasks that it has assumed over the course of its history. It is the interpreter of Christian doctrinal tradition — a great heritage, but also a burden that it cannot lay aside; these traditions and texts, however, also represent an important interpretation of human life and history. The doctrine of the mystery of the Trinity is in its way a brilliant formula for plotting the experience of faith onto the map of history. God is a subject who transcends history, who is "above" and "in front of" it; Jesus is a subject who represents God's will as unconditional truth and asserts it within history, so that it can be relied on for orientation; and the Holy Spirit enters into the very heart of human beings, into human subjectivity. In the Holy Spirit, God reaches into the human "I" itself. He is extremely close to each human person and understandably extremely difficult to identify. For this reason it is necessary to "examine the spirits" to see whether they acknowledge that Jesus has come in the flesh (see §3.7.2 below) and thus whether they are from God. Trinitarian thinking thus moves between testimony and critical self-reflection, and the classic creeds are at the same time a scheme for the world — a scheme that earlier mediated between myth and philosophy and today mediates between myth and the analogical or metaphorical language of the contemporary world.

Theology came into being as a systematic reflection on the basic experience of faith. Unfortunately, some theological conclusions that assumed a special authority (i.e., dogmas) effectively came to be seen as revelations of the basic experience of faith, rather than as a reflection on it, and were thus often simply handed down. It is therefore necessary today for the interpretation of these dogmas to return to the roots of experience from which they have sprung. Theology must thus often return to the past, both for its own good and for that of society as a whole, but formulating new schemes, this time consciously left open, does not cease to be its calling. In view of the many dimensions in which it operates, theology in this connection sometimes allocates some of its tasks to fundamen-

What Is Hermeneutics?

tal theology,[4] but this does not alter its basic task of examining openly the possibilities that faith offers for orientation in the "life-world."

It remains to define the role of Christian philosophy. It can be defined as that part of philosophical reflection that, in terms of the themes it deals with, overlaps with the basic task of theological reflection, but that in so doing makes use of other traditions and the texts linked with them (from the history of philosophy) in such a way that it communicates its reflections primarily on the basis of, and with the help of, these traditions and texts.

This parallel status of theology and philosophy, along with, to a certain extent, the competition between them, constitutes a certain degree of complication in hermeneutical work, as it is a field in which both sides are involved. At the same time, however, it presents a great opportunity for the two sides to show they are open to mutual dialogue.

---

4. Fundamental theology should not be confused with fundamentalism. Rather, the former is concerned with the contribution made by theology to resolving the fundamental problems of philosophy. It is a Catholic academic term, adopted for hermeneutics by D. Tracy, *The Analogical Imagination* (New York: Crossroad, 1981), 62ff.; cf. 183, nn. 241ff. In fundamental theology, systematic theology publicly (and not just for internal church circles) gives an account of the methodology used in its interpretation of Bible. See Jeanrond, *Text und Interpretation*, 130ff.; and M. Kirwan, "Theological Hermeneutics," *Communio viatorum* 43 (2001): 103-26.

2. The World of Language

BIBLIOGRAPHY

Jack, Alison M. *Texts Reading Texts, Sacred and Secular.* Sheffield, Eng.: Sheffield Academic Press, 1999.
Patočka, Jan. *Tělo, společenství, jazyk, svět.* Prague: OIKOYMENH, 1995.
Saussure, Ferdinand de. *Cours de linguistique générale.* 1916; Paris: Payot, 1982 (edition with commentary by T. de Mauro). ET *Course in General Linguistics,* ed. Charles Bally and Albert Sechehaye (New York: Philosophical Library, 1959).

A text is communication expressed in language. If we are to understand a text, we must understand the function of language.

If in this section we shall refer primarily to the Bible, it is because (1) the Bible is a classic text (or collection of texts) in the European and American cultural heritage, which leads us to ask questions about it through its cultural authority alone. At the same time we must remember that (2) the long history of biblical exegesis is the largest reservoir of hermeneutical experience, a fact it would be foolish to ignore.

We address these observations in two directions as the starting point for study and discussion. First, we would like to point out to the broader public and particularly to students that the Bible is the basic text that was and is interpreted in European history. Without the Bible, we shall be unable to understand the principles of European culture, including some practical aspects of Western traditions that were suppressed in our country during the period of the totalitarian regime but were never completely conquered (such as a critical view of one's past, overcoming the inevitability of fate, the awareness of personal responsibility, and taking for granted the care of the weak and the sick). The Bible has also been used many times to justify terrible deeds. However, a hermeneutical analysis indicates that such a use can be criticized from the point of view of the way the biblical texts are constructed, and it is possible to defend the view that they have been misused in these cases.

Second, we need to remind Christians that there is essentially only one hermeneutics *(hermeneutica generalis)* — the hermeneutical dimension of a single common universal human question. There is one hermeneutics, just as there is one basic system of communication, which is the system of language, and just as there is one world in which we understand each other. Of course we do have something like "regional hermeneutics" — the interpretation of texts linked by a common genre — which requires certain specific methodological approaches that have been formed over the course of history. In this sense it is also possible to talk of biblical hermeneutics. Essentially, however, the interpretation of the Bible is not a hermeneutical operation for which fundamentally different rules of interpretation apply than for other texts. If there is something unusual about biblical texts, it is the fact that we mentioned in our introduction: in them we are confronted with the issue of hermeneutics in a profound and extreme form, which can help to reveal its essential nature better than is the case with the analysis of most other texts. That is, historical existence in time is pertinent to the understanding of something that fundamentally transcends it. Only in this way does *hermeneutica sacra* stand out in comparison with general hermeneutics.[1] And because the interpreter must take the claims of the text seriously, the interpretation of biblical texts is concerned with a more universal and profound series of questions. But this special characteristic can be convincingly revealed only if we interpret biblical texts working from the assumptions of general hermeneutics. Otherwise we would constantly be faced with the objection that results obtained by using a different, biblical-hermeneutical strategy cannot be convincing. (Incidentally, even from the theological point of view, attempts to establish a special biblical hermeneutics or interpretational tendencies that might lead in that direction are suspect undertakings. This is because by using a different hermeneutics they are denying Jesus' full humanity, which is a Docetic heresy.)

---

1. It is in this sense that we must understand Schleiermacher's statement that general hermeneutics does not exist, and that the art of understanding *(Kunst des Verstehens)* exists only in special hermeneutics (F. D. E. Schleiermacher, "Hermeneutik," in *Werke in Auswahl*, ed. F. Lücke, vol. 4 [1927-28, repr. Aalen, 1967], 137). In saying this, Schleiermacher wanted to emphasize that an interpretation must respect the pragmatics of the individual texts.

The World of Language

The interpretation of a text is something very relevant to the present, something that impacts the whole of the interpreter's existence. The very fact that we read and listen to a certain text constitutes an **indirect challenge to us to express our opinion on what it is saying and on its quite different world,** and to react to it.[2] The alien "I" who speaks to us from the text expands our horizon and becomes our partner in dialogue, enabling us to begin looking at ourselves through different eyes and thus helping us to better understand ourselves.[3] And **as soon as we start talking "about something," then what we say is an interpretation or, more accurately, an attempt at an interpretation.**[4]

2.1. Language as an Encoding System

We cannot understand contemporary linguistic theory without some knowledge of *Course in General Linguistics,* by Ferdinand de Saussure (1857-1913), first published in French in 1916 as *Cours de linguistique générale.* In saying this, I do not wish to disparage discoveries that were made and described before this work was published, nor what has followed it. Nevertheless, Saussure's work is the most systematic and most frequently quoted expression of what became the starting point for later discussion. The terminology that he used is also well known among experts, and the translations of his main work include an overview of appropriate renderings of the individual terms he uses in other languages. We shall see that his opinions have been subjected to criticism and his terminology has been modified, but overall research reached an irreversible stage with Saussure, without which it would be difficult to imagine the current models for resolving the basic issues. And because linguistic theory does not yet have a standard terminology, it is convenient to make use of his terminology in specialist discussion in the field.

Ferdinand de Saussure reflected on the fact, already well known, that language (which he referred to as *langue*), as the background and supporting structure for speech *(parole)* — what we say — is the hidden but indispens-

---

2. B. Waldenfels, *Der Stachel des Fremden* (Frankfurt: Suhrkamp, 1990), 16/III.

3. G. Figal has demonstrated how, even when it is hostile, something alien is a reality that helps shape the way people understand themselves ("Fremdheit und Feindschaft," *Wort und Dienst* 18 [1985]: 229-55, esp. 239).

4. P. Ricoeur, *De l'interprétation. Essai sur Freud* (Paris: du Seuil, 1965), book 1, chap. 2.1.

Hermeneutics as a Theory of Understanding

able basic model for a specific language such as English or Czech *(langage)*. We should note that *langage* is a comprehensive term when we are referring to the general signs of speech and of the function of *langue* as a system. If we are dealing with specific vocabularies and grammars, then we must talk about *langages*. In the narrower, specialist sense of language, however, *langue* is for us to a certain extent an unknown dimension of *langage*. It indeed grows out of specific needs of *parole,* but it is concealed behind it; when speaking, we are not aware of it, and when reading a text, we do not see it. Nevertheless it is something concrete; it can be reconstructed in explicit grammatical outlines, and individual words can be written down in dictionaries. While *langue* is the child of *parole,* we can also say that it is the model for *parole* that has turned out to be the best in practice; above all, it is in fact the organizer of our experience.

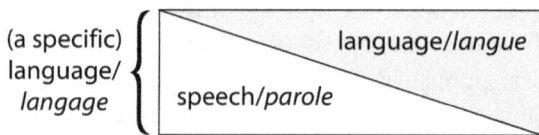

Saussure's scheme for the relationship between language (*langue* — abstract, general principles of language) and speech (*parole* — language actually used) in a specific language (*langage* — e.g., English, Czech, Greek).

2.1.1. Vocabulary

Ferdinand de Saussure presented a coherent demonstration of the function of language as a system. It is an encoding system in which ideas that relate to entire groups of individual phenomena (i.e., what is signified; Latin *significatum*) are transferred to a system of signs incorporated into certain external manifestations of the human individual. One of the main forms of such manifestations is the broad range of consciously created and differing sounds (phonemes), which can be built up into words and sentences and written down using agreed graphic signs. If we group phonemes together according to certain rules, they can signify individual ideas *(idées)*. In this function we call them "signifiers" *(significants)*. Such groups of phonemes usually do not have any connection (either graphically or in terms of sound) with what they signify. They are an "agreed" and arbitrary signification, and therefore essentially they do not have to have any connection with the signi-

The World of Language

fied groups.⁵ They have become established as such by the practice in certain areas (such as Great Britain) or certain settings (such as a British family living abroad) in which one language is spoken. The same idea can thus be called different things in different languages (table, stůl, Tisch, trapeza, etc.). Here we can see the advantage of language in everyday communication. It enables us to talk about something that is not directly in front of us, that we cannot point to or bring from somewhere else. However, we can make it present using the agreed code. We become aware of this when (usually in a foreign language) we do not know a certain expression, and there is a gap in the index of our code. Then we have to point to the object in question and say, "What do you call that?" We can observe the same thing with children who are learning their mother tongue. Once, when one of my grandsons was three years old, he was in our house and saw a plate of cakes. He did not know what they were, but he found them tempting. He wanted to take one, but he did not know how to say this. So he had to take the whole plateful from the kitchen and carry them carefully through to the room where my wife was so he could ask her: "Grandma, can I eat one of *these?*" Knowledge of the correct vocabulary would have saved him having to undertake this "operation," including walking from one room to another.

A condition for two speakers to understand each other using vocabulary is that they must both know the same "encoding table" — in other words, speak the same language. However, this is only the first part of the much more complex lexical dimension (the dimension relating to vocabulary) of each language system, in which the meaning of individual signs depends on their relationship to other signs.

Excursus on Semiology

The discovery of language as a system led to the development of semiology — the science of signs in the life of a society. In this connection language turned out to be, while far and away the most complex system of signs related to life on

---

5. The fact that they do not have to have a connection does not mean that they cannot or must not. Onomatopoeic words have a direct relationship to what is being signified, even if it has often become a formal one (a Czech dog goes "haf, haf," an English one "woof, woof," and a Russian one "vau, vau"). Some encoding systems (e.g., the sign language of the deaf and dumb — see Phyllis Wilcox, *Metaphor in American Sign Language* [Washington, D.C.: Gallaudet University Press, 2000]) consciously aim to emphasize such elements. In a certain sense, poetic forms in different languages also aim to do this.

Hermeneutics as a Theory of Understanding

earth, nevertheless not the only one. All such systems have their **encoding register** (registering the relationship between signs and things), their "**grammar**" and their **pragmatics**. Grammar (including syntax) can be understood as a strategy whereby language (a system) makes use of words (signs; in the case of language, lexemes) in a pragmatic way — in other words, so as to achieve something. Semiology thus becomes a general self-reflection: by means of semiology science reflects on its own hypotheses and thus searches for its own theory. At the same time, this general theory is open — it is itself a process, in the course of which terms used in the exact sciences are tested out as possibly being capable of having other, more complex meanings (see the use of terms such as "isotopy,"[6] "synchronization," "paleontology," and "generative" in literary science and philosophy). Philosophical hermeneutics is a more general discipline in the sense that it also reflects this function of semiotics.

* * *

When we discuss vocabulary, we should not forget that this is only the first dimension of language as an encoding system. However, it turns out that even the creation of vocabulary is not such a simple matter as we had thought. Our everyday experience with the use of vocabulary creates the impression that vocabulary is a collection of designations for various phenomena that we can stick on them like labels designating the various items exhibited in a laboratory. In reality, the development of vocabulary is creative work, and here language starts to be more than just a means of communication. Language organizes experience; it is the center (not just the means) of interaction with the human "life-world" and thus contributes to shaping it. It is not a question of communication but of doing something actively.

Excursus on Experience

In the previous excursus we used the term "experience." It is a term that philosophy and theology did not trust at the end of the twentieth century. Philosophy, because its extent could not be defined, and theology, because it was suspected of tending toward subjectivism. Nevertheless, it is a concept that plays an impor-

---

6. "Isotopy" is a set of signs (or words) relating to a particular area of meaning; in a literary text, it forms a layer that repeatedly emerges. See J. Schulte-Sasse and R. Werner, *Einführung in die Literaturwissenschaft*, 7th ed. (Munich: Fink, 1991), 68ff.

The World of Language

tant role in hermeneutical theory. In Hans-Georg Gadamer's view, experience in itself has a hermeneutical value. It is something that comes to us from outside, something "alien," but it is "something different" that affects us personally, and somehow we have to work with it.[7] Experience disturbs the tendency toward individualism, the narcissism[8] of the postmodern world, and compels us to try to find our bearings in the things that experience forces upon us. It leads us to attempt to communicate and evaluate in dialogue. Experience thus already contains within itself the tendency to capture things in words and texts. In other words, language is not something that has been imposed on reality from outside and is not an "invention" in the common sense of the word. Language comes from experience, and it can even be compared with instinct, which accompanies human beings and is their internal dimension.[9]

* * *

Before our excursus on experience we were talking about language as an organizer of experience. By now, however, it is clear that simply giving names to experiences would not help us. Vocabulary cannot classify all the phenomena of our world using separate terms. There are an infinite number of them. No person is the same as any other person, no flower is the same as any other flower of the same species (just compare two dandelions), and even no two hairs on our head are the same. The idea that language is able to classify every phenomenon is mistaken. We have already said that language designates groups of phenomena, which we can work with as with ideas. If language had to designate each individual phenomenon, it would be no good to us. Everybody would have to know everything, and we would have to see everything in advance before we would be able to talk about it. Nobody would be able to learn the infinite number of expressions. Even if someone came close, it would be exceptional. And even then it would do them no good, because there would be nobody else with whom they could make themselves understood. In addition to the infinite number of experiences and phenomena, everybody would also have to master an infinitely

---

7. H.-G. Gadamer, "Text und Interpretation" (1983), reprinted in *Gadamer Lesebuch* (Tübingen: Mohr Siebeck, 1997), 141-71, here 143ff.

8. O. Bayer, "Hermeneutical Theology," in *Philosophical Hermeneutics and Biblical Exegesis*, ed. P. Pokorný and J. Roskovec (Tübingen: Mohr Siebeck, 2002), 103-20, here 104.

9. The fact of the consistency and translatability of language demonstrates the limits of postmodern deconstructivism; see Jack, *Texts Reading Texts,* 30ff. 141ff. (she interprets Jacques Derrida).

extensive language code. In practical terms, for example, it would mean that we would have to know the name of every other person. That would be an absolutely precise code, but at the same time a completely unnecessary one. It would mean superfluous work. And in any case it is something that would be impossible to achieve. Vocabulary must therefore incorporate fairly radical generalization, enabling us to find our bearings in the infinite field of experiences by using a limited number of different words. Usually our vocabulary does not exceed four thousand words, while the number of words that we use actively is considerably more limited still. This is because, as we have said, vocabulary creates categories, ideas, so that the expression "dog" can include both a St. Bernard (which a short-sighted person might mistake for a calf) and a dachshund, which from a distance might be mistaken for a cat. Their common characteristic is that they manifest themselves ("function") in a similar way: they associate with humans, keep guard, and so on, not to mention the fact that they are capable of having viable offspring together (though not always very magnificent ones). A St. Bernard and a calf cannot manage this. The tendency toward generalization is therefore very strong indeed. We might call it a tendency toward the maximum possible reduction in the number of vocabulary expressions while maintaining the maximum practical ability to distinguish between phenomena. Of course, vocabulary does not just include designations for groups of phenomena that are essentially of equal value. Some expressions are linked by hierarchical relationships: they designate phenomena that are superior and subordinate to each other. There are some terms that cover the whole of our experience (are coextensive with it), such as the terms "world" or "experience," and at the other end of the spectrum the most subordinate terms in the hierarchy are specialist expressions known only to small groups of speakers. A special group consists of proper names, where effectively no generalization has occurred. Vocabulary is thus created by speech searching for a balance between the lowest possible number of expressions and the most perfect coverage of experience.

In this way, language forms a net with the gaps in the mesh being of varying size, or, to put it another way, a system of coordinates. These are the various expressions in the vocabulary. We place this net or system of coordinates over our experience, over the world we live in, in order to be able to find our way around it. Because language codes are created by agreement, this net has a different structure in each language. The space covered by the gaps in the mesh will be different from one language to another. We encounter the most well-known example of this difference between different lexical nets when using dictionaries, where for one expression in the source language we usually find several expressions in the receptor language.

Excursus on Phenomenology and Hermeneutics

Bibliography

Dilthey, Wilhelm. "Die Entstehung der Hermeneutik." In *Gesammelte Schriften*, 4th ed., 5:317-38. Leipzig: Teubner, 1964. Quoted in *Philosophische Hermeneutik*, ed. Hans-Ulrich Lessing, 33-48 (Freiburg: Alber, 1999).
Fink, Eugen. *Sein, Wahrheit, Welt*. The Hague: Martinus Nijhoff, 1958.
Koch, Dietmar. *Zur hermeneutischen Phänomenologie*. Tübingen: Attempo, 1992.
Mathauser, Zdeněk. "Edmund Husserl." In *Hermeneutika jako theorie porozumění*, part 2, chap. 4. Prague: Vyšehrad, 2005.

If in what we said earlier we talked about something "appearing" or used phrases such as "the way" and "forward," then we in fact abandoned the way of thinking that is characteristic of the exact sciences, especially in the form in which the theory of these sciences took shape in the nineteenth century. The present classification of sciences has gradually become established through a process whereby the individual disciplines worked out their methodology, defined their sphere of validity, and separated themselves off from philosophy. As late as the mid-nineteenth century the natural sciences came under the remit of the philosophical faculties at universities. In fact, however, they had already made themselves independent of the field of philosophy at the beginning of the modern age. And as they emancipated themselves, each of them introduced their own exact and verifiable methods of carrying out research. This meant in most cases that they could be verified by repeating them on a small scale — that is, by experiment. This indispensable exactness of the natural sciences, without which they would not have been able to develop, was achieved at the cost of separating them from philosophy and thus from the study of human experience in broader contexts. History cannot be verified by experiments. The Battle of Hastings cannot be verified by a small-scale experiment, for example, with twenty or fifty people on each side. (In such an experiment, the Normans might lose the battle!) History is too complex a phenomenon to be able to repeat it. And above all, we are part of it and thus are unable to step outside it and examine it in a truly unbiased way. We must find some way of dealing with our own bias.

The crisis in scientific theory that preceded this recognition was described in 1936 by the Austrian philosopher (born in Moravia) Edmund Husserl

(1859-1938) in his treatise *Die Krisis der europäischen Wissenschaften und die transzendentale Phänomenologie* (The Crisis of European Sciences and Transcendental Phenomenology).[10] The fragmentation of the sciences with their exact methods meant that there were no longer any appropriate categories for the experience of the broader whole. "The world" in all its variety and complexity, as it appears to us when we look around us, is something that cannot be captured using the tools of the exact sciences, even though we are constantly faced with it and, in a certain sense, we know it intimately. For this reason Husserl took as the starting point in his philosophy things that "appear" to us. The world understood as a phenomenon (*Lebenswelt*, "life-world") is what we encounter through direct contact and in a natural context. For this reason we also talk about the natural world. This world is a complex phenomenon, and for phenomenological philosophy its decisive level is the analysis of human existence *(Dasein)* — in other words, the perception of one's own existence in the midst of this "life-world." The results of this study can be communicated by means of language, and a comparison can be made of the conspicuous common elements that appear in the functions of the partial phenomena that make up the whole, as observed at different times and under different conditions by different observers. In this way a certain idea *(eidos)* can be uncovered. This discovery can further be stored in the memory and communicated later on. Husserl wanted to lay the foundations of a scientific, almost empirical philosophy. Indirectly, however, he also opened up the way to studying language as a phenomenon of a special type. Later on, phenomenology also inspired the theory of the literary text.[11] This cognition of reality, an integral part of which is the cognitive subject, uncovers more than might appear at first sight: the distinctive nature of both sides that enter into the cognitive process, both the cognitive subject and the phenomenon about which knowledge is acquired. Furthermore, phenomenology made it possible to study the whole of the world (the "life-world" that we have mentioned) as a phenomenon.

One reason phenomenology is important for our purposes is that it is an approach that enables a text to be understood, not just as a historical source or as an aesthetic object that impacts in various ways, but as something that can be considered as a whole and whose meaning can be understood as a whole, even if it is a text that we cannot retain in our memory in its entirety. Phenomenology does not reject or exclude the historical approach but creates a framework for it

---

10. Published in Edmund Husserl, *Husserliana*, vol. 6 (Dordrecht: Nijhoff, 1954).
11. The groundbreaking work of this type is the monograph by the Polish philosopher Roman Ingarden (1893-1970) *Das literarische Kunstwerk* (Tübingen: Niemeyer, 1931).

in that it understands the text as a phenomenon whose overall meaning is not qualified by its other functions (see §§3.6 and 5.3, on reference). It would be difficult to understand linguistic theory without some knowledge of the phenomenological approach.

* * *

Vocabulary is thus a basic means of organizing the "life-world." The organization is indirect, without any direct intervention in the world that surrounds us. **Speaking is not a direct communication of ideas, but the process of selecting expressions from the range of signs — that is, from the world of meanings — that is encoded in the vocabulary of the language used.**[12] **The interpretation of a fixed text will in principle be an attempt to express what the text is concerned with, with the help of signs and structures different from those used in the text itself.** This could be a provisional definition of interpretation.[13]

2.1.2. Grammar (Syntax)

Grammar is the second and fundamental part of the organization of experience, experience now reduced to a finite number of concepts represented by individual words.

2.1.2.1. The Sentence — the Basic Bearer of Meaning

It is not just the sound aspect of language codes that is not directly connected with the phenomena that are represented by them. The same applies to the extent of the fields in those codes. The field of meanings covered by individual words differs from one language to another and is created on the basis of different plans, so that when translating, we encounter constant overlaps in meaning. When interpreting texts that readers know only from a

---

12. M. Merleau-Ponty, *Phénoménologie de la perception* (1945), ET *Phenomenology of Perception* (London: Routledge & Keagan Paul, 1965), 193. Merleau-Ponty draws attention to the fact that meaning is not implicit in a word but comes from the intention of the human subject, who attempts to express a certain thought and creates or searches for its primary (sound) or secondary (graphic) code.

13. P. Ricoeur, "The Canon between the Text and the Community," in *Philosophical Hermeneutics and Biblical Exegesis,* ed. Pokorný and Roskovec, 7-26, here 13.

translation, there is a great danger of underestimating these overlaps. We have already mentioned the situation we find in dictionaries, where a certain term in the source language usually has its counterpart in a number of terms in the receptor language, even though its field of meaning is rarely completely identical with some of them. This was very well described by Jan Blahoslav in his *Czech Grammar,* written in the year 1571, in the section "de verborum et phraseon proprietate." In it we find a diagram resembling two parallel rows of stones of various sizes in a wall. It represents a sentence containing the same communication in two different languages: "the words of one language" (A) and "the words of another language" (B).[14]

A
B

The author comments on it as follows: "The rectangular stones joined in these two rows are not identical, but some are broader, others narrower, so that a certain stone placed in the upper row may be so large that several stones must be placed in the second row to fill up the space, and nevertheless both the first and the second rows are full. It is similar if you place the speech of one language on one side and that of a second alongside it, such as Greek and Czech or Latin."[15] The basic bearer of meaning is thus not simply a word alone but must be at least an entire sentence, or indeed a broader context. But a sentence itself may be the bearer of a message that makes sense.

As an example, we can take the following sentence from the New Testament — 1 Timothy 6:6:

> Estin de porismos megas hē eusebeia meta autarkeias.
> But godliness with contentment is great gain.
> Now there is great gain in goodliness with contentment.
> Est autem quaestus magnus pietas cum sufficientia.
> Die Frömmigkeit aber ist ein großer Gewinn für den, der sich genügen läßt.

Here the Greek original has eight words, the King James Version (1611) seven words, the English Standard Version (2007) nine words, the Latin transla-

---

14. Jan Blahoslav, *Gramatika Česká* (1571; repr. Vienna: Hradil & Jireček, 1857), 219.
15. *Gramatika Česká,* 219-20.

tion (the Vulgate) seven words, the German translation (Luther, 1984 revision) thirteen words. In almost every case the words are in a different order.

From this comparison we need to immediately draw a conclusion that is an irrefutable contribution of structural linguistics and an important rule of exegetics: the basic **bearer of meaning is not the word alone, but the sentence,** in some cases even a longer section of the text, whose meaning can be deduced from it without taking into account the context. When we translate, we translate at least a sentence. If we interpret a text, again we base ourselves on a sentence. We determine the meaning of an individual word from its position in the sentence, because language is not just a code register but a system, a structure.[16] Only within contexts like this does semantics, which deals with changes in meanings of words, have its place. Even words that sound the same but have different meanings (homonyms) can be precisely distinguished and told apart with virtual certainty in the context of a sentence. If we say "Her hair needs cutting" and "Her hare is ill," we can say straight away which hair (or hare) we are talking about. We can also recall the example we used to illustrate the differences in the lexical nets in different languages. The English word "seal" does not just mean a wax seal or a seal on a bottle. It can also mean an animal. But this is a homonym and does not fall into the category of expressions with overlapping meanings. Here too the context will reliably help us to distinguish between the two meanings. Artificially breaking through this contextually created boundary is the basis for a certain type of joke (e.g., "No matter how much you push the envelope, it's still stationery").

We have paused to consider this phenomenon and the functions of language that are connected with it because in philologically oriented exegesis and in some formalistic literary theories in the twentieth century, terminology was sometimes understood as an autonomous phenomenon (e.g., the issue of metaphors was dealt with only within the framework of semantics),[17] and the role of context was not given sufficient importance. The meaning of individual expressions was not derived from the context but from their meaning in another place (following the concordance) and usually in another setting. The pitfalls of this approach can be illustrated in the New Testament by the different meanings of the word *kyrios* (lord, master). It can take the place of the word "God," it can be a sovereign title for Jesus, and it can simply be a polite form of address (like "sir" in English).

---

16. Vilém Mathesius, *Řeč a sloh* (Language and Style) (1942; Prague: N.p., 1966), 50ff.
17. See below, §2.4.

There are certainly words that have become set terms and are capable of functioning like sentences on their own. But even they must be recognized from the context. We read the request by the father of a sick child "Lord, have mercy on my son" in Matthew's gospel (17:15), and at the end of the same gospel we read: "Go therefore and make disciples of all nations, baptizing them in the name of the Father and of the Son and of the Holy Spirit" (28:19). Even if we only hear these words and do not have the guidance of the relatively late distinction between lower case and capital letters, we understand that in the first case "son" designates a male child, whereas in the second it is a sovereign title for Jesus, expressing his unique relationship to God, or God's relationship to him, as it is stated in the Christian creed. In contrast, the form of address "Lord" in Matthew 17:15 is intentionally polysemic. In the original narrative it was a polite form of address, but in the context of Matthew's gospel, it can and should also be regarded as a sovereign title for Jesus, which when spoken is also an appeal to a power that is not indifferent to the father's wish. This meaning sees Jesus as a representative of God's will; like any other son, he had full power to represent his father in legal matters.

It is therefore the sense of the sentence that must be preserved during any form of transformation of a text, whereby a translation is a basic transformation and an interpretation is a more complicated one. Frequently used terms without a direct equivalent in the receptor language and whose meaning can be gradually discovered from the context do not have to be interpreted and sometimes can remain untranslated. They are specialist expressions that all readers of or listeners to the text in question can learn to understand if they read or listen to it over a lengthy period. An example of this in the New Testament might be the Hebrew "amen" ("so be it!").

More modern examples might be "perestroika" or "tsunami."

After what we have just said, it is no longer necessary to comment in any greater detail on the assertion that the sentence is the minimum basic element in the scheme of the total wider text (the macrotext), its internal strategy, and its literary genre.

The observation of lexicological aspects has itself thus led us to consider the issue of grammar.

2.1.2.2. *Grammatical Persons*

Grammar is no longer concerned with mapping out experience, but with transforming phenomena into a structure that is tailored to fit human needs.

The World of Language

In personal pronouns and the conjugation of verbs, language uses "persons," where every speaker is the relative center of his or her world. This corresponds to speakers' elementary experience: their physical existence connects the first person ("I") with the present tense ("now"). From the viewpoint of their personal experience, human beings stand constantly in the center of the world and live constantly in the present. "I" is a basic grammatical category, which is quite understandable. We have spoken about the phenomenological view of the world. I, you, he, she, it, we, you, they — these are pronouns that express basic relationships free of all randomness. They form the coordinates of the map of our lives. It is not a question of any particular person proclaiming himself or herself to be the center of the world. It is simply that every person sees himself or herself as the center of the world and cannot look at the world in any other way; they see it with their own eyes, and they are therefore its relative center, just like any creature that sees. Of course, unless they are mentally ill, people know that this center is only a relative one, but they also realize that they must reckon with the fact that their cognition has this characteristic.

In addition, human beings are creatures that are capable of expressing the fact that they perceive themselves as the relative center of the world, linking this fact with unique personal experiences and thus becoming individuals. And because a genuinely social organism, a society in the true sense of the word, can only be made up of unique individuals (just like a machine is made up of different parts),[18] so the human being as an individual is at the same time the basis of a community, the basic link in the socialization of life. "It is not necessary to be a human being in order to perceive objects and forces spread out all around us. All animals can do this just the same as we can. The special quality of human beings is that they assume a position in nature in which the convergence of lines we have referred to is not just something visual, but also has a structural basis."[19] In other words, human beings see reality from their viewpoint, and language enables them to evaluate this image of reality and to reflect on it. They are even able to reflect on it to the extent that they learn to distinguish between the egocentrism of personal experience and grammatical structures, on the one hand, and, on the other, the egoism of personal ambition.

---

18. A series of parts that are all the same cannot be the basis for a machine but is just a collection of objects; a group of organs that are all the same does not make an organism.

19. P. Teilhard de Chardin, *Le phénomène humain* (Paris: du Seuil, 1947), 7, along with the whole opening essay, "Voir."

Hermeneutics as a Theory of Understanding

The identity of the human person is given by the unity of a subject represented by the first person and collecting experience (Paul Ricoeur speaks of "ipseity"), even in cases where the appearance and beliefs of the person change.[20] A change of attitudes is also part of people's inner identity in the sense of being themselves — their subjectivity remains the same. However, people must also assess how they appear to others (and indirectly to themselves) from outside, in the role of the third person, which involves an objectivity whose identity is measured by the extent to which its manifestations remain constant (*mêmeté*, sameness).

Human beings can and should recognize for themselves, and understand by means of their conscious "I," that that "I" is by no means the final authority. However, they can work toward this recognition only from their own point of view. They must follow the circuitous route to the recognition of themselves seen in the mirror of external relations as a subject, and they must speak about this in the first person. This is a different world to the one presented to us by natural science. The world of natural science (or, rather, the worlds of natural sciences) is only one of the phenomena of the linguistic world in which we really live. The great importance of the natural sciences with their theoretical and directly applicable discoveries is simply underlined by the fact that they have defined themselves as an area of research that operates with exactitude, but that on principle does not aspire to knowledge of reality as a whole. Perspectives on life are formed in the area of society and history. Our "I" must encounter a different "I" that approaches it with a promise, an expectation, and a claim. This, for example, is the function of Jesus' "I am" in the Johannine texts (such as John 10:7, 11). On the one hand, his authoritative form of address puts into perspective the listener's (or reader's) egocentric linguistic tendency; on the other, it offers a firm guiding principle. It speaks to us personally, but at the same time it gives instructions connecting true humanity with certain objective moral viewpoints.

These reflections are not motivated by some kind of morality that attempts to humanize science. They are simply reflections on the functions of language that are associated with a precise phenomenological analysis. Such an analysis examines words in their various relationships and forms and thus ascertains their nature and effect as lexemes. A lexeme, in the basic sense in which this term is used, is a word in all its grammatical (morpho-

---

20. On this question, see P. Ricoeur, *Soi-même comme un autre* (Paris: du Seuil, 1990; ET *Oneself as Another* [Chicago: University of Chicago Press, 1992]), 140ff.

logical) forms and syntactic (grammatical and stylistic) connections — that is, a word as a phenomenon.

At this point we can once again emphasize the active function of language: not only does it enable communication, but at the same time it helps shape the world. It creates an analogous linguistic world that enables speakers to find their bearings in the world and to intervene in it as subjects.

2.1.2.3. Grammatical Tenses as Constructs of Reality

The quality of language as a structure that makes possible an active orientation in a world that human beings do not have in their power, because they live in it (i.e., they are within this world), can best be seen in the function of grammatical tenses. It may seem to us that the terms "past," "present," and "future" designate a universal experience, but this is an illusion. Only the present is directly attainable. This is not a "chronological" present, which in fact does not exist, because it continually, without any time lapse, sinks into the past before we are able to be conscious of it. Consciousness, in this sense of time, lags a long way behind reality. What in practice can be considered as the present is what we perceive directly for a certain time and maintain in our consciousness. We thus reckon with a certain limited fixed character of the present. It is possible to speak of a present that also has a "retention" and a "protention" (anticipation). This is the present as a phenomenon, the present seen phenomenologically.

We come up against an obvious problem, however, when we ask what the past is. We know that the past used to be, that it was. But what does it mean to say that it "was"? "Was" and "will be" are linguistic categories. Let us first examine the past. The fact that something was cannot be defined by direct verification. From experience we know that some things in our mind can no longer be verified using the senses. They cannot be made part of the present, although we are still able to imagine them. In the present we capture the past through the image of memory and the future in a vision that expresses our expectation. I am able to describe our house and my room; I know what they looked like this morning. But as such they cannot be reached by the senses; they live only in my memory. Things are here only as they are now. The past is the past of something that in some way impinges on the present and affects us; without this link with the present, it vanishes into the darkness.

If we express in words an image of the past that, in some way difficult to define, is part of human consciousness, then language creates appropriate grammatical categories for this image. Grammatical tenses make it possible to classify those things that appear in our mind and are no longer the present. The past, too, can be captured, provided its traces (objects that originated in the past, memories, or records) are preserved in the present. They can be preserved either in a form that is directly accessible (buildings or nature are relatively unchanging parts of the past that carry on into the present), or they can be "wrapped up" in our memory, from which they can be brought into the present by a conscious act of recall (this also applies to searching in archives, looking at old texts or letters, and so on). However, the way in which we classify these data and phenomena, the way in which we speak about the past or the present, is to all practical purposes a matter of intentionality and language. The separation into a grammatical past ("was") and future ("will be") is a classification, a pattern, by means of which language expresses a certain important experience in our orientation in the world, one that is independent of language itself. When we speak of the past, we know that we are concerned with something real, something that is not just an illusion but that is no longer accessible. We also know that what we count on as the future has many features that are derived from our experience, and that it "can" become the present. However, neither past nor future can be captured in objective records. From the viewpoint of our present experience, they are things that are no longer or are not yet, but that can be captured by means of memory or can be "expected."[21]

> Yesterday is but today's memory
> and tomorrow is today's dream.
>
> (Khalil Gibran, 1883-1931)

Assigning things to the past or the future, this grammatical classification forms a working image of the world in which we can place things that come to our mind in different places, where we will be able to find them again in our memory. It is an indispensable support for our life, and we have clear notions that we associate with it. We imagine time as moving further behind us, the future as being in front of us. In some cultures we come across other notions, but spatial notions, which are inspired by language (referred to as quasi-spatial images),[22] can originate only in a setting where there is a

---

21. See J. Ebach's interpretation of the relation between present and past according to W. Benjamin, "Vergangene Zeit und Jetztzeit," *Evangelische Theologie* 52 (1922): 288-309.

22. Lat. *quasi*, "as"; *spatium*, "space."

certain elementary linguistic culture.[23] Quintilian, a Roman rhetorician and contemporary of the apostle Paul, recommends, as an aid to remembering things, that people use the image of a house, and that they place individual events and facts into the different rooms (*Orat.* 11.2.18-22).

Excursus: Augustine's Reflections on Memory

Seizing hold of time, which passes us by into the past, which cannot be directly grasped — this is a question that the great theologian Augustine (354-430) devoted his attention to in his *Confessions*. All later aphorisms about time, including the one by Khalil Gibran that we have just quoted, are influenced by him directly or indirectly. In his reflections, Augustine considered the fact that the division of time into past, present, and future, which we take for granted, becomes a problem as soon as we have to express it and explain it to someone else. The future is not yet here (it exists only in our expectations), and the past, from our vantage point, tends toward not being (it exists only in our memory, in our recollections) — every event "vanishes" into the past *(tendit non esse)*. It is as though the whole of reality came out of a mysterious hiding place and immediately disappeared back into it. This is a way of observing things that is most obviously similar to that of twentieth-century phenomenology.

But since past and present are preserved in our minds, then they must be "something" (*quae si nulla essent, cerni omnino non possent* — if they were nothing, then it would not be possible to distinguish them — *Conf.* 11.17). For us, this means that language "takes place" (is spoken) now, but at the same time it is possible now, through the medium of language, to perceive our own life as moving from the past into the future. This linguistic span, this extension of the present, also enables us to recognize the borders of our lives and to live with them. We live with an awareness of our own mortality, and with this awareness we are able to plan our lives. Animals are also aware of threats to their life, but only if they encounter something which they have already experienced as being life-threatening (such as beasts of prey, hunters, or the elements), or possibly if they remember it in dreams. It is not very likely that a dog warming himself in the sun in front of his kennel spends any time wondering how many days or years of life here on earth are left to him.

Augustine develops what we would today call phenomenological observa-

---

23. The description of these concepts is one of the most important philosophical contributions of Henri Bergson (1859-1941).

tion when he examines how the past is preserved in the human mind and how the human mind is directed toward the future. He demonstrates this with the example of somebody singing a song that he or she knows: the whole of the song is present in the singer's mind as a phenomenon — we might say "as if it were wrapped up" — but its reproduction (unwrapping) is transformed into expectation. We know that a song that we start to sing is something that is "in front of us." It becomes the present only for an instant, and then a larger and larger part of the song disappears into the past again as we sing it (*Conf.* 11.28).

The first part of resolving this problem lies in the observation that people measure time in their mind and thus in fact measure the effect made on them by what they are measuring (*Conf.* 11.27). The mind is thus present passively (perceiving) but also actively (preserving), and its intention includes various parts (or various degrees) of reality. In this way the past becomes the present in the mind's intention. But as soon as we no longer devote any attention to it, it disappears again into the darkness of the past, as is the case with singing the song. This is a problem. Does the reality of something that is not the present depend only on us? Here Augustine's thinking seems for a moment to be close to some trends in modern philosophy of existence or consistent constructivism. In the end, however, Augustine does answer the question after all, even if only in a roundabout way, in the form of a concluding prayer in which he abandons the genre of critical reflection on time in order to reflect on the whole issue with a greater sense of detachment in a relation of prayer with God. This greater sense of detachment has both an advantage and a disadvantage in that the author can reproduce his new viewpoint only in the form of a personal testimony, not as a conclusion that has been arrived at logically:

"What is man that you are mindful of him [O God — P.P.]?" (Ps. 8:4, quoted in Heb. 2:6). The eternal nature of God is his hope, his future, toward which his life is directed: . . . *donec in te confluam purgatus et liquidus igne amoris tui* — until I am united with you, cleansed and transformed by the fire of your love — *Conf.* 11.29. Let us pause and consider what this means: his spirit turns to God, to the one in whose mind ("memory") live the past, the present, and the eschatological (ultimate, final) future. Our time is thus an unfolding of eternity. From God's viewpoint the things that lie beyond our horizon can be seen. God's word (the Word) not only makes these facts present in the memory (i.e., in God's memory) but also creates and guarantees their existence (§4.3.1). Only God's present is so "extended" that it includes the whole dimension of time (i.e., is eternal).

For Augustine, then, the reality of the time construct is rooted in God. His experience with his own memory encourages him to follow this line of thought,

The World of Language

although he does not see it as an analogy. God certainly does not experience things in the same way as people do, because he is the Creator (*Conf.* 11.32). The inherent human understanding of what the time construct relates to and what gives it its inner justification is a question of a personal, existential relationship directed toward something that includes overcoming previously fragmented perspectives *(until I am united)*. And because it is a personal relationship, it is possible and necessary to speak of this relationship as a matter of trust (faith), and of its counterpart as a person, as someone who goes beyond previously fragmented perspectives — in other words, as God *(until I am united with you)*. The linguistic egocentrism remains authentic: the writer speaks in the "I" of the first person. But he yearns to be transformed (remolded) into God's present: his human memory and expectation thus reach fulfillment in something that is not — not because it is an illusion, but because it is "not yet" our present. Faith here imagines itself as a heuristic (searching) passion that counts on experiencing doubts and risks as well. God is not just the source of personal hope but is also truth — the one who guarantees the meaning of existence (the Creator).

This reference to Augustine's solution is in a certain sense a premature attempt at a solution. We shall see that other schemes do not say anything about the question of the reality of past and future time but concentrate on a timetable for the human life in time limited by the foreseeable horizon of death. In our context, however, Augustine's examination of memory indicates a problem with a scope that goes beyond what is admitted by, for instance, philosophy of existence. The question of understanding, which any interpretation of old texts must inevitably lead to, goes right to the very essential issues of philosophy and theology. We will deal with this fundamental problem of hermeneutics in chapter 4.

We have taken language as our starting point because the linguistic milieu in which we live is the wider framework for the written and printed text, to which we will of course have to keep in the following chapter. And because language is a more general phenomenon than the world of the text, it is necessary to start with at least a brief description of its structure and the basic possibilities for understanding it.

Before we start with these reflections, it is important to stress something that, while it is a generally known fact, is often in fact overlooked. This is that language is not only a means of communication but also a means of thinking.[24] Thinking people become knowing people only when they speak their thought in

---

24. In the introductory paragraphs of his "Hermeneutik," Schleiermacher defines the act of speaking as the outward dimension of thinking (p. 137).

their mind.[25] Everything that we have said about its active function in ordering human reality leads inevitably to the basic conclusion that language is not only a means of external communication but also a means of internal, unspoken, monologue, and thus of human deliberation, thinking, and reflection.

2.2. The Question of the World of Language (or, From Syntax to Pragmatics)

BIBLIOGRAPHY

Greenwood, David. *Structuralism and the Biblical Text*. Berlin: Mouton, 1985.
Güttgemanns, Erhard. *Einführung in die Linguistik für Textwissenschaftler*. Vol. 1. Bonn: Linguistica Biblica, 1978.
Patte, Daniel. *Structural Analysis for New Testament Critics*. Minneapolis: Fortress Press, 1990.
Ricoeur, Paul. *Du texte à l'action*. Paris: du Seuil, 1986. ET *From Text to Action* (Evanston, Ill.: Northwestern University Press, 1991).

2.2.1. From Speech to Language, from Narration to Structure

In the context we are considering, the question of grammatical tenses is important because the separation of experience into present, past, and future is also a basic precondition for narration, which is the genre used for many important texts and which is, as we shall see, quite crucial for the structure of the biblical canon.

We already know that the construction of grammatical tenses and literary forms is concealed below the heard or seen "surface" of a text.[26] This is a feature of language that is a hidden part of speech and cannot be read from it directly. Linguistic structures, which enable us to organize events, narrated stories, and images that appear in human thought (memory and projection), are imposed on human experience from within human thought, from historical tradition. They are not an immanent part of reality. They are spectacles through which we view reality. Or we could say that linguistic structure is an outline that can be aligned to any text so that we can orient ourselves in

---

25. Merleau-Ponty, *Phenomenology of Perception*, 177; cf. J. H. Charlesworth, "Polanyi, Merleau-Ponty, Arendt, and the Foundations of Biblical Hermeneutics," in *Interpretation of the Bible*, ed. J. Krašovec (Sheffield, Eng.: Sheffield Academic Press, 1998), 1531-56, here 1542.

26. Greenwood, *Structuralism*, 6.

it. The opposite is not true; for example, a narrated story is not an illustration of the time axis. That is just a backward reflection of the function of language, an attempt to uncover the "unconscious logic of speech" formed by language. By analyzing it we can come to know one elementary, intersubjective (shared between people) and at the same time complex dimension of experience, which can connect us with the world of the text. Paul Ricoeur has pointed out the basic similarity between the role of the unconscious described by Sigmund Freud and this hidden dimension of language.[27]

Uncovering the unconscious logic of speech starts by phrasing it and separating a written text into paragraphs, sentences, and words. We do all this ourselves subconsciously. How deeply this phrasing is rooted in human experience with language can be seen in critical editions of texts from antiquity. Manuscripts in antiquity did not use punctuation to separate words and sentences. Nevertheless, reconstructing them does not usually cause any great problems, and in critical commentaries we find only a small number of significant alternatives in punctuation. The situation changes only when we are concerned with the overall literary strategy and meaning of the work as a whole — with structures formed intentionally and specifically for a particular text. What we call the meaning of the work cannot be examined without an attempt to reconstruct the pragmatics of the text (see below, §2.2.2), which can be uncovered only by means of systematic interpretation.

We said at the beginning that language is concealed behind speech, of which it is the internal organization, and we now need to state (or in fact just remind ourselves of the fact once more) that speech, especially dialogue and narrative — in other words, the consciously shaped dimensions of a text — in its turn influences language.[28] From this follows an important rule for interpretation: **When interpreting any text, it is necessary to have in mind an analysis of its content, that is, to consider what is being talked about in the text. An important part of interpretation, and in most cases its starting point, is therefore to paraphrase what is related in the text (if it is a narrative one) or its argumentation (if it is a discursive one).**

From what we have just outlined about the basic function of language, we can derive observations that call into question certain aspects of some concepts of language and especially of literature, above all the concept known as constructivism, a consistent structuralism. Constructivism bases itself on the assumption that language is a set of generally valid structures.

---

27. Ricoeur, *De l'interprétation*, book 3, chap. 1.3.
28. Saussure, *Cours de linguistique générale*, 54.

They might be described as something analogous to formalized Platonic ideas. This sort of theory, which in the twentieth century was called the theory of universal grammar, has parallels in the ideas of the Sophist Protagoras (486-416 B.C.) and in medieval Scholasticism.[29] Constructivism fits the whole area of human experience into a framework of systems that are constructed by the structures of our perception. Apart from the linguistic construction, which we have already mentioned, the main one is the construction of the senses. Our senses are not a direct mirror of reality, but they transform it by means of the central nervous system in a similar way to that in which a digital recording transforms the reality to which it relates. Well-known examples are pictures that reconstruct how a certain phenomenon, accessible through the senses, is seen by a horse or an ant, in contrast to the way a human sees it.

It therefore cannot be denied that our perception is indirect and constructed, just like our communication. It almost seems as though the construction is more real than the world it relates to. Postmodern constructivism is correct inasmuch as, when interpreting a text, the question of the syntactic "how" often becomes part of the answer to the question "what": grammar directs itself at the basic relations and dimensions of human life, what are known as anthropological universals. What is important is not how we make use of this basic linguistic ability (its "performance") but the fact that we have it, that we live in a linguistic world and are capable of communicating with others in it (what is known as linguistic "competence"). Such a view of a system also has a certain tendency to seek out the most universal features in what the text says: a piece of age-old wisdom rather than a story. A consistently structural concept of language (known as the C-paradigm) leads exactly in this direction.[30]

We have already indicated that language is not only the setting for our human life but is also capable of referring outside itself, to speak "about something" (see §§2.2.2, 3.7.2, 4.4, 5.4 — on reference) and thus to qualify its own autonomy and to reveal that its structures are simply functional (i.e., perform a service) in relation to reality. This is an argument that must cause systems theory to look at things differently, too. From what we have said, we cannot infer that when interpreting a text we must look only for a grammati-

---

29. E. Güttgemanns, "Linguistisch-literaturwissenschaftliche Grundlegung einer neutestamentlichen Theologie," *Linguistica biblica* 13-14 (1972): 2-18, here §46.

30. This approach is associated with the work of Noam Chomsky, the father of generative grammar. In the Czech context his work has been followed up by E. Hajičová.

cal or rhetorical structure in it. Basically, we already know that such a structure does exist, and we also know that it has its logical "broad dimensions" in the syntax and, to a certain extent, in the literary genre of every text. But we shall have to deal with a further aspect of the text — the question of whether and to what extent the text has a referential function (in that it refers to certain events), and in what way this function is connected with its reflective function (considering things retrospectively).

Excursus: Structures and the Human World

Bibliography

Corvez, Maurice. *Les structuralistes*. Paris: du Seuil, 1969 (a critical essay on structuralism).
Eco, Umberto. *A Theory of Semiotics*. Bloomington: Indiana University Press, 1979.
Greimas, Algirdas J. *Sémantique structurale*. 1986; 2d ed., Paris: Larousse, 1995.
Luhmann, Niklas. *Soziale Systeme. Grundriss einer allgemeinen Theorie*. Frankfurt: Suhrkamp, 1984.

We have already said that language is not the only encoding system (in the excursus on semiology in §2.1.1). But nor are encoding systems the only structure that people are able to define, help shape, and make use of. All this is not obvious. Only after language had been analyzed as a system was the crucial stimulus and inspiration provided for examining structures more generally and the way they functioned with other phenomena. We need to pause a moment to look at this phenomenon, which represents structures as being from a certain point of view a superior category to encoding systems. Research in the twentieth century discovered certain analogous features in various fields that were often far removed from each other.

In the literary field, for example, we can point to the work of the Russian folklorist Vladimir Yakovlevich Propp (1895-1970), who defined folktales as systems combining a limited number of functions, of which he found thirty-one in his study "Morphology of the Folk Tale."[31] In §2.4.2 we shall mention similar analyses of the functions of myth.

The Austrian doctor and psychologist Sigmund Freud (1856-1939) devoted considerable thought to the structure of the human unconscious, which plays the

---

31. Vladimir Y. Propp, *Morphology of the Folk Tale* (trans. from Russian; 1st Eng. ed., 1928; repr., Austin: University of Texas Press, 1968), part 1, chap. 3, table of folk tales; part 1, appendix 1.

role of intermediary between basic archetypes linked with the beginning of life and the longed-for adventure of certain situations in life. His work influenced European thought in the twentieth century, and Paul Ricoeur devoted critical attention to him in relation to grammar and problems of interpretation.[32]

The French sociologist Claude Lévi-Strauss (1908-2009), influenced by linguistic structuralism, developed a theory of thought in native societies and the related social relationships; the Chilean biologist and philosopher Humberto R. Maturana (b. 1928) developed an analogous theory of the system of natural chains, which included the observer "I"; and the German sociologist Niklas Luhmann (1927-98) formulated a systems theory as a general hypothesis on the nature of reality, which protects itself from chaos and entropy by means of systems. He concentrated on the "life-world" and especially on social systems. These come into being through an "agreement" between at least two links, for example, husband and wife, allies, producer and customer. Their relationships grow into a chain and network of relationships creating systems and subsystems that merge into one another. Each of them serves its environment; for example, a communication system serves vehicles or boats that travel along roads, railways, or rivers. A system reacts to stimuli in its environment and assimilates them as a system, as a chain, in which we cannot work in a clear-cut way with the terms "cause" and "effect."

In this context, language should be defined as a specific system that facilitates communication between society and the systems of intellectual life.

On closer inspection of the complexity of such a system, which language undoubtedly is, we see that the structure in such a case is indeed a system of paths in the extensive space of our consciousness, paths that resemble each other in their arrangement, and the most interesting feature of which is their unique surrounding. We therefore cannot hope to create exact methods in the humanities and social sciences on the basis of structuralism.

When the structuralist Noam Chomsky describes the creativeness of language — the fact that every speaker of a certain language is able to form a sentence that has never been formed before, but that is still a signal that other speakers of the same language can understand, although they have never heard it before[33] — he is at the same time formulating the function of linguistic struc-

---

32. Ricoeur, *De l'interprétation*, book 3, chap. 4.1. Freud's theory had already been applied to language by F. de Saussure; see E. Güttgemanns, "Der redende Mensch als unbewußter Schachspieler," *Linguistica biblica* 47 (1980): 93-130.

33. N. Chomsky, *Current Issues in Linguistic Theory* (The Hague: Mouton, 1964), 212; a similar statement had already been made by Ernst Fuchs, *Hermeneutik* (Bad Cannstatt: Müllerschön, 1954), 129.

tures: it is a fundamentally open system, capable of indicating new experiences.[34] In a certain sense language can be said to be in advance of direct perception of objectively perceptible reality, but it is here because of that reality and returns to it. This is clear and logical, but so far it has not been sufficiently appreciated as a significant function of language. It might be said that it was already foreshadowed in the thinking of the Johannine writings in the New Testament. We can recall these two statements from the first chapter of the Gospel of John: "In the beginning was the WORD. . . . And the word became flesh" (John 1:1, 14).

2.2.2. Pragmatics

In the elementary form of a statement, we can distinguish its pragmatics as well as its lexical and grammatical aspects. In some academic literature pragmatics is defined as the intention behind the utterance or writing of a particular statement. When analyzing structures, we prefer to speak about function, that is, about how particular texts work. This is because intention is not something we can verify; indeed, the kind of structural analysis that aspires to come as close as possible to the exact sciences avoids the category of intention on principle. Thus — every linguistic expression has a function. We have already talked about this in connection with the sentence, and even the larger text (the macrotext) can be defined according to its genre, that is, according to whether it is a text supposed to entertain or to teach, to warn or to please. Often, however, there is also a need to locate the text in a particular environment, to establish its function in a concrete situation. In all cases we must be aware that every statement and specifically any written statement came into existence for a particular reason. It wants to convey something (it has a communicative function) and also wishes to change something. It is not an activity guided by a reason but rather by a motivation.[35] We say only what "is worth saying." This is true of such banal words as "I'm going to buy some bread rolls" as well as of serious statements such as the text of a constitution, for example, or a declaration of faith. The concepts of language that are primarily interested in the pragmatics of the text are sometimes classified together as the P-paradigm Group (matrix P).[36]

---

34. Cf. P. Ricoeur, "Structuralisme, idéologie et méthode," *Esprit,* May 1967, 801-21, here 812-13.

35. Ricoeur, *Du texte à l'action,* 189.

36. The other attitude, concentrated on the structural dimension of a phenomenon (construct), is called C-paradigm.

Hermeneutics as a Theory of Understanding

One fact must be borne in mind, however — that to fulfill their basic pragmatics, texts must convey a certain amount of information. This information can be exploited in other contexts as well and so contains a certain "surplus" meaning. Interpreters must be aware that a surplus of this kind exists even if they lack knowledge of all its dimensions. They can even exploit it, because we can ask texts questions that the author himself or herself was not trying to address and that are only the unconscious margin of the author's pragmatics. Nonetheless, interpreters must not forget the nature of the pragmatic of the text, and the contexts in which the text came to speak of other phenomena. For example, the gospel story of the suffering of Christ can incidentally provide us with some information on the topography of the Jerusalem of the time or on execution by crucifixion, but we must keep in mind that we are learning this in a particular context that may have affected the secondary information by overshadowing it in terms of importance. As far as the topography of Jerusalem is concerned, we are learning only what would have been enough to localize the events related for the reader of the time. Furthermore, this is a narrative governed by the narrator's idea, which is above all his idea of where the events must have taken place. Then again, the description of Jesus' death on the cross is to a certain extent influenced by interest in having the reader recognize in it the fulfillment of certain expectations of the day associated with the arrival of the Messiah. In the oldest layer, Jesus at his interrogation is silent as a sacrificial lamb in accordance with Isaiah 53:7 (Mark 14:61), while the inscription above the cross bears the paradoxically true title "King of the Jews" (Mark 15:26 and par.). According to the Gospel of John, Jesus' bones were not broken, as was the usual practice to ensure that the convicted died a quicker death, because Jesus died before the point at which this would have been done. The reader is supposed to understand by this that Jesus died a true paschal lamb, for the paschal lamb's bones were never broken (Exod. 12:46). Yet again, the soldier pierces the side of the dead Jesus, and it gushes with water and blood, which is a clear symbol of the two main sacraments, baptism and the Table of the Lord (Eucharist), based on Christ's sacrifice (John 19:33-34).

Thus the decisive role of the pragmatics of a text does not entirely invalidate the other functions of the text that the interpreter can uncover, although usually the latter functions are indirectly once again in the service of the pragmatics.

2.2.2.1. The Author and the Pragmatics of the Text

We have already said that it is not easy to verify what the author was thinking, "what he meant."[37] Indeed, according to thoroughgoing structuralism, it is impossible and is known as the "intentional fallacy." Yet, it is almost always possible to tell how the text worked on its surroundings. These two aspects cannot be separated (as some linguistic theories demand), but it is still necessary to make a distinction between the intention of the author and the pragmatics of the text. The intention of the author, which can be reconstructed only indirectly, is usually close to the pragmatics of the text but is a fundamentally broader concept. "I am going to buy bread rolls" might mean simply that the speaker wants to satisfy his own hunger, but he might, for example, be wanting to offer them to a guest. All that is certain is that he is going to buy bread rolls. Just as it is fundamentally evident to us that the intention of the author is close to the pragmatics of the text, it is equally evident that we can never fully excavate the intention of the author from analysis of the text itself. Readers can reconstruct it for themselves in any way that is not contradicted by other knowledge about the text, but they can never exclude a different reconstruction that meets the same criterion.

At the end of the last section we spoke of the significance of internal analysis, and we can now take another step and state that **the basic aim of content analysis is the identification of the pragmatics of the text**. *Pragmatica,* actually "practical intention," is the impulse that the text (and in smaller measure, of course, the separate parts of it) introduces into human experience. If we are exploring pragmatics, we ask in which direction, in which way, and with what intensity a given text wants (wanted) to intervene in the world and change it. In some way it changes the world in any case. Its actual effect, however, does not always correspond to its pragmatics. A text may be abused or unintentionally placed in contexts that are alien to it. This is why it is important to look for its original, peculiar pragmatics. The basis of pragmatics is already given in the elementary units of argumentation: an invitation and its acceptance expressed in simple phrases (exchange), for example, already involve an easily perceptible shift in relations.

37. I must refer here to the famous passage in J. Žák's book *Študáci a kantoři* [Pupils and Teachers], 19th ed.: "The teacher forces the children to explain in plain and simple words what the poet actually wanted to say, although it is an open secret that the poet usually does not know this himself. The poet is just simply singing away to himself" (Prague: Československý spisovatel, 1968), 58-59.

In order to be able to grasp the pragmatics of a text, we need to have a good knowledge of the time and conditions in which it originated, for otherwise we shall fail to identify how it actually functioned at the time.

2.2.2.2. Communicative and Noncommunicative Texts

In the light of these observations, there seems to be no justification for the division of texts into the categories of communicative and noncommunicative, that is, written for the author's own needs, such as private notes, for example, or private poetic or philosophical reflections on the self. The author and reader are one and the same in a case of this kind — an elision that might seem to support the idea of the noncommunicativeness of this type of text — but since we think in language, it is still first necessary to objectify our own thought in text in order to create it at all and be able to remember it. A written text is also in principle accessible to other people, since otherwise the question of noncommunicative texts would never arise. The notion of noncommunicative texts in fact assumes that someone other than just the author often encounters such texts.

In considering the hermeneutic process itself (§§3.8–5.5.2), we shall learn that any text can in some way serve our understanding of ourselves, and so even interpretation of purely private texts has meaning.

2.3. Hermeneutics, Transformational Grammar, and the "Future" of the Text

BIBLIOGRAPHY

See bibliography for §2.2.

At the start of this paragraph we shall define further steps that will get us closer to the problem of hermeneutics itself — to the problem of interpretation and the theory of interpretation. From the hermeneutic point of view it is clear that the interpretation of a text means above all the explanation of its function. From the point of view of positivism, which had a major effect on our thought in the nineteenth century and part of the twentieth, the main problem of interpretation was to answer the question, "What really happened?" This, however, is not of itself interpretation. Not only is it often an impossible task ("What really happened to Red Riding Hood?"), but above all it does not address the question of why things happened in one way or another, and in what contexts they happened. Even so precise a visual record as a photograph needs to be selected and interpreted.

If we continually point out that in interpreting a text it is impossible to get away from the field of language, this is not because we want to interpret statements and texts as no more than some kind of linguistic constructs, but because language is also necessarily a medium of interpretation. The conclusion that follows from the identification of language as a construct necessarily leads on the one hand to the finding that we reached earlier: that we can see interpretation inter alia as the linguistic transformation of the macrotext (the coherent textual whole, part, or segment) that we are interpreting (§2.1.2). At the same time, we cannot but notice one significant fact, namely, that **language itself has the power to indicate that the world of structures in which we live is not entirely autonomous**. It has its own extraterritoriality. It is capable of speaking "about something," of opening up to the reality that is the "environment" ("surrounding") of its structure.

We have therefore established that the text incorporates both concrete stories and statements and at the same time structures — general and nonaccidental.[38] **What is the relationship between these two sides of each text?** This question is one that we shall answer in the chapter on the text, after analyzing several other phenomena of linguistic communication.

2.4. Symbol and Metaphor

BIBLIOGRAPHY

Lotman, Jurij M. *Major Issues in Narrative Theory.* Vol. 1. London: Routledge, 2004 (Russian original, 1964).

Ricoeur, Paul. *L'herméneutique biblique.* Introduction and translation by F.-X. Amherdt. Paris: du Cerf, 2001.

———. *La métaphore vive.* Paris: du Seuil, 1975. ET *The Rule of Metaphor in Language: Multi-disciplinary Studies of the Creation of Meaning in Language* (Toronto: University of Toronto Press, 1977).

———. "Le symbole et le mythe." *Le Semeur* 61, no 2 (1963): 47-53.

Stern, Josef. *Metaphor in Context.* Cambridge, Mass.: MIT Press, 2000.

Wimsatt, William. *The Verbal Icon.* 2d ed. Lexington: University of Kentucky Press, 1967.

38. Previous discussion of this fundamental issue in hermeneutics is reviewed by William Wimsatt, *The Verbal Icon,* 2d ed. (Lexington: University of Kentucky Press, 1967), 69-83. Wimsatt himself is more inclined to the view of W. Blake, that generalization is not objective (73-74).

Hermeneutics as a Theory of Understanding

The symbol is a special linguistic phenomenon — "an expression with a double meaning, where the literal, immediate, physical meaning refers to a meaning that is hidden, metaphorical, existential, ontological, and so forth."[39] The symbol thus "summarizes" (Gr. *symballō*) information about a certain phenomenon or idea and a statement about its import or meaning. For example, a flag and state emblem (graphically formed and visual phenomena) are abbreviated statements of the reality and self-conception of a certain state. Generally symbols are classified among the stylistic devices consisting in the substitution of the meaning of words and used in poetry, rhetoric, and many complex literary genres. These are analogical means of expression, which originate from similarities between what is ostensibly expressed or stated, on the one hand, and, on the other, a thought (in Plato *dianoia*) or idea *(idea)*. The symbol is, then, a means of analogical expression.

Unlike allegory (from Greek *alla agoreuein* — to speak of something other), which does not just make substitutions for individual words but transposes whole episodes into a different environment (often telling a story about animals instead of people),[40] the symbol is concentrated on one emphasized feature about which the reader or listener also has a certain idea, and so its use presupposes an unwritten agreement on its meaning (a convention). This is because symbols draw their images from the basic experiences of the human being standing on the ground (fall, rise [up], receive, reject, overcome, fight, see, ahead, upward, grasp, leave, eat, drink, sleep, wake, and so on). To understand these as allegories means to tear them away from their basic and universally known meaning.

Usually symbols are replaceable by other, short verbal phrases. For example, if English soccer fans say, "Come on, you Blues!" they are expressing their support for Chelsea and at the same time alluding to the blue strip Chelsea players wear.

Today scholars talk less of symbol and more of metaphor in similar contexts. For a long time symbol was considered a concept only indirectly

---

39. Ricoeur, "Symbole et mythe."

40. Allegory is used in fables. The best-known teller of fables in ancient times was the semimythical Greek Aesop in the sixth century B.C.. The pseudo-Homeric hymns ("The War of the Mice and the Frogs" as a parody of the *Iliad*) date from almost the same time (seventh-fifth century B.C.). In modern times, allegorical fables have been written by the Frenchman Jean de Fontaine (seventeenth century) and the Russian Ivan Andreyevich Krylov (early nineteenth century), while in the twentieth century George Orwell wrote his famous *Animal Farm*.

The World of Language

connected with metaphor, or indeed superior to it. The academic terminology of linguistics, literature, and philosophy is insufficiently settled for us to be able to give a precise definition of the line between symbol and metaphor. Like symbol, metaphor is the use of a word in a figurative sense, in a sense different from its encoded function, its "literal" meaning. This is not, however, a generally familiar shift, but often a new combination, the metaphorical function of which consists precisely in its unexpected character. Metaphors also for the most part relate to words and cannot be visual emblems, as in the case of symbols. Together with metonymy (the use of a word objectively close to the literal meaning, for which it is substituted, for example, "I drank a whole glass") and allegory, metaphor in literary theory is classified among what are known as the tropes (the expression used by the Roman rhetorician Quintilian, who lived in the years A.D. 35-96).[41] In the Anglo-Saxon world the term used in this connection is "figurative language." Metaphor was defined in this broad sense by Aristotle (384-322 B.C.) in his *Poetics* (chaps. 21 and 22: 1457a-1459a). Aristotle supposes that metaphor is an alternative mode of expression, that it is "seeing the similar" (Gr. *to homoion*, *Poet.* 1459a). He seems to regard this kind of expression above all as a form of variation, a matter of adornment. Very often metaphor conveys an experience of intensity that is difficult to express in another way. For example, in Ancient Greece people used to say that someone had a "sea of money." This was not a symbol, with which metaphor can indeed sometimes overlap, but an established metaphor.

Because contemporary linguistics and literary theory have discovered the important role of metaphor in language and in thought, metaphor is now being talked about in a wider sense and is sometimes used metaphorically to denote analogical and figurative speech in general.[42] The Greek verb *metapherō* in its basic sense means "I transfer." (As a note of interest, in modern Greek *metaphora* means "transport.")

More often than other tropes, metaphor relates to experiences that need not be familiar to the hearer or reader of the metaphor and are represented precisely by the metaphor as a component of artistic speech (see

---

41. Quintilian's main work is *Institutio oratoria*, a textbook of rhetoric in twelve books (scrolls).

42. The famous German philosopher Immanuel Kant made the category "analogy" subordinate to that of metaphor in his *Kritik der Urteilskraft* (1790; ET *Critique of Judgement* [Oxford: Clarendon Press, 1978]); see H.-G. Gadamer, *Wahrheit und Methode*, 2d ed. (Tübingen: Mohr Siebeck, 1965; ET *Truth and Method*, 2d Eng. ed. [London: Sheed & Ward, 1989]), 71.

§3.8.2). Metaphors relate to something that cannot be defined in another way and thus also have a certain cognitive function; the use of metaphor can serve as an alternative orientation in the world. Sometimes metaphors of this kind are considered to be special symbols ("tensive," or open-ended, symbols),[43] which unlike true (i.e., substitutable) symbols ("steno," or narrow, symbols) are the messengers and representatives of a new reality.[44] This reality can be conveyed poetically.

At the end of the last chapter we said that it would be necessary to define the relationship of the deep structural, conservative, systemic, and archetypal functions of language to its ability to express new reality. In metaphor, then, we can most clearly demonstrate the mutual, dialectical nature of this relationship. Metaphor draws primarily on the basic experience of human beings and their bodily perception of the surrounding world and themselves as the relative center of the world, as we have just said in relation to symbol.[45] Metaphor, however, is better able to relativize this linguistic ego-centrism, for example, by speaking of what is counterposed to the human being in terms expressing dominance and at the same time a certain surplus that benefits all the rest. These are the metaphors of sun, light, or spring. Sometimes these are characterized as universal metaphors. In contrast to this kind, there are metaphors referring to crafts, machines, or specific social configurations that are characterized as metaphors associated with a particular culture (i.e., *culture-bound* metaphors). Even among these metaphors there is a group of metaphors that are relatively established, and one of their basic features is that they remain potent long after the circumstances in which they originated cease to apply. This is the case for example with metaphors originating in a clearly patriarchal environment (God as the father) or an outdated social structure (kingdom).[46] In these we can observe how a kind of "surplus of meaning" is part of the essence of the metaphor, and so it can work as metaphor with an altered emphasis even in the framework of another worldview. "Kingdom of

---

43. N. Perrin, *Jesus and the Language of the Kingdom* (Philadelphia: Fortress Press, 1976), 30. Perrin adopts the concept of the symbol held by P. Wheelwright, *Metaphor and Reality* (Bloomington: Indiana University Press, 1962), 130.

44. P. Ricoeur also assigns this duality to symbols conceived of in a broader way. See his "Existence et herméneutique," in *Interpretation der Welt*, FS R. Guardini (Würzburg: Echter Verlag, 1965), 32-51.

45. M. Johnson, *The Body in the Mind: Bodily Basis of Meaning, Imagination, and Reason* (Chicago: University of Chicago Press, 1987).

46. Anna Wierzbicka, *What Did Jesus Mean? The Lord's Prayer Translated into Universal Human Concepts* (Duisburg: Linguistic Agency University of Duisburg, 1995), 3.

God" is a fascinating metaphor of hope to this day, even when most political power is concentrated in democratic bodies.

We have already indicated that, in metaphors, familiar expressions or concepts and the experiences connected with them are set in new contexts and thus signal an as yet *un*common or even *non*existent reality hidden in an *in*accessible future, which influences us only *in*directly (metaphors then appear as "spaceships" in the spiritual realm). They break through the borders of our ordinary experiences, which are — as the reader may just have noticed — often conveyed by negatives.

The problem of metaphor resides in the fact that both written texts and speech are full of metaphors, and for precisely this reason language cannot be understood (only) as a coding system. Elements of a coding system are contained within language, but these are insufficient as a basis for explaining its function. Metaphor is a "strange phenomenon." Furthermore, because it is used where a great deal is at stake (in philosophy, religion, and — as we shall see — scientific hypotheses and theories), we need to devote special attention to it. It might appear that the generally religious environments in which metaphor so often appears compromise metaphor, and so it can have no place in a critical process such as theological or philosophical thought. We shall see, however, that metaphor is an essential part of language, and so the difference between science or faith on the one hand and dubious religions or ideologies associated with self-delusion on the other hand lies not in the use or exclusion of metaphor but in the way that metaphors are treated.[47]

Let us look first at the basic anatomy of metaphor. When we read in the Book of Judges (15:4-8) that Samson caught foxes, attached torches to their tails, and released them in the grain of the Philistines, we may wonder at the callousness and the ingenuity of the methods of war of the period, but it is clear to us that we are reading about a fox *(Vulpes vulpes)* or some imprecisely designated jackal — that is, this is about an animal. In contrast, when in Luke 13:32 Jesus says, "Go and tell that fox," which follows a comment to him by some Pharisees about Herod (Antipas), it is clear that this is a metaphor having the basic form "Herod is a fox" and that the statement in fact relates to a man. Why is it "clear"?

Views of metaphor have recently been diverging. On one side Donald Davidson denies any linguistic function to metaphor over that which is its literal (and false) meaning and, insofar as it is a disturbing phenomenon, regards

---

47. E. Jüngel, "Metaphorische Wahrheit," in *Metapher. Zur Hermeneutik religiöser Sprache,* by P. Ricoeur and E. Jüngel (Munich: Kaiser, 1974), 71-122, here 121.

it only as a kind of provocative impulse, something like a poke in the ribs.[48] On the other side Nelson Goodman emphasized that metaphor creates a new likeness, the creation and use of which is work, activity, and that, as such, metaphor has a cognitive function, is a linguistic phenomenon, and conveys a certain perception and message.[49] Goodman approaches metaphor in the framework of his concept of language as an autonomous structure, and so the relation of metaphor to reality is something that lies outside the range of his argument, but his work is inspiring as a starting point for further reflection.

2.4.1. The Cognitive Function of Metaphor

We have already shown that, just as no word can be precisely semantically defined outside the framework of the sentence (see above, §2.2), so a metaphor can be clearly identified as such only from the context and type of statement. Aristotle believed that the main function of metaphor was as ornament. It is certainly true that it is an aesthetic object, but as such it can also communicate a certain message (i.e., it has a cognitive function). It is used in poetry, but even there it is in many cases the bearer of a communication that is irreplaceable, that is, otherwise impossible to communicate at all, or only clumsily.

One situation in which metaphor appears is in relation to things of which the hearer has no direct knowledge. For example, when the first automobiles appeared (and naturally most people had no experience of them whatsoever), they were referred to metaphorically (apparently in a contradictory way) as "horseless carriages." This seems to be a calculated mistake in the categories used.[50] The basic metaphor was, then, "the automobile is a carriage without a horse." This was a precise expression of its appearance and function, but of course a metaphorical expression, because objectively what is distinctive about the automobile is above all the engine.[51] Soon,

---

48. D. Davidson, "What Metaphors Mean" (1978), reprinted in *Inquiries into Truth and Interpretation: Philosophical Essays of Donald Davidson* (Oxford: Clarendon Press, 1984), 245-64, esp. 246-47; a coherent interpretation of Davidson's views appears in Stern, *Metaphor in Context*, chap. 2.

49. N. Goodman, *On Mind and Other Matters* (Cambridge: Cambridge University Press, 1984), 71.

50. Ricoeur, *La métaphore vive*, chap. 4, part 2.

51. Consider the fact that a metaphor cannot be "converted." A carriage cannot be defined as an automobile drawn by horses.

however, automobiles because so common that the word "automobile" immediately conveyed to everyone what it means to every reader of these lines. In the Czech language "auto" was first an indeclinable foreign noun, but then it became naturalized to the extent that it even came to be declined as an ordinary Czech noun.

Some metaphors, then, are really irreplaceable. They do not summarize something that can be expressed in another way but are themselves part of the otherwise not fully expressible reality that they help to create.[52] Jesus' teaching developed around the metaphor "the kingdom of God." This is explained by other linguistic means that are narratives about something apparently different — Jesus talks of what the metaphor expresses in parables: "With what can we compare the kingdom of God, or what parable will we use for it?" (Mark 4:30). The parable can be understood as an elaborated metaphor. Most of Jesus' parables have a present part and at the same time a perspective into the future. Their pragmatics consist in the fact that they lead the listener to take into account a new horizon that can influence his or her decision making. The internal pressure that leads to the creation of the metaphor is a part of that which the metaphor represents: "Blessed are you who are poor, for yours is the kingdom of God," says Jesus to the people who stand before him (Luke 6:20). The change in their status has not yet occurred, but an alternative vision of the world is already in the world, and this is not just an "idea"[53] but a vision that genuinely influenced the present actions of many of those who took the metaphor "kingdom of God" seriously. Here we have reached an extreme case of the functioning of metaphor — its pragmatics (§2.2.2).

The communicative and cognitive function of metaphor includes its capacity to refer to phenomena and realities that go beyond ordinary experience and are hard to communicate by the lexical codes familiar to both sides. These are experiences that are particularly intense, experiences that are hard to test by ordinary forms of knowledge, experiences relating to the whole of which we ourselves are parts and that we therefore cannot grasp by objective description, with detachment, and experiences with new phenomena that have not yet or cannot be encoded in the lexicon. Metaphor connects sense and non-sense by suggesting the potential transfer of experience from one

---

52. Some scholars speak about replaceable and irreplaceable symbols (i.e., metaphors in a broader sense, including metaphors and parables).

53. See H. Weder, *Neutestamentliche Hermeneutik* (Zurich: Theologischer Verlag, 1986; 2d ed., 1989), 173-74.

area to another, but at the same time demonstrates that an exercise of this kind is dangerous unless we try to identify the true function of the new contexts. In this way metaphor impels to thought, to reflection. Among the phenomena that must be expressed by metaphor, Paul Ricoeur also classifies realities in which personal relationship, above all love, plays the crucial role.[54] From this point of view it is understandable that all religious speech is full of metaphors (God the Father, Son of God, Shepherd, redemption, sacrifice, rebirth, and so on).

This does not mean that such speech is for that reason unscientific or even antiscientific. The point is for theologians to be aware that they are working with metaphors and to work with them with precision — that is, to critically investigate their pragmatics in the given context. Let us therefore remind ourselves of some properties and possibilities of metaphor.

1. *Similarity and provocation.* In considering the anatomy of metaphor, we cannot but have noticed already that metaphor usually has or presupposes the form "subject — link — (metaphorical) predicate." Let us go back to the metaphor "Herod is a fox," which we mentioned earlier. Unlike a comparison (or parable as elaborated comparison), here the statement is not that Herod is *like* a fox.[55] The readers (or listeners) are taken aback. They know that there must be a certain resemblance here, and because they also know that Herod does not walk on all fours, they can quite easily deduce that Herod is *as cunning as* a fox. Or to put it more precisely, cunning as a fox is cunning in ordinary people's ideas and traditions. We can analyze the metaphor "Achilles is a lion,"[56] widespread in classical literature, in a similar way. Despite all its closeness to comparison and parable, metaphor differs from these kindred literary devices by its quality of provocation. It provokes the reader by not declaring the analogical character of the combination of words, by suppressing the connection "like," which is an essential part of comparison. Achilles was not an animal. "Is" is therefore ambiguous; in the literal sense it is false, but the metaphor has only to be spoken, and it demands attention. Metaphor also has certain features of the puzzle. If Achilles is not a lion in the sense of an animal, then he is a lion in the sense of pos-

---

54. P. Ricoeur and O. Bayer, *Liebe und Gerechtigkeit = Amour et justice* (Tübingen: Mohr, 1990), 64ff.

55. A sentence with "like" says almost the same thing as a metaphor, but it does not function the same way, since it does not provoke. See N. Frye, *The Great Code: The Bible and Literature* (New York: Harcourt Brace Jovanovich, 1982), 115-16.

56. Frye, *The Great Code*, 81, quotes from the Testament of Jacob in the Book of Genesis: "Issachar is a strong donkey" (Gen. 49:14).

sessing some qualities that we attribute to the lion. In the statement about Achilles as a lion, these are so material that the whole weight of the unexpected "is" is shifted onto them.

The theory of metaphor, which as we have noted was founded by Aristotle, distinguishes between different types of similarity — according to attributes: (fox, lion); according to quantity: (sea, beans on a plate), and so on. We have also noted that Aristotle classifies the other tropes (irony, the substitution of the individual for the species and the species for the individual, the substitution of the part for the whole and vice versa) as metaphor. For our purposes, these distinctions are not so important. What is crucial is that the unexpected "is" draws attention to similarities so urgently that it actually creates an affinity otherwise not perceived. In the theory of metaphor today there is much discussion about how metaphor arises. On one side of the debate are those who claim that the similarity or semantic affinity presupposed by metaphor is hidden in the lexical meaning and is just an unexpected application of its range stretched to the extreme limit. In this case the origin of metaphor would be essentially lexical. After all, we know (see §2.1) that the lexicon is a collection not of designations of individual phenomena but of whole categories, into which individual phenomena may be classified only at the price of considerable abstraction (a bird is an ostrich and a humming bird, an owl and a hen). Opposed to this approach is the view that metaphor is a matter of syntax, structure, and that practically any kind of expression can be exploited metaphorically (some linguists use the word "usurped") by appropriate use in context. It would seem true that the strategy of the creation of metaphors is basically a matter of structure. While it cannot be said that any word at all could be used metaphorically, when we are looking for metaphors the main consideration is not to identify a similarity that would occur to anyone and is extremely obvious, but rather an unexpected similarity — a similarity drawn to our attention only by the use of the metaphor itself.

Unexpected combination then produces a new meaning (what is known as "innovation"). Speech resists every new metaphor, fights against it because it offends against its ordinary logic, but in the end speech accepts it, uses metaphor, and so metaphor can then function as a usually returning expression for phenomena that are hard to codify. Metaphor thus intensifies perception, is directed to the fundamental, and draws attention to new phenomena and experience. This is the source of its cognitive function.

2. *The openness of metaphor.* For all its power and truthfulness, metaphor indicates that the reality that it represents transcends what the metaphor can express. Everyone knows that Achilles is not a lion in the sense of having

become an animal. Yet metaphor can transform this weakness into strength. It is obvious to the "recipients" (listeners or readers) that the reality suggested by what the metaphor describes cannot be expressed by the metaphor in full, that is, that the reality itself has an advantage on the metaphor. Metaphor can therefore (surprisingly!) encourage critical thinking. This has been a part of the Christian biblical tradition ever since the Jewish Bible (the so-called Deuteronomist's source) began to take shape in the period of the crisis of the ancient kingdom of Israel. In the pericope on the consecration of the temple we read, "But will God indeed dwell on the earth? Even heaven and the highest heaven cannot contain you, much less this house" (1 Kings 8:27; see also Isa. 66:1). In ordinary usage the temple was spoken of metaphorically as the house of God (e.g., Ps. 5:7), but where it was necessary to define its function precisely, another metaphor was employed — "a house for the name of the LORD" (1 Kings 5:5; see also 1 Chron. 22:8, 10). Although most readers of the Bible took these pictures "almost" literally, authoritative teachers were aware of their metaphorical nature. Here we have the beginnings of the critique of myth (§2.4). Metaphor is a fragment of myth that carries in itself the potential for the interpretation and relativization or secularization of myth. Metaphor can be replaced and defined as having only an indirect, analogical relation to reality.

3. *Replaceability.* There is a great deal of discussion today on the replaceability of metaphor. We have considered the way in which some metaphors have a cognitive function, and are analogical speech,[57] and it is only possible to paraphrase them briefly using another analogy. The simplest explanation is to replace the metaphor by a comparison: Achilles is *like* a lion. In the biblical example that we cited we would be able to explain Jesus' calling Herod a fox ("Say to the fox") by saying that Jesus regarded Herod as a man who was as cunning as a fox. Jesus would then had to have said, "Say to Herod, who in his cunning reminds me of a fox. . . ." This would already be less replacement than something close to explanation. Metaphor can therefore be explained, as we have just tried to do, but it can be concisely paraphrased only using another analogical statement. We have already shown that Jesus explained the nature of the "Kingdom of God" by speaking in parables: "The Kingdom of God is as if . . ." In so doing he is actually elaborating what the metaphor merely suggested, signaled, as a surplus of meaning. This

---

57. Some scholars, like J. M. Soskice, draw the line between metaphor as model and analogy (e.g., "God is gracious") (*Metaphor and Religious Language* [Oxford: Clarendon Press, 1985], chap. 6). From the literary point of view, we have a metaphor in both cases, with one of the tropes employing analogical language.

is why the tradition about Jesus is full of parables that suggest different features of the "Kingdom of God" — that is, the basic metaphor. The basic metaphor of the "Kingdom of God," however, links these together drawing attention to the fact that they all relate to one basic reality.

4. *Metaphor and technical terms.* Although at the beginning we talked about the fact that metaphors are often useful for expressing new experiences or a new phenomenon, we should point out that this is just a potential, not a rule. Not every new phenomenon needs to be expressed by a metaphor, or rather not every new phenomenon needs to be expressed by a metaphor that retains its metaphorical character. In cybernetics, for example, "chip" is a word that rapidly lost its original meaning of "splinter" and in untranslated English form has become an international specialist term that many computer users neither know nor need to know. It is enough just to learn how to work the computer. For this kind of new phenomenon it is necessary that a linguistic code should be found fast. Often these codes are derived from an original metaphor, but this plays only a short episodic role in their introduction. Such a phenomenon can be rapidly encoded precisely because it does not have to be known to a wider circle of users. There is no need to inform the public about it and spend time laboriously convincing people that it is useful to know the expression. It is enough for it to be known to the experts who already have experience of what it is that the code designates. It suffices that they can use it to communicate with each other, while others happily live without a knowledge that they do not need from day to day. The vocabulary of individual languages multiplies enormously with the inclusion of academic terms, but none of the speakers of any particular language either know or need to know it in its entirety. They know only what they need for their overall orientation in the world and what they need for their occupation. The argument from new codes in specialist technical language is therefore not an argument against the indispensability of metaphor.

We have already mentioned[58] that more frequently used metaphors can change into a word with a specific meaning, into a "term" or even a "technical term." "Tongue," "horsepower," to "grasp" the problem — all these expressions are actually metaphors just like "the Milky Way," "rebirth," or "enlightenment," but they are already "well-worn" metaphors that we do not notice as being metaphors because not even those who use them consciously work with them as metaphors. Yet even these words, when combined with other metaphors (e.g., "the Milky Way, that mysterious belt of light girdling

---

58. See point 1 above, "Similarity and Provocation."

our horizon") or pointed up by a context in which we focus on their metaphorical character (Nicodemus answering Jesus' words on rebirth with the question, "Can one enter a second time into the mother's womb and be born?" John 3:4b), can reveal the depth and importance of the metaphorical layers of our thought. These moments show that we are aware of only a fragment of the metaphors with which our linguistic world is woven through. The specific value of the social sciences (which today include philosophy and theology) is that they are aware of the role of the world of language in our orientation in the world and our understanding of ourselves and are conscious of its specific features, including its basic metaphorical nature.

A metaphor changes into a technical term everywhere that a certain community uses it repeatedly (in religious groups above all liturgically), as for example Christians use the metaphor "the kingdom of God" in the Lord's Prayer. The transformation of metaphor into technical term, however, is not irreversible. Some theorists claim that when metaphors reach the lexicon, they die, but this is not the case. In the middle years of the twentieth century a teacher who had acquired the nickname-metaphor "Erasmus" was teaching at a Czech grammar school. It soon became his name and a summary of all the marks of his character for most of the pupils. They therefore started to call one particularly gifted pupil "Little Erasmus." Especially the younger boys, who entered the school at eleven, had no idea of the original meaning of this nickname term. They thought that the strange-sounding name was just some exotic form supposed to distinguish him from the other teachers with the same surname. It was only when the history teacher in a lesson on humanism talked about Erasmus of Rotterdam and told his pupils that this was the origin of the nickname of his older colleague, the professor of Czech with his enormous range of learning, that the expression "Erasmus" reacquired the function of metaphor in their minds. In the same way, for example, Paul of Tarsus started to reinterpret Jesus' words on the kingdom of God when they had become ordinary terms of Christian teaching: "The kingdom of God is not food and drink but righteousness and peace and joy in the Holy Spirit" (Rom. 14:17). This is an interpretation of the term that once more engages with its metaphorical character. It is not to be ruled out that Paul was here correcting the enthusiastic expectations of the poor who saw the kingdom of God as a land where cake would fall into your mouth (see the beatitude of the hungry according to Luke 6:21), but the context suggests that some Christians in Rome had identified the faith with the observance of religiously motivated dietary prescriptions, which they believed opened up the path to the heavenly kingdom (Rom. 14:14a; Col. 2:20-22).

When interpreting the metaphor "the kingdom of God," Paul's pupils took a further step of a kind not taken, and clearly impossible to take, in the case of the "Erasmus" metaphor. Paul had decided to replace the teaching on the kingdom of God with a new interpretation, in which he usually spoke instead of a new age (Eph. 1:21 and elsewhere). This had the effect of making "the kingdom of God" a rarer, captivating guest in Christian vocabulary, one that retained its richness of meaning. In other words, it did not succumb to inflation. Claims that as metaphors become commonplaces they die as metaphors are therefore one-sided. A metaphor carries with it a lasting potential to manifest itself as an alternative project of the world. While in most cases metaphor relates only to a tiny slice of reality, if accepted and surviving in usage, it is the visible footprint of a world that envisages something of the kind. Moreover, the desire to create such metaphors is not only testimony to the confines of language as structure. "Its imperfection has, however, another aspect in that it positively creates the true infinitude of the spirit that aims above itself in an ever new spiritual process and precisely in doing so finds the freedom for ever new projects."[59]

5. *Metaphor in science.* It is good to be aware that, from the very outset, metaphors have found their way into the world of exact science, where, in terms of the ideas of the architects of that science, there ought to be no place for them. This is because while there is indeed little room for metaphor in the measurement or recording of individual experiments and observations, when the scientist has to interpret this data, metaphor emerges, often without its users even being aware of the fact. Thus not only does the astronomer, for example, speak of "black holes" and the zoologist or anthropologist of our position as "relatives" of the anthropoid apes and distant relatives of the half-apes, but even in the prefatory words to a scientific paper we often hear that research has made an important "step forward" but that there is still "a long way to go." These, of course, are metaphors that we no longer experience as metaphors and could be included in any conventional dictionary of style, but they have not entirely lost their metaphorical function. When combined in several statements, they put together a project of the world that is figurative (unverifiable in exact terms).[60] This is influenced to a great extent by the very structure of the language and the ideas that it conjures up in

---

59. Gadamer, *Wahrheit und Methode*, 403.
60. Some scholars call this phenomenon conceptual metaphor. This is the overall focus of the study by G. Lakoff and M. Johnson, *Metaphors We Live By* (Chicago: University of Chicago Press, 1980).

our culture (the future conceived as "ahead," the passage of time as a "path") and that differ fundamentally from scientific method. Where is "ahead" in the Einsteinian universe? How does one measure the length of the "path"?

The same applies to the fields of philosophy and theology. Here there is no need for everyone to be familiar with some of the technical terms, even though work in both these fields relates in principle to all human beings. Not everyone needs to know what a Qumranologist is (an expert on the texts from Qumran), or to know what soteriology is (a field of research that compares and interprets the various different ideas and concepts of human hope and salvation from alienation [sin] and death that derive from basic religious experience — in our context, most probably Christian or Hebraic). What is crucial is for people to gain a proper understanding of the texts that the experience of the church tells them are fitting expressions of the grounds of their hope.

Above all, these are all metaphors through which we communicate new experiences relating to the fundamental dimensions of human experience.

6. *The success of metaphor.* The question of the credibility or the authenticity of metaphor is one that arises on the margins of the discussion. Tomáš Kulka makes the claim that all metaphors are true and make a certain sense. What he actually means is that they are successful and convey something that is relevant and comprehensible to listeners, not that they are true in the sense of truth as normativity. They may in fact be parts of propaganda or the bearers of perverted ideals. Yet this is the case with any language that functions. What is decisive is that every metaphor is successful.[61] But even this is not an entirely precise definition. People can simply play with language and so produce a nonsensical, incomprehensible metaphor. That the rightness — or, to put it better, the success — of a metaphor is measurable only by its usage (i.e., by the fact that a poem in which such a metaphor is used, for example, is a success with the public, or the fact that it continues to be used as a metaphor in itself) means that we can really say that an unsuccessful metaphor does not exist. An unsuccessful metaphor does not survive. In this sense it is the same with metaphors as with jokes. Someone can think up a bad joke, but no one else will tell it again. A bad joke does not get into circulation.

7. *Metaphor as a project of the world.* Here we are approaching the character and function of metaphor in the widest sense. We have already

---

61. Davidson, "What Metaphors Mean," 113; T. Kulka, "Jak metafora vytváří své divy," *Filosofický časopis* 42 (1994): 403-20, esp. 405 and 418a (reply by N. Goodman).

seen that metaphor concentrates the attention of the listener on a certain phenomenon, placing it in the foreground and presenting it as something with a meaning that goes beyond the immediate context — as something that potentially provides orientation in broader connections. For example, if we say that Teresa is a little ray of sunshine, we are drawing attention to a certain good quality of Teresa's that has an influence on her environment. This quality is more important than the fact that Teresa is the daughter of Mr. Svoboda the butcher, that she is a blue-eyed girl, that she lives in the village, and so forth. We are saying even more, however, for we are saying that it is precisely on this phenomenon that we should dwell, that it touches more people, just as the sun shines on everyone, that here before us we have a phenomenon of importance — as it were, a part of another reality. This may be exaggerated, but literary theorists try to think through the implications of certain phenomena by taking them to the extreme, and metaphors really have arisen from dissatisfaction with the possibilities of the ordinary use of speech. We should be aware that the serious element of an alternative project of the world is present for example even in so banal a metaphor as the "slumbering forest." It is a figure of speech that today hardly gives anyone pause, but it is nonetheless an alternative to the approach to nature as the age-old setting of the struggle for life, at once source of subsistence and perpetual threat. Nature as terrifying environment — this is a picture that accompanied man for practically the whole period of his existence on earth as an animal species right up to quite recent times, and in some situations it survives to this day (storms, floods, harvest failure). At the same time, however, the metaphor of the "slumbering forest" has the potential to express protest and an alternative to the hard scientific approach to the world (the forest as a source of raw materials, the forest as an ecosystem). Thus metaphor shows a dimension of knowledge that is at the least as consequential as the undoubtedly essential critical scientific understanding. It is a dimension of knowledge filtered by the individual approach, which changes the accessible world, the whole "field" open to human perception, depending on the "mood" of whoever is perceiving it.

The statements in the first verses of the biblical Book of Genesis, concerning God as the creator of heaven and earth (1:1), originally had a similar function. This was not yet a matter of metaphor but was a "new" myth, a new image of the world that radically transformed the older mythical traditions. The new myth proclaimed the earth and cosmic phenomena, hitherto considered to be the fundamental deities, to be the creation of the God already encountered by Father Abraham according to earlier accounts, that is, as realities dependent on God in their being and their purpose. A new myth of this kind already starts to function in a way analogical to metaphor.

8. *Metaphor as analogy.* To understand this function of metaphor it is useful to think of metaphor as analogical to real models in physics, such as the well-known models of the nucleus of the atom,[62] where protons and neutrons are made out of wood or plastic and fixed together on wires, The replaceability of metaphor, which we considered in an earlier section, is the most marked manifestation of its analogical function. The wood and wire model of the atomic nucleus is not a picture of the nucleus but an analogy expressed by a symbol that works on the user in a way that is to a certain extent similar to the thing represented by it — that is, its metaphor.[63] The individual parts of the atomic model do not at all correspond to the shape, size, or distances of the phenomena in the real atomic nucleus, and their symbolic representation also excludes entirely a real speed of movement unimaginable to us. In point of fact this model has nothing in common with depiction, just as the fox running in the forest has nothing in common with Herod Antipas. Yet at the same time it is a model that expresses some fundamental features of the function of the atomic nucleus, just as the statement about Herod as fox shows us what we need to concentrate on when assessing his personality and government, what his most dangerous characteristic is, and what is evidently crucial in judging any political power.

One reason for the power and lasting appeal of the biblical metaphor of the kingdom of God lies in the way that it concentrates attention on the fundamental characteristic of credible hope: it must be a hope that is social in the deepest sense of the term. There has to be a similarity here between the last, eschatological future, which is always the main issue in relation to the kingdom of God, and the earthly kingdom, once a common form of government that now we know only from history textbooks. It is not that there would be soldiers and officials in the kingdom of God, or that there would be different social classes and estates. The poor will not be poor there, no one will be master or serf, and so the only thing in common between the earthly and heavenly kingdom is that the latter will be a social reality, social in the deepest sense of the word. God will rule in such a way that everyone will spontaneously do his will. This is a message of great importance, which distinguishes hope in the Christian traditions (in Judaism starting with the

---

62. See H.-G. Gadamer, "Sprache und Verstehen," in *Gesammelte Werke*, vol. 2 (Tübingen: Mohr, 1986), 364-77, here 371-72.

63. Ricoeur, *La métaphore vive,* chap. 4, part 4.

Hellenist period, and to some extent in Islam as well) from the concept of hope in other world religions, especially Buddhism, where hope consists in the denial or dissolution of individuality and, with it, suffering and care, and Hinduism, where the doctrine of reincarnation seriously relativizes the notion of the unique character and identity of the personality. In the metaphor of the kingdom of God, this conception is coded into the period picture of the world (heaven, earth, the underworld; the present age, the future age that will mean a cosmic transformation, etc.), which today we also see as metaphor, but the function is nonetheless evident: the human being with his or her unrepeatable face (see the metaphor of meeting "face to face" in the "new age"; 1 Cor. 13:12) and his or her own name (see the statement-metaphor of names recorded in the book of life; Phil. 4:3; Luke 10:20; Rev. 3:5) is the goal (definitive) value, and it may never be used in the name of God as a means to the achievement of anything else, such as progress or the classless society, nor may the value of the individual be relativized by the notion that he or she should prepare for merger with God. Apparently purely religious ideas can then be interpreted concretely and topically if we look at their original functions. This interpretation is by no means exhaustive but is an illustration of how metaphor can be explained and elaborated, and how we can enter into the "surplus of meaning," the presence of which is signified by the metaphor. Here the kingdom of God itself is just as similar and just as dissimilar to the familiar concept of a kingdom in the sense of a monarchy as the atomic nucleus is similar and dissimilar to models from the physics teaching closet.

According to the metaphor of the kingdom of God, the future of man is community with God, the possibility of entering into his presence, which is the enlargement and deepening of human sociability, and so also the confirmation of genuine individuality. We have already mentioned the fact that structure, machine, organism, and society can be created only from unique irreplaceable parts; when identical elements are put together, all that is produced is a mass.

On this basis we can now take a further step that can get us closer to the problem of interpretation. **To interpret a momentous text full of metaphors means to seek to understand the alternative project of the world that they presuppose and intimate. If we succeed in explaining the specificity of the alternative world concerned and its difference from our own notions, this is the decisive step that will allow us to subsequently provide a direct explanation of the meaning of the whole statement.** The continuing relevance of the thought of Rudolf Bultmann, about whom we shall have more to say at a later stage, lies in his demonstration that reconstruction of the period ideas that accompanied the creation of a text is the precondition for persuasive explanation. He did not fully appreciate the metaphorical character of text and spoke only of myth, but in terms of methodology he made an irreversible advance.

The critical interpretation of a particular text (in the interpretation of the Bible, the texts of its separate "books") means that we explain in modern speech how such a text functioned in the period when it was written and how it reflects its own function, while its systematic philosophical or theological interpretation means that we explain in the words of the present how it might and ought to function today.

2.4.2. Metaphor and Myth

Myth — Greek *mythos* "word, speech" — means a narrative, and in its more formal literary sense a narrative about the gods, how the world came into existence and how it will end, the foundation of societies and the origins of certain human activities and institutions. In contemporary religious studies, myths are divided into several basic groups. The most widespread classification is more or less pragmatic, that is, there are vegetative myths (representing the cycle of nature, on which man depends for his survival, e.g., the originally Egyptian myth of Isis and Osiris), dynastic myths (telling of the origins of the ruling power, e.g., the epic of Gilgamesh or Aeneas), and etiological myths (concerned with the origin of new activities, institutions, and their names, e.g., the Prometheus myths). The myth offers a view of the world that goes beyond ordinary experience, relates to the whole, and is accepted by the wider community. Like every narrative, a myth is a linguistic system, but in its claim to universality it is at the same time an interpretation of the meaning of all the expressions that can be created in human speech.[64] It is through the linking up of separate narratives into a continuous myth or cycle of mythic tales and their transmission from generation to generation that a society stabilizes, a common internal experience develops, and so myth becomes the internal anchorage of life. Its narrative form allows it to offer insight into the contexts and connections transcending everyday experience, while at the same time forming the frame of the everyday.

---

64. R. Barthes, *Mythologies* (Paris: du Seuil, 1957; ET *Mythologies* [New York: Hill & Wang, 1972]), 199; Barthes understands the function of myth as principally negative, as a deformation of reality (217-18).

The World of Language

Myth is the basic "matrix" through which sense can be made of individual life stories; it is the archetype, the ur-foundation of reality. The Greek philosopher Sallustius, a friend of the Emperor Julian, fourth century A.D. (not the Roman historian Sallust, or Sallustius), defined myth as something that "never happened, but always is" (*egeneto de oudepote, esti de aei;* from *De diis et mundo* 4). This is the basic feature of myth: enduring, ever-valid, approximating to the fundamental structures of life expressed by elementary grammatical relations. This insight was behind the efforts of the cultivated emperor Julian to establish a new interpretation of pagan cults to counter the victorious Christian campaign of his predecessor, politically backed by the church. He precisely identified the complete opposite to Christian faith. Myth relates to a sort of time above time *(illud tempus).*[65] It assumes that time moves in a circle, ever repeating and returning, thus giving the events narrated the character of reliability. To abandon this solid mythical base is perilous, and it can be rejected only with impunity, allowing man to enter into history, when our philosophy of freedom does not exclude God, when it has the grounding and with it the courage to be creative in a way that resists the dangers and tragedies of history and refuses to succumb to despair — so has written the Romanian-born American scholar of religion Mircea Eliade (1907-86) in one of his first major books.[66] Otherwise, to step into history is to step on perilous soil that disappears under one's feet. In addition to dreams (see above, §2.2.1), then, myth, fairy tale, and folk wisdom constitute the storehouse of the basic models of human behavior. This led the German religious writer Eugen Drewermann to the unambiguous conclusion that the point of interpretation of old texts is to reveal these archetypes, in which "God the Father," for example, represents the psychoanalytically verifiable "Super-Ego" — the hidden depths of being.[67] Behind historical incident he looked for examples and models of universally human-divine events. For the most part he was only repeating the penetrating structuralist analyses of biblical texts offered by the classics of this method.[68] But this fact itself confirms that Drewermann, a very popular writer in the 1980s, had identified several

---

65. Eleazar M. Meletinskij, *Poetika mifa* (Moscow: Nauka, 1976; ET *The Poetics of Myth* [New York: Garland, 1998]), chapter on structuralism.

66. Mircea Eliade, *Le mythe de l'éternel retour* (Paris: Gallimard, 1949; ET *The Myth of the Eternal Return* [New York: Pantheon Books, 1954]), closing paragraph.

67. Discussion of an author's psychology may serve as an escape from literary criticism per se; thus Wimsatt, *The Verbal Icon,* 57.

68. For example, Jean Starobinski, "Le démoniaque de Gerasa," in *Analyse structurale et exégèse biblique,* ed. R. Barthes et al. (Neuchâtel: Delachaux & Niestlé, 1971), 63-94.

authentic features of the hermeneutic process, specifically the way that the "figural" part of the metaphor mediates understanding, signifying the area to which a metaphor can refer. The statement itself, however — the *novum* — eluded him.

From today's perspective, myth is analogical speech and close to metaphor or parable in its function. It is also a picture of reality presented through a narration. The creatively reproduced myth — for example, in classical drama — could be experienced as the model of the ostensibly hidden framework in which the life of every spectator unfolded. In contrast to individual ideas and pictures of metaphors, the myth is an ordering of the world as a whole. Myth relates to something that has the same dimension as that to which language relates: an area in which we locate all our experience. Myth is coextensive with language. The disadvantage of myth lies in the fact that the narrator of a myth is not aware of its analogical function; because myth presupposes that the narrator identifies with it, we can see that myth itself denies us the possibility of standing back from it. It does not suggest its provisional nature, because its authoritative narrative style differs from the consciously artificial creation *(poiēsis)* that is intentionally only an imitation of reality (the novel or history book). The result is that a certain model of reality, useful at a particular time, is handed down by myth in conserved form and gradually changes into ideology. It becomes a dike against the uncovering of new realities and the creation of new projects of the world. The Homeric epics already display this kind of crisis of mythology. This is why it has often been supposed that myth was replaced by theology and philosophy (which is true only of the particular schools of thought that did not cease to put the question of the meaning of the whole), and the adjective "mythical" has become, inter alia, a synonym for "archaic" or "dangerously conservative." The role of archetypal stories understood in this way as obstacles to a true view of God and so credible self-knowledge was already criticized by the Israelite prophets of the biblical period and the first Greek philosophers.

Plato first used the word "theology" *(theologia)* in his Laws 318, 379, where he warned against the bad moral consequences of the Homeric stories of the gods, all too human in their behavior and thus not corresponding to the "theologically" formed image of the divine. The critique of myth was thus already born in antiquity, specifically in philosophy, starting with the Ionian natural philosophers.

We have shown earlier that one of their premises was that metaphor could not be taken literally. It is more powerful and effective if it remains metaphor. We have also suggested that critical work with metaphor is based

The World of Language

on the premise of its replaceability by another metaphor. This finds a striking analogy in the critique of myth, already expressed indirectly where different mythical narratives relating to the same event were set side by side in a literary record, forcing the reader to concentrate on their common features and to note the relativity of the differences, that is, to challenge the literal character of the individual versions of the same mythical story. One major example is in the first chapter of the Book of Genesis, with its Israelite adaptations of the myths of the creation of the world, which were given a new meaning in new conditions. Over and above what we noted in §2.4.1, the different versions of these myths were linked up (Gen. 1:1–2:4a = Priestly Codex: relativization of the pagan myths of nature gods; Gen. 2:4b-25 = Yahwist: the mission of man).[69] Neither this nor the similar doubled-up narratives that can be found in some other parts of the Bible can yet be considered conscious critique of myth. That would be to force the thought of the time into the mold of our own ideas (i.e., an anachronism), but the mere fact that the two versions have been left side by side reveals that the author of the literary records was conscious of a certain provisionality about the stories. A more conscious relativization of mythic narrativity seems to be reflected in the multiple versions of mythical interpretation of the world presented by a single author, as we encounter them in ancient Christian Gnosis (in the case of Valentinus, a project preserved in the first book of the Irenaean treatise against heresies, its variant recorded in Hippolytus of Rome, and a project represented by the Nag Hammadi *Gospel of Truth* [NHC I.3]). Not even here do we yet have a systematic concept of mythical elements as philosophic metaphors, but the philosophical project already takes clear precedence over the narration.

For interpretation of the Hebrew-Christian tradition, it is significant in this context that after Easter Jesus' followers used different metaphors on different occasions to express their religious experience with Jesus (coming down to earth; incarnation; redemptive death, crucifixion, and resurrection). Although these were soon linked into the single basic narrative that religious scholars term the "Christian myth," most Christian theologians of the ancient world were aware of its metaphorical elements, despite the fact that the majority of Christians understood them objectively as an account of events that formed the basis of their salvation. The Christian myth connected the heavenly plot "above" with the terrestrial story of Jesus: Jesus

---

69. See Jan Sokol, "Der zweifache Schöpfungsbericht als hermeneutischer Schlüssel," in *Philosophical Hermeneutics and Biblical Exegesis*, ed. Pokorný and Roskovec, 238-44.

Hermeneutics as a Theory of Understanding

"came down" to earth, and after his crucifixion and resurrection he was once again "raised up" (see Phil. 2:6-11). We can see just how radically different could be the ways in which the scheme was handed down when we compare the hymn about Jesus' incarnation, suffering, and resurrection from the Epistle to the Philippians with the presentation of the Christian myth in Revelation 12.

> [Christ Jesus], though he was in the form of God,
> > did not regard equality with God
> > as something to be exploited,
> but emptied himself,
> > taking the form of a slave,
> > being born in human likeness.
> And being found in human form,
> > he humbled himself
> > and became obedient to the point of death —
> > even death on a cross.
> Therefore God also highly exalted him
> > and gave him the name
> > that is above every name,
> so that at the name of Jesus
> > every knee should bend,
> > in heaven and on earth and under the earth,
> > and every tongue should confess
> > that Jesus Christ is Lord,
> > to the glory of God the Father. (Phil. 2:6-11)

A woman clothed with the sun . . . was pregnant. . . . Then the dragon stood before the woman who was about to bear a child, so that he might devour her child as soon as it was born. And she gave birth to a son, a male child, who is to rule all the nations with a rod of iron. But her child was snatched away and taken to God and to his throne. (Rev. 12:1-2, 4-5)

Jesus' entire life, which in terms of the view "from above" in Philippians appears as his "incarnation," is reduced in the second passage merely to the fact of his birth. The Book of Revelation indicates his death only indirectly (in the image of Jesus as the slain lamb), and attention is concentrated on his ascent into heaven. There is no direct reference to his crucifixion.

Thus the early Christian traditions already contain the preconditions

The World of Language

for the critique of myth, and these were developed in the work of great theologians such as Paul of Tarsus, the apostle Paul. Paul's response to statements about Jesus' death as a redemptive sacrifice of cosmic scope was to elaborate the doctrine of justification by faith: anyone who trusts in God will be freed at the last judgment (justified — Rom. 3:21–4:25). For former pagans, to whom the idea of God's judgment was alien, he reinterprets this image of justification as a statement about reconciliation (2 Cor. 5:18–6:10). This is already a higher level of interpretation.

From our point of view, then, myth is elaborated metaphor, and metaphor is "secularized" (i.e., open and replaceable) myth. Mythic narratives are still relevant today as a source of metaphors, but myth itself is alien to contemporary man. Nonetheless, in myth we understand how metaphor tends to sketch an alternative project of the world, and in metaphor we see how myth, if it is still to fulfill its function today, must not be understood ideologically as a binding account but precisely as metaphor.

Myth is so important that, before we embark on a critique of it, we must try to grasp its positive significance and to recognize all the mythic elements of the picture of the world that is supported by the text under interpretation. It will become clear that myth genuinely held up the world of the old texts as a vault supports a Gothic cathedral and that statements that we have set in our own contexts suddenly become remote from us. The **remythologization,** which we have already mentioned, **is the beginning of interpretation, which ought to alert us to mythic elements, to interpret the mythic elements alien to us** (to explain how they functioned in their time) **and to recognize as such** (to diagnose) **mythical elements close to us** (still functioning).

From the point of view of the Christian, it may seem that to use the term "metaphor" for some statements regarding our basic orientation in the world, which are indeed fundamental articles of Christian faith, is to express disrespect for them. In fact, metaphor in these statements is the expression of a meaning that it is beyond the capacities of ordinary speech to express. As we have seen (§2.2.1), every separate entry of a dictionary of a particular language contains the expression of a meaning. In metaphor this simply comes to the fore. What kind of reality is being evaluated in this way is something metaphor does not indicate. In every case metaphor expresses the meaning of something (see §2.4). If we then say that a statement about Jesus' sacrifice on the cross is a metaphor, this does not mean that it is *only* a metaphor. All that is meant is that Jesus really died on the cross and not on the temple altar like the sacrificial lambs in the Israelite cult, to which the statements from the tradition of the Last Supper relate (see the institutions of the Lord's Supper in 1 Cor. 11:23-26 and Mark 14:22-24 and par.). The greatness of the story of Jesus, which undoubtedly exceeds that of the lamb, can nonetheless be suggested by comparison with this tradition and events. Thomas Aquinas reminded us that we can only speak analogically about fundamental realities. We cannot, however, base our argument on the claims of Aquinas, because he shows a lack of systematic thought concerning the other side of the new experience: the testimony that directs attention to the importance of the individual event.[70]

If we were to deny the metaphorical character of statements about the foundations of human orientation in history, such statements would become ideology and would become self-contradictory. The oldest Christian thought already worked with several metaphors or mythic models in parallel; to elevate one to the status of basic teaching of the church would mean to shunt the others onto a secondary track or else to harmonize them and so create a pious amalgam that hurts no one but also helps no one in spiritual orientation and in dialogue with contemporary thought. This is the kind of spiritual amalgam that fundamentalists of every stripe offer us.[71]

Having once become aware of the role of metaphor and succeeded in recognizing elements of demythologization in the past, as mentioned above, we cannot step back into the world of myth, for the seeming return to old values actually means to enter the world of ideology, which demands the repetition of certain statements without any kind of critical examination. In a 1941 lecture on mythology in the New Testament, Rudolf Bultmann (1884-1976) described the contradictions to which this kind of ideologization of faith leads.[72] In Bohemia the problem was defined by the Old Testament scholar Slavomil C. Daněk (1885-1946), when he argued that in the Bible mythologies are being exposed to criticism — in the Bible myth is in *statu liquidationis*, it is being suppressed.[73] We have certain reservations about

---

70. Ricoeur, *L'herméneutique biblique*, 143; cf. F.-X. Amherdt, "Paul Ricoeur et la Bible," in Ricoeur, *L'herméneutique*, 43 (opening study).

71. Fundamentalists link their religion with some historically conditioned expression, which they consider to be divine. As minorities, they are represented especially in Judaism, Christianity, and Islam.

72. Rudolf Bultmann, "Neues Testament und Mythologie" (1941), in *Kerygma und Mythus*, vol. 1, 5th ed., ed. Hans W. Bartsch (Hamburg-Bergstedt: Reich, 1967), 15-48.

73. See Josef B. Souček, "Die Entmythologisierung in der tschechischen Theologie," in *Bibelauslegung und Theologie*, by Petr Pokorný and Josef B. Souček (Tübingen: Mohr Siebeck, 1997), 51-64, here 54.

Bultmann and Daněk's approach to a problem that we shall be discussing further, but their critique of attempts to suppress myth instead of seeking to interpret it represents an irreversible advance.

2.4.3. The Double Face of Metaphor

The figural, "attributive," and essentially unexpected part of a metaphor (Herod is a *fox*; the *slumbering* woods) directs attention to familiar phenomena. It seems to convert historical experience (Herod Antipas) or experience typical of certain conditions and a certain era (the woods as background and inspiration of a comfortable life) into universal experience, accessible to all, and already anchored in the past. This is understandable, because it seeks to elucidate for all that which it knows or suspects is not the experience of all.

Only metaphor is not bound to the inertia of tradition and clearly signals to every listener that he or she should focus attention on its "objective" part (fox, woods). Metaphor can convey that the objective part has a meaning that goes beyond the place and time of the event referred to, but it is precisely this concrete event, person, or phenomenon (e.g., a woods) on which the metaphor concentrates more intensively than would follow from mere straightforward reference.

Metaphor can then also function in a way that differs from ordinary expectation. Indeed, a good metaphor genuinely works first and foremost in the opposite direction to that which is assumed. In this way it shows that certain realities that have functioned on a long-lasting basis or are still valid can be revealed or grasped only through a concrete historical event, only through nodular points that provide a mode of orientation in the wider field of history. Usually we draw general conclusions from frequently repeated similar phenomena and events, but we must also suppose that some momentous realities may manifest themselves in events with which we meet only rarely, in some cases perhaps even only once in history.

If the protagonists of the dialectical theology of their time underlined the role of Jesus' story, including all its historical contingencies (chance, unrepeatable elements),[74] their aim was not to belittle Jesus' story but instead to stress it; they wanted to come to grips with the claim that one needs to look behind the chance and fleeting truth of history.[75] They were convinced that

---

74. Karl Barth, *Kirchliche Dogmatik IV/1*, 2d ed. (Zurich: EVZ Verlag, 1960), 202ff.

75. The thesis regarding the necessary insight into the deeper and more or less con-

it was through such historical fleeting truth that we would reach the most momentous of realities. We shall be returning to this insight in chapter 5, but here we need to point out that Jesus' appearance and the Easter events are not something that God, as it were, just whimsically happened to use to address man so that we, against all conjecture, should simply posit that this event was the center of history. No, the biblical texts presuppose that we are speaking of the manifestation of a reality that, in its scope, goes far beyond the moment of its happening. In the Christian tradition (first in 1 Cor. 8:6, less prominently in John 1:1-16), they even conclude from the Easter experience that Jesus is the mediator of the creation of the world and that his story is the revelation of the deepest nature of God, the internal axis of all things.

Here we are arriving at a second, deeper answer to the question posed at the end of §2.3. Much of what we have said earlier suggests that the path to the deep layers of consciousness and the fundamental structures of the story — to the "grammar" of the human world isolated from the concrete communication — is not the way to the goal. Yet such a path still enriches us if through it we get to the permanent sediment of human experience. **The deeper we dig down below the story told or the argumentation developed, the more we get to the less changeable and longer-lasting level of reality.**[76] This is the background against which the concrete events of our history and lives unfold. We shall see that the life of society and every individual constitutes a part of this great stream of tradition (§3.4), from which that which we encounter as something new diverges.

The deepest level of tradition, the level that we call tradition in a somewhat metaphorical way, includes, inter alia, the basic structures of language. This level too is something that we should not overlook. We have seen the importance of the structures of language in the whole of our being-in-the-world (Dasein). But this deep level is still not the goal, the main thing that we look for in a concrete statement. **The deeper we descend to the sublexical deep layer of basic relations and structures, the less meaning we find, and this is quite logical.** If we find some deeply grounded experience, such as "everyone has his or her own experience," it is a quite reliable piece of knowledge but at the same time entirely banal. In contrast, if we say

---

stant level of history has been supported by German poet and playwright Gotthold E. Lessing (1729-81), esp. in his study "Über den Beweis des Geistes und der Kraft," reprinted in *Sechs theologische Schriften Gotthold Ephraim Lessings*, ed. Wolfgang Gericke (Berlin: Evangelische Verlagsanstalt, 1985), 114-18, here 116.

76. Ricoeur, *L'interprétation*, book 3, chap. 1.3.

The World of Language

that, evidently in the fourteenth century B.C., nomadic groups of worshippers of the God Yahweh, despite fears of the power of the Egyptian divinities and repression on the part of the pharaohs, went into the desert to search for the land they believed had been promised them by God himself (the story we read in the first part of the biblical Book of Exodus), this is a statement that is hard to verify and for many recipients means nothing but a marginal episode of world history. At the same time, however, it is a story linked with concrete history (every sentence links the statement with a concrete event), and above all a story charged with a meaning that can become an inspiration for our own hope. The individual metaphorical statements that can be derived from it (Egyptian captivity, the exodus, the crossing of the Red Sea, "Cross Jordan!" the Promised Land, but also the Egyptian "fleshpots" [Exod. 16:3], the golden calf, etc.) are key expressions of hope and temptation. The individual metaphors (and other tropes) and the Exodus story itself understood as metaphor use familiar images to draw attention to events associated with a particular time and place in history. These are its actual content, and they give substance and meaning to history and lives.[77]

The principles of the mutual correlation of the fundamental and the universal structures of life are summed up in the examples of exegesis. Here we might refer to a passage from the tradition of Jesus, "Those who try to make their life secure will lose it, but those who lose their life will keep it" (Luke 17:33 and par.). Here Jesus expresses the meaning of his own unique life, using a well-known saying. Through the story of Jesus the reader starts to understand the potential implications of universal folk proverbs.

A "**revelation**" of this kind, which belongs to the past on the time axis, **can be a signal of the future**. We have shown several times that metaphor can function to signal a new experience with which the recipients of the communication are not yet familiar ("iron bird" for an airplane, for people who have never seen an airplane before; "virus" for deliberately introduced parasite programs in computers, causing "an infection" leading to an avalanche of breakdowns [epidemics]; "good news," gospel, for the content of Christian teaching, etc.). Likewise, metaphor can function for experience that cannot be expressed without emotional involvement ("Honey" for a beloved person, "Lord" for Jesus as a figure mediating hope), or for something from which we cannot detach ourselves because it concerns something of which we are a part ("the linguistic world," divine "paternal care," as an ex-

---

77. On the role of archetypes, see esp. Northrop Frye, *Anatomy of Criticism* (Princeton: Princeton University Press, 1957), 131ff.

pression of Christian experience). Here we are no longer talking about the deep levels of consciousness, but of metaphors linked with concrete phenomena and events, metaphors that express the universal meaning of something unique and thus connect the two extreme levels of experience: the level of the unique, and the deep level of the permanent.

From all this it follows — once again generally logically — that metaphorical speech is employed to express that last, meaning-generating future (Lat. *novum ultimum*): "paradise on earth" (the worker's movement in its initial phases), "heaven" (various religious movements), "the kingdom of God," and "the New Jerusalem" (Christianity and some schools within Judaism). Such a metaphorical signal of a new experience may be aesthetically and existentially extremely effective. In the Revelation of St. John, God, who has "the key of David" (3:7), announces to the church in Philadelphia, "Look, I have set before you an open door, which no one is able to shut" (3:8). It is a language full of surprising tropes (microstructures).[78] The "door" opens the way to the "New Jerusalem," and God announces its opening via an "angel," who represents the Philadelphian Christian community before him.

Excursus: Inside Metaphor

When in the fifth century B.C. Menenius Agrippa (according to Livy *History* 2.32.8ff.) told the rebellious plebeians a parable of the human body, explaining that no limb was inessential, he changed their image of the world. They allowed themselves to be calmed and so actually "entered into" his parable and took on the role that he offered them (whether rightly is not our subject here). The Syro-Phoenician woman whom Jesus refused to help (Mark 7:24-30 and par.) entered into a metaphor more creatively. According to Mark, Jesus replied to her plea that he heal her daughter by saying, "It is not fair to take the children's food and throw it to the dogs." He used the image of the family at table. Evidently he wanted to concentrate entirely on the reform of Israel so that this people of God should be able to accept the coming arrival of the pagans to Mount Zion (centripetal mission). But the woman did not give up. She entered into Jesus' parable and took on herself the role of a dog and puppies — animals that also belong to the household and receive their food — that is, their life — there. As presented by the evangelist, the whole story becomes an etiology, or justifying narrative,

---

78. Some structuralists speak about microstructures instead of tropes (metaphors, synecdoches), since the expression "trope" suggests that it is rather only a literary decoration.

The World of Language

for the equal participation of former pagans in the Christian celebration of the Eucharist, to which only those who were also Jews had initially been invited. In a similar way baptism, which the apostle Paul calls a death or burial with Christ (Rom. 6:1-11), transformed the view of life as a whole. It was a break by which a life acquired a new horizon: "resurrection" with Christ.

For the concept of metaphor it is important in our present context to note that, as an alternative picture of the world, it not only can function as the basis for an orientation in history and in personal life but can also lead to a change in behavior.

Ostensibly, the "chance," unique story and its metaphorical treatment are as heterogeneous as the two parts of any metaphor: the material and the figural. In fact, they are still also "alike." One of the basic problems of interpretation that can be well demonstrated in the mystery of metaphor lies in the way metaphor and then narrative influenced by metaphor actually work with this likeness. One of the most important theological interpretations of classical Christological statements speaks of Jesus as the parable of God (see §5.5.2).

Let us return to the question posed at the end of §2.3: the horizon of hope is something that the repeatedly perceived deep forms of our experience — basic personal relations, the classification of experience, orientation in time — help to outline. The reason that we turn to it, however, is that we need to express the extent of the implications of particular events and experiences that surprise us by their singularity. It is the background to the universally oriented stabilizing tradition, the background against which the particular becomes striking and changes into an appeal to the listener or reader.[79]

---

79. Rudolf Bultmann, "Allgemeine Wahrheiten und christliche Verkündigung," *Zeitschrift für Theologie und Kirche* 54 (1957): 244-54, here 254.

3. Text

BIBLIOGRAPHY

Bayer, Oswald. "Hermeneutical Theology." In Pokorný and Roskovec, *Philosophical Hermeneutics and Biblical Exegesis*, 103-20, esp. 115ff.

Bonnard, Pierre. *Anamnesis. Recherches sur le Nouveau Testament*. Geneva: Revue de Théologie et de Philosophie, 1980.

Egger, Wilhelm. *Methodenlehre zum Neuen Testament*. 3d ed. Freiburg: Herder, 1987.

Gadamer, Hans-Georg. *Wahrheit und Methode*. 1960; 2d ed., Tübingen: Mohr Siebeck, 1965. ET *Truth and Method*, 2d Eng. ed. (London: Sheed & Ward, 1989).

Ingarden, Roman. *Das literarische Kunstwerk*. Tübingen: Niemeyer, 1963.

Pokorný, Petr, and Jan Roskovec, eds. *Philosophical Hermeneutics and Biblical Exegesis*. Tübingen: Mohr Siebeck, 2002.

Pöttner, Martin. "Sprachwissenschaft und neutestamentliche Exegese." *Theologische Literaturzeitung* 123 (1998): 929-42.

Ricoeur, Paul. *La mémoire, l'historie, l'oubli*. Paris: du Seuil, 2000. ET *Memory, History, Forgetting* (Chicago: University of Chicago Press, 2004).

———. *Temps et récit*. 3 vols. Paris: du Seuil, 1983-85. ET *Time and Narrative*, 3 vols. (Chicago: University of Chicago Press, 1984-88).

Robbins, Vernon K. *The Tapestry of Early Christian Discourse*. London: Routledge, 1996.

Wellek, René, and Austin Warren. *Theory of Literature*. New York: Harcourt, 1949.

3.1. The Graphic Character of the Written Text

Unlike the spoken word (the orally transmitted text), the written text has certain properties that have enabled it to exercise a fundamental influence on human culture. Indeed, the invention of printing at the end of the Middle

Ages only increased that influence. The interpretation of written text nonetheless involves a number of new problems.[1]

As is obvious, written text is handed down by means of symbols and not sounds, unlike spoken text. Hearing gives way to sight as the crucial sense. Written text can of course be read out loud, that is, returned to its oral form. This was the usual practice up to the Middle Ages, when only isolated learned individuals owned books or knew how to write, but in fact any reading out loud is only a partial return to oral form. For example, it has lost the freedom of reproduction typical of oral narrative. It has lost the large sections presented in direct speech, the phrasing has changed, and the vocabulary too has been modified. What was earlier rendered present by narration, even though the narrator spoke in the past tense, has become document.

Of course there are gains too: the text has become accessible to a wide circle of readers, in principle universally accessible and "permanently present."

3.2. The Silence of the Text

BIBLIOGRAPHY

Dihle, Albrecht. "Platons Schriftkritik." *Jahrbuch der Akademie der Wissenschaften in Göttingen,* 1995, 120-147.

A text fixed by being written down has one fundamental unpleasant characteristic: if we need to ask it about something in it that is not clear, it cannot answer. It attracts us, and we expect something from it, but when we want to ask it something, it is silent. Unlike the spoken word it is not directly open to dialogue, and the most common attempts to make up for this deficiency provide only very partial substitutes.

We have mentioned the reading out loud of text — secondary orality. Not only is this not a full return to oral communication, but it reanimates the text together with all its obscurities, the person performing the reading being in most cases unable to explain such obscurities, and as mere reader unable to play the role of interpreter of obscurities of content. At the most he or she can leave out the unclear passages when reading. The essential point,

---

1. Some studies on communication with computers mention the use of text messages on mobile phones and in e-mail as a kind of renaissance of orality. The icons (pictograms) employed as instruction for how to use computer programs also recall the preliterate period of humanity. See W. Ong, *Orality and Literacy* (New York: Routledge, 1982).

however, is that the text read out loud cannot answer questions posed in immediate response to it. Rephrasing the text appears as the best alternative. Narrative as paraphrase of the text is a different form of a new orality and allows the listeners to identify those particular momentous features of the text without which it would cease to fulfill its function.

Another form of animating the written text — translating it — functions in a similar way. With old texts translation is essential, and we are in these cases dependent on translation, but there are no grounds for expecting that this process will also explain obscurities (see §4.2.1). It is true that translation removes obscurities arising from the difference between the two languages concerned. As we know, where the two languages concerned are entirely different, only those who know something about the interpreted text, at least from indirect information, or who understand the language of the "transmitting" text can have even a provisional grasp of the meaning of the individual statements contained in it. General mistakes and slippages in understanding can arise only with languages that are close (e.g., Czech and Slovak), with translations from older forms of the language (e.g., the translation of some texts by Petr Chelčický into modern Czech) or in translation of texts known in translation into an earlier form of the recipients' language (e.g., Sládek's Czech translation of Shakespeare plays and the translations of E. A. Saudek, the ecumenical translation of the Bible compared to the Kralice Bible, etc.). Such translations can remove some misunderstandings (e.g., in the sixteenth century *důvod*, which means "reason" in modern Czech, had the meaning "proof," which is important in translating Greek *elenchos* in Heb. 11:1), but otherwise translations only bring out the problems and obscurities inherent to textual interpretation. The better the translation, the more evident are the obscurities associated with the difference between the environment and period when the text was created and the contemporary world. Translation, then, is only the first step in interpretation.

Plato devoted part of his dialogue *Phaedrus* to this problem (274e-275e; see also *Philebus* 18bff.). In his view written text "maintains a dignified silence" in the places where we would like to ask it a question (275d).[2] It is only "medicine for the memory . . . and wisdom" (275a). The word used here for "medicine" is *pharmakon*, which can also mean "poison." For this reason Plato warns against writing and appeals for direct dialogue. We find a similar fear of the silence of the text in Heidegger. The very fact that the text has a

---

2. See Günter Figal, "On the Silence of Texts," in *For a Philosophy of Freedom and Strife* (Albany: State University of New York Press, 1998), 1-12.

certain autonomy that cannot be canceled, even by its author, constitutes a warning. This is a serious challenge. Socrates did not write his opinions down, and in the same way there is no record of a single line written by Jesus of Nazareth, even though he evidently knew how to write (see John 8:6 according to manuscripts D, G, and others). **If we get over the silence of the text by creating an interpretation** (verbal commentary, notes to a critical edition, monographs, commentaries, homilies, meditation on the text, etc.), **that is, a metatext, this is a substitute for dialogue.** Dialogue as concrete interchange or as literary genre presupposes the possibility that the result may be a new opinion, if not on the part of the participants in the dialogue, then at least for those who can follow their dialogue. Dialogue had a critical and cognitive function and challenged what had been accepted as a fixed tradition. Sometimes it even had a comic dimension, thus suggesting that listeners and readers should take a detached view of the different speakers and their views. This is true in the case of Plato and Xenophon in the dialogues associated with Socrates, but also in some comparable texts from ancient Israel (the Book of Job). Plato's definition of the problems arising from the need for interpretation is based on the priority of dialogue over the written word.

A dialogue can be conducted with a text only in a roundabout way. We can get to know something of the character of the text by reconstruction of its environment and its time. Just as we are, so the interpreted text is to some extent (but never entirely) a "child of its time." Or to put it more precisely, it is the author who is a child of his or her time. Admittedly we have no path to the author except through the text, but the text indirectly stimulates us to ask questions about the author. To accept the text as a partner in dialogue is therefore to get to know the time and conditions in which it was produced.

3.3. The Possibility of Misusing the Text

What we have just indicated about the relative autonomy of the text, separated as it is from its original author (speaker), has an even more unfortunate aspect: this kind of text is less resistant to any false interpretation that may be attached to it than the spoken text, whose author can directly defend himself or herself in dialogue or polemic. Sometimes interpretations of a text can become widespread, even though they are at odds with its pragmatics and may on occasion even function in a directly contrary way. We shall be considering this problem later, but for now we at least need to consider the possibility of a false conception of a text that arises because of the distance in time between us and the period when the text was produced — that is, misunderstanding of a historical kind. For example, the fact that in his epistles the apostle Paul addresses slaves as well as free men as members of the Christian community was understood by nineteenth-century Marxist critics of Christianity to signify his support for a social order based on slavery, to suggest that the apostle was evidently resigned to that order and even justified its acceptance by appeal to the will of God. In fact, in Paul's epistles we encounter a new, unprecedented phenomenon: slaves are being addressed as equal members of Christian communities, to which his letters were read out loud. They found their real home in such communities, which was leading to a more thorough transformation of their status than could have been achieved by any revolution.

The history of the function of the text (in German, *Wirkungsgeschichte*) therefore needs to be considered and pinpointed but cannot provide the norm for understanding the text. On the contrary, analysis of the pragmatics of the text and of its historical interpretations needs to create a feedback relationship that can expose implausible interpretations.

3.4. The Fixed Character of the Text

The separation of the written text from its author is a function of the fact that the record (handwritten, printed, electronic) is conserved. It is why a text cannot be a direct partner in dialogue. This is an aspect of the difference that we have already mentioned, but we need to give this, the most momentous characteristic of written text, separate treatment.

If we are to derive basic conclusions for interpretation from what we have established so far, we must first be aware of the advantages of the written text. We have already mentioned one — namely, that the written text can be preserved for many centuries and even millennia and is in principle open to deciphering and conversion into contemporary language. It opens the way to information and ideas from the past, sometimes even the strikingly distant past. Script enables speech to be emancipated from its original context. What was written for people who lived in the past can be preserved by script and become current for us. But be careful! This does not mean that differentiation in terms of chronology is unnecessary or that script as the most widespread of symbols is a timeless system, with a status in time that cannot be defined. The long-lasting character of script does indeed to a certain extent render the dis-

Hermeneutics as a Theory of Understanding

tinction (differentiation) of time less absolute, but the difference between present and past remains (see above, beginning at §3).³

This is without prejudice to the fact that language is more persistent than other expressions of social life. A society can be transformed from its very foundations but can still be defined in the same language. Some new expressions will be added (codes; §2.1), interpretation of which may usually be derived from the context of the kind of narrative concerned, but the whole will be comprehensible to both sides of the social or political conflict. Some will protest against such a narrative, others will agree with it, but everyone will understand it. If language were an entirely autonomous reality, there would be no dispute about what this speech, comprehensible to both sides, expresses.

Of course language is also something that evolves. We have firsthand experience of the phenomenon when we meet Czechs living abroad in Czech communities, for example. In such isolated conditions the language scarcely develops at all, and its speakers are often living documents of Czech of the period when they left their homeland. It is unreliable, however, to use their speech as a historical guide, not only because the principle of conservation works only over the few generations in which the community preserves its language at all, but also because the language of such groups is influenced by the language of the host country. Generally, because language evolves much more slowly than the whole cultural and social environment, its development is better studied using fixed texts.

The relative inertia of language is truly striking. When Stalin published his *Marxism and Philology* in 1950 (it was evidently the last work in the canon of Marxism-Leninism), it caused a sensation. This was not just because an aging dictator had produced a new tome, but because the work departed from some of the basic teachings of the ideology that he himself had implemented with ruthless violence. The sensation consisted in the fact that Josef Vissarionovich Stalin (Dzhugashvili, 1879-1953) had done nothing less than exclude language from the long list of social phenomena and institutions dependent on relations of production for their genesis and development. According to Stalin the author, language did evolve in history but was not directly contingent on social development. Clearly it was some specialist rather than Stalin himself who composed the book, but the dictator himself

---

3. Jakub Čapek demonstrates the difference by analogy to space. From our position we can see other places, but the difference remains between (1) our place and our view and (2) other places and areas. See his "Diference a přítomnost" [Difference and Present], *Filosofický časopis* 46 (1998): 741-52 (English summary).

must have approved it. He seems to have suspected some fundamental shortcoming in Marxist theory, and the book was a symbolic milestone after which Marxism had to start admitting its problems. This episode is not directly related to our purpose here, but it confirms the fact of the internal autonomy of language and so the usefulness of the written record for conserving information about the past — or to put it better, for preserving the information that language itself classifies by assigning it to the category of the past formed by itself.

In any case, from what we have established so far, we can already draw one conclusion: the disadvantage of the written text — that is, that it can be abused and there is no direct way to clarify statements not entirely clear to us (we cannot ask) — is balanced by the fact that this is fixed text that can be interpreted (by comparison with other texts, investigation of the time of writing, analysis of internal structure, etc.), so that indirectly, with an interpretational loop, its real pragmatics may be found. This is text that does not disappear in the way live speech disappears in memory.

3.5. The Reduction of Redundancy

When characterizing written text, we also need to draw attention to some of its less overt properties. In its original sound form, language requires a certain percentage of superfluous bearers of meaning, that is, words that repeat (known as "fillers"). Acoustically, listeners are usually able to catch only a certain part of an utterance and often have to fill in the gaps for themselves. For this reason some information has to be repeated to assist listeners in filling in the gaps. The idea is false that it is best to speak in such a way that no word is superfluous. A certain degree of redundancy is essential, for otherwise the message would be practically incomprehensible. The ability to fill in acoustically unidentified sounds and meanings develops separately from the ability to speak and write in a particular (native or foreign) language. It is important that someone listening to a speech (e.g., a lecture) in a foreign language should try to catch as much as possible acoustically (e.g., by sitting close to the speaker), even when he or she knows the language very well and understands every word. Understanding a whole set of words is a peculiar mental capability that we acquire over a long period in our native language and that we require special practice to master in a foreign language. If a Czech man spends just a few months away from his homeland, his ability to follow the spoken Czech word is temporarily diminished when he returns.

Of course, too much redundancy is distracting. A speaker can be "too wordy" or "garrulous," but this tends to be a recognizable condition and is generally considered a fault.

A written text can allow itself less in the way of redundancy because the reader can reread the unclear words and has the entire context in graphic form "before his eyes." Even in a written text, however, a certain redundancy is inevitable, for otherwise reading would require too much attention and, in terms of difficulty, would be the equivalent of deciphering a crossword puzzle.[4]

3.6. The Successive Surface of the Written Text

Unlike visual artifacts, neither in verbal nor in written form can a text be directly perceived as a whole. We may have a prior idea of such a text as a whole and have certain overall expectations of it (see the account of phenomenology), but we are always hearing or reading (with the text in front of us) only a part of it. The order of words indicates their meaning in the framework of the sentence and their mutual relationships.[5] Professor Jan Firbas from Brno, who has devoted much of his work to the investigation of the sentence from the functional perspective, has explored translations of the Bible in this light. He has studied the sentence from Matthew 14:8b in the Czech Ecumenical Translation (CEP: "Bring me the head of John the Baptist on a platter") and its parallel in Mark 6:25b in twenty-two English translations, with a view to establishing how the sentential function, stress, and aesthetic effect of the different versions reflect their respective word order. Later, at a meeting of the International Academic Forum of Associated Bible Societies in Bratislava, he did a similar analysis of a sentence from Ecclesiastes 11:9b, "Yet know that God will bring you to judgment for all these things" (CEP). The shifting of the word "God" to the end of the sentence, which occurs in some English translations, makes it clearer that the judgment is the judgment of God, distinct from human courts. Given the original context, this is clearly a more precise translation.

---

4. On the spatial dimension of the text, see Ferdinand de Saussure, *Cours de linguistique générale* (Paris: Payot, 1982), 59.

5. Jan Firbas, "A Case-Study in the Dynamics of Written Communication," in *Linguistics across Historical and Geographical Boundaries*, ed. D. Kastovsky and A. Szwedek (Berlin: Mouton, 1985), 859-76.

Text

A text of this kind may also be referring to different events distributed over a long time period. It can reproduce these in just a few lines. In the Gospel according to St. Luke (15:13-14), several years in the life of the protagonist of the parable of the Prodigal Son are described in just two sentences: "A few days later the younger son gathered all he had and traveled to a distant country, and there he squandered his property in dissolute living. When he had spent everything, a severe famine took place throughout that country, and he began to be in need." Yet even so laconic an account is spread over time; it takes the reader a certain time to read it — incomparably shorter than the time to which the words refer, but still a time that can be measured and increases with the length of the text. In a written text this is reflected in the extent of the written space, which in longer texts exceeds the visual field. The scroll must be shifted several times, the page turned, or the page-down button pressed if we are to follow it.

The graphic record of the text is essentially one-dimensional. Whether we read from left to right or continuously in alternating directions, as in some ancient (Greek, Ethiopian) texts,[6] the reading always follows a line that possesses only one dimension; this is the linear surface of the text.

Following the text is thus a successive (progressive) task. Of course, the linear progression is only the surface of the structure of the text. The succession of the narrative events need not necessarily be linear. The time of the narrated story usually runs faster than real time but can be slowed down in such a way that the description of certain situations is longer than their course itself. This is a signal that in itself draws attention to a nodal point of the narrative.[7] Note how in the passion story of the gospel, the time earlier given in terms of days (e.g., "after some days" — Mark 2:1) starts to be

---

6. The so-called boustrophedon way of writing — following the pattern of an ox plowing; see the graphic above.

7. As early as 1949, Wellek and Warren analyzed the difference between real experienced time and time in narration (*Theory of Literature*, chap. 16).

counted in hours (Mark 15:25, 33, 34), or note how carefully the evangelist describes the decision of the prodigal son (Luke 15:17-19), whose preceding story he has summed up in one sentence (v. 13). The difference between real time and narrated time is, however, just the first level beneath the surface. The narrative may be interrupted and an interpolated passage may appear. Such "sandwich" compositions are typical of St. Mark's Gospel. For example, the story of the healing of the woman suffering from bleeding is inserted into the narrative of the healing of Jairus's daughter (Mark 5:21-42). We find similar examples in Mark 3:20-35, 6:7-30, 11:12-24, 14:1-11, and 14:26-72. Alternating prolepses (anticipations) and analepses (evocations of preceding events) may form another level.[8] The linear surface of the sentence may relate to the past and refer to the future ("And so John remembered how he had felt the day before. As he walked on, he met a farmer working in the field and thought that he might help the man out and then find a bed for the night at his house. He greeted him . . ."). After a moment's reading, the text may return to the narrated past, and the level of reading may intersect with the level of narrated time in various different ways. The narrative is structured in complex ways under the level of linear succession.

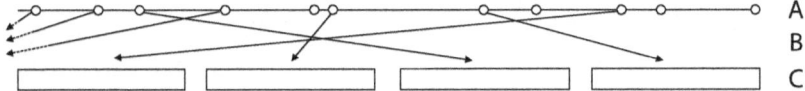

A. Linear surface of the text
B. Grammatically deciphered and differentiated layers of references and meanings (the sequence in real time)
C. Spreading layers of the "sediment" of general experience and archetypes[9]

We need at least to mention the fact that the text can capture (fix) a narrative in which the story narrated in the simple past tense is, from the point of view of the people who appear in the story, their present, such that the conditional represents their future and the pluperfect their past (retrospect). Here we have a shift in the grammatical expression of the past, the purpose of which is to suggest a detachment from what is narrated. Basic removal from our historical time frame can be indicated by a clear signal such as "Once" or "Once upon a time."

---

8. Ricoeur, *Time and Narrative*, 2:103-18.
9. See below, §3.7.5; in literary theory the term "ideology" is sometimes used for any kind of teaching or reflection, including reflective thought in theology and philosophy.

One important expression of the complexity of the inner structure hidden under the successive structure is what is known as the internal monologue *(soliloquium)*, which in Luke's texts (the gospel and Acts), for example, integrates theology with structure. Thus in the parable of the Rich Man and the Barns (Luke 12:15-21), the reader hears something no one had ever heard before: the internal monologue of the rich farmer, and actually even a doubled monologue — a monologue within a monologue: "The land of a rich man produced abundantly. And he thought to himself, 'What shall I do, for I have no place to store my crops?' Then he said, 'I will do this: I will pull down my barns and build larger ones, and there I will store all my grain and my goods. And I will say to my soul, "Soul, you have ample goods laid up for many years; relax, eat, drink, be merry."' But God said to him, 'You fool! This very night your soul is being demanded of you. And the things you have prepared, whose will they be?'"

This is a beguilingly simple text. It takes place in what for the reader is an unlocalized past ("a rich man . . ."), but a time in which the protagonist of the story, for whom the time is present, looks forward to an undefined long future ("many years"). But his plan is cut short in the present ("this night"). The expression "soul" in Greek *(psychē)* is ambiguous. It can mean life (as in v. 20, "is being demanded of you"), but also the soul in the sense of the bearer of a person's identity (v. 19, "I will say to my soul"). In his retelling of Jesus' parable, the author's intention is for the two meanings to penetrate each other. Thus the reader can recognize that what is at stake is truly "life" and ceases to perceive the protagonist's next "night" as the past, with the result that the parable intervenes in his own life project. Jesus in fact immediately provides an interpretation of this kind within the narrative ("Therefore I tell you . . . ," v. 22). We have seen, however, that this kind of deep view toward the most distant horizon, to which the reader is led by successive following of the text, does not interfere with the surface narrativity, the form of which is essentially successive.

As we have seen from the preceding diagram, primary orientation in the text is superficial, successive, and is so from the linguistic and the literary points of view, especially from the point of view of the phenomenology of reading. Linear succession is the basis of the subdivision (segmentation) of the text and the starting point for numbering for the purposes of orientation (verses and chapters, sections, and so on). Only through the linear surface do we get to the depth of the text; to represent this graphically we have to use a three-dimensional model (see p. 78).

Hermeneutics as a Theory of Understanding

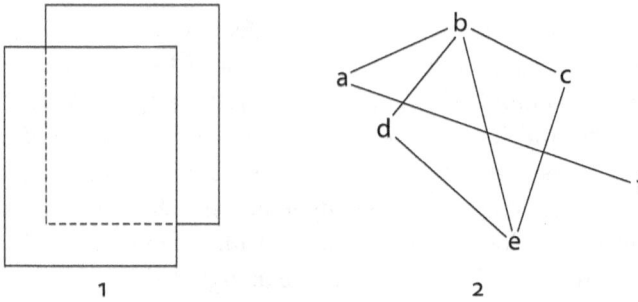

Diagram of a three-dimensional model of a text (see Egger, p. 75): the meaning is not hidden behind the text (1) but is revealed in the structures of the text (2). The lines express grammatical and substantial relationships; the letters, the sequence on the linear surface of the text.

The interpretation of the text must, inter alia, respect the successive character of the individual segments in their linear progression and must be based on this progression in the identification and interpretation of other layers.

This statement is not self-evident. Interpretation can and must involve a distance from the text; it is not bound to the text's literary form. Yet at the same time, interpretation must enable the reader to return to the text and facilitate direct reading. Moreover, because an interpretation is a metatext,[10] which must be logical, verifiable, and systematically related to its object (i.e., the basic text), the literary form of the metatext must first and foremost follow the linear dimension of the text interpreted. In interpretation of the Bible, commentaries (interpretations with notes to the individual smaller sections) proceed by "chapters" (these were for the most part introduced only at the beginning of the thirteenth century) and by "verses" (introduced in the sixteenth century). In the period of the early church Christian preachers and teachers adopted the same procedure in their homilies, although they divided the text into different wholes, in most cases pericopes (sections read out liturgically).[11] This is because interpretation must bring the text sufficiently close to the reader for the reader to be able to cope with the text in the form in which he or she usually encounters it. In practice this means, as we have already established, that interpretation must get to the "deeper" lev-

---

10. For the problem of a metatext, see J. Schulte-Sasse and R. Werner, *Einführung in die Literaturwissenschaft*, 7th ed. (Munich: Fink, 1991), 43.

11. Homilies are sermons that systematically explain the biblical text.

els through the linear surface. It does not mean that the interpretation (commentary) should not also include an overview of the structure of the work (its surface and internal arrangement) as a whole. The advantage of such an overview is that it can take graphic form in which the basic features of one dimension of the structure can be viewed all at once, as with a visual work of art. The graphic overview indicates the basic relations between the individual protagonists (actants) in narrative texts, and of arguments of two or more pages in argumentative (discursive, explicatory) texts.

The schema of actants in the parable of the Prodigal Son (Luke 15:11-32) might, for example, be represented by the accompanying diagram.

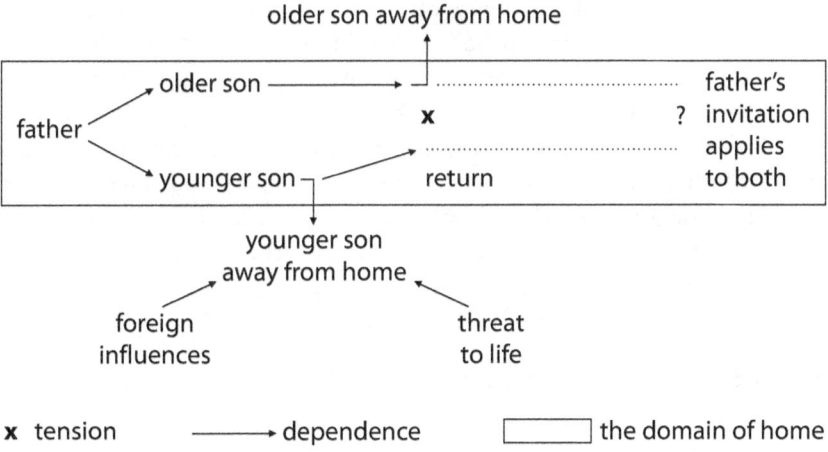

The relationship between the two brothers is here revealed at first glance, even though when reading the text, the reader uncovers it only after a certain point.

In the same way, using a schematic depiction of Paul's argumentation in Romans 6, we must indicate how sin pays those in its service with death, whereas God does so with mercy and eternal life, even though in actual verbal interpretation this comes as the culminating point to which the whole argumentation rises.

In a commentary, therefore, it is good to present some features of the basic structure at the beginning and the end. It is also essential that the commentary should provide a view of the linear arrangement of the text right at the beginning. This should go to the depth to which it can be assumed that the text was consciously formed by the author.

All this, however, is only the groundwork for an interpretation that should mainly consist of commentary and continuously bring the reader to a new reading. Its surface, on which we move, and which we read successively, is, in aesthetic, psychological, literary, and "ideological" terms, the gateway to the other levels of the text.

The projects for structuralist commentaries that appeared in the 1970s proved impossible to carry out. Wolfgang Schenk's 1984 commentary on the Epistle to the Philippians of 1984[12] and Bas von Iersel's 1998 commentary on the Gospel according to Mark[13] ultimately do not differ strikingly from classical commentaries, and in my view, this is precisely why they are useful.

One more comment in conclusion: in the preceding chapter (§§2.3 and 2.4) we spoke at several points about the unconscious logic of speech and the deep levels of reality that may be reflected in the organization of speech, in systems affecting every human being or in the psychological presuppositions of human experience in general, but now we need to bear in mind the fact that in written text these dimensions of the text, or the connotations (i.e., the indirectly indicated connections) contained in them, play a smaller role. Their identification should not overshadow the literary strategy, which is first and foremost the conscious work of the writer and only secondarily draws on generally shared traditions.

3.7. The Text between Tradition and the Future

BIBLIOGRAPHY

Gadamer, Hans-Georg. *Gadamer Lesebuch*. Tübingen: Mohr, 1997.
———. *Wahrheit und Methode*. 1960; 2d ed., Tübingen: Mohr Siebeck, 1965. ET *Truth and Method*, 2d Eng. ed. (London: Sheed & Ward, 1989).
Hejdánek, Ladislav. "Hermeneutik und die Zeit." In *Philosophical Hermeneutics and Biblical Exegesis*, ed. Petr Pokorný and Jan Roskovec, 42-48. Tübingen: Mohr Siebeck, 2002.
Mathauser, Zdeněk. "Verständnis und Gültigkeit. Zu kunstlerischen und biblischen Texten." In *Philosophical Hermeneutics and Biblical Exegesis*, ed. Pokorný and Roskovec, 29-41.
Sokol, Jan. *Člověk a náboženství*. Prague: Portál, 2004. Ger. trans. *Mensch und Religion* (Freiburg: Alber, 2007).

12. Wolfgang Schenk, *Die Philipperbriefe des Paulus* (Stuttgart: Kohlhammer, 1984).
13. Bastiaan M. F. van Iersel, *Mark: A Reader-Response Commentary* (Sheffield, Eng.: Sheffield Academic Press, 1999); see the review by Petr Pokorný in *Theologische Literaturzeitung* 125 (2000): 284-85.

3.7.1. Tradition as Our Bedrock

Analysis of the historical dimension of the text must start with an account of tradition.

A text that has already been written down is lasting (§3.4) and is therefore always bound to the past. The recorded past is thus part of the present in a double sense. First and foremost it is a dimension of the present because it is an integral part of the language with which we speak and think. We live in a linguistic world that recognizes the past tense and is adapted in its structure to bringing the past into the present. The fact that in the present we speak and write in the past tense and are able to make the "past" present by other linguistic means[14] is in itself already proof of the potential actuality of the past. Interest in the past is a part of our nature as human beings.

Yet, second, from childhood and especially from our school years, we absorb a great deal of information associated with the past, which creates the firm framework of our thinking and whole life. This information is passed down from generation to generation by means of language and writing and so is part of our world. It is tradition.

Part of *Truth and Method* (1960), by Hans-Georg Gadamer (1900-2002), which is the fundamental work of modern hermeneutics, is devoted to the analysis of tradition and its role in the life of society. Tradition is a living stream of experience passed on (Latin *trado* — I pass on) primarily in texts, most of them written. The medium of tradition is therefore speech, and in this way tradition becomes a part of our linguistic world. It possesses an authority given by its characters as a persisting dimension of the past, filtered by memory that is preserved and known in the present. In a certain sense it is more persistent than the present, which is always vanishing. It is the result of "sedimented" history, the genesis of which is veiled in obscurity.[15] It is the buttress of our praxis and our thinking. Its authority may degenerate into a pressure that constrains critical thought and free decision making, but all this can be established and expressed only on the basis of awareness of its importance as a stabilizing force.[16] This is social in the broadest sense of the word. When people speak of traditions today, they usually mean folk traditions, old rural customs. In fact, the basic schemata

---

14. For example, using the present tense after explicitly localizing a certain story in the past (the *praesens historicum*, or historical present).
15. Ricoeur, *Time and Narrative*, 1:110.
16. Gadamer, *Wahrheit und Methode*, 265ff.

and conventions of our life, the division of the day, the periods of work and rest, the mode of eating and dressing, the life of the family, the role of education, and so forth are all also part of tradition.

Tradition, especially tradition captured in literary form, is in this sense the "great" memory of humankind. One of its spiritual forms is myth, which we have already considered (§2.4.2) and to which we shall be returning (§4.4.2), but in our present context we need also to connect tradition with a phenomenon as universally literary as the literary genre (type), defined by a number of common literary characteristics, as well as a phenomenon as minor as literary conventions.

It is self-evident that tradition is something we perceive as a present whole — it functions synchronically. New texts are inserted into the order of the present, together with all the other experience to date. They themselves, however, always have a diachronizing effect (they set their original context on the time axis). In practice this means that, even if not works of history, most texts speak about a certain period (they set their action somewhere), but at the same time they directly or indirectly betray to the reader the time of their production and encourage the reader to notice them in a certain chronological relation to other texts.

Texts, then, must be interpreted in their relation to other texts, and we must not forget that some texts actually come into existence as interpretations of other texts — for example, commentaries. This is a phenomenon that we call intertextuality (see excursus below). In cases of this kind it is particularly necessary to know not only the time of which the texts alluded to speak, since a commentary relates to the time about which those texts speak, but also the time of the commentary's own origin, which can sometimes be determined only indirectly.

Let us return, however, to reflections on tradition as a whole. If tradition is in fact the product of human experience rendered continuously present, and the sediment on which we walk as on a solid floor, tradition is the fundamental form of the lasting and the noncontingent, from which metaphors borrow their figural part and which we have spoken of as the subconscious layer of history.

This insight might seem to offer support to the structuralists, rather than to our interest in events and history in all their unrepeatability. This is a superficial view, however. We have spoken of the way that tradition structures itself diachronically, on the basis of chronological distinction. We already know that, without knowledge of what is older, what it "sedimented," it is impossible to express what is new. What is new is new in relation to tradition, and differentiation from tradition is how novelty and the unique character of the new is defined. Innovation is the correlate of sedimentation.[17] Tradition determines the rules without which communication with the surrounding world would be impossible. It is a certain model, formula, or paradigm. Its classical manifestation is the archetypal role of myth (§2.4.2). But be careful! The content and extent of a new expression, a new text, and a new work cannot be derived from traditional assumptions any more than a concrete literary work can be derived from grammar.[18]

Excursus on Intertextuality

In any account of tradition we need to consider the special case of an older tradition explicitly recalled in a later text itself, that is, a tradition that then becomes a part of the text. Texts are often linked up in this way, and this internal connection between texts is known as intertextuality (a term originally used in French: *intertextualité*). The references to Odysseus in one of the classic modern Czech satirical dialogues of Voskovec and Werich constitute intertextuality, as do the quotations from old Jewish literature in the writings of early Christian authors — in church language known as quotation from the *Old Testament* in the *New*. Since we usually quote something that is an authority for us, it is necessary to know what in the text is its older cited part — that is, to know the dating (the period of production) of the cited text. Otherwise we would be entirely unable to understand the intertextuality. If we were to hear a reading of the section concerning Stephen's speech from Acts of the Apostles 7 and then later, for example, the story of Joseph from Genesis 37–47, we might think that the much older story from Genesis was in fact a new version of what we had heard "from the lips" of Stephen. In reality, Stephen's description is just a slightly one-sided abridgement of the long narrative in Genesis. Then, of course, anyone who was tempted to believe that the long literary version of this story in Thomas Mann's trilogy *Joseph and His Brothers*[19] was the oldest version, they would be very much mistaken, for it is a modern reworking of the classic biblical story. As it happens, just because our cultural traditions lead readers to classify individual texts chronologically (i.e., to look for their diachronic relations), there is less misunderstanding in this area than might be expected. In the case of narratives

---

17. Ricoeur, *Time and Narrative*, 2:111.
18. Ricoeur, *Time and Narrative*, 2:111.
19. In German, *Joseph und seine Brüder*, 4 vols. (1933-43).

about Joseph, the problem is worse if we read them in the moving Jewish Hellenistic novel *Joseph and Aseneth*. This was written roughly in the New Testament period or a little before, and even scholars have had problems determining its relationship to some Christian texts.[20]

We would not, however, expect any serious difficulties to arise in the interpretation of the Voskovec and Werich satirical dialogue mentioned above, which refers to the story of Odysseus catching a ram to escape from the cave and the clutches of the giant Cyclops. We have already mentioned that the operative theme here is intertextuality, with the action relying on an older text and the even older tradition embodied in the *Odyssey*. Only those old enough to remember the period of the dialogue or scholars, however, will understand the reference in the dialogue to the prime minister under the Second Republic (whose name was "Beran," which means "ram" in English), which, at the performances of the Liberated Theatre just before the war, drew the greatest applause. Any interpretation must note such information if the text is to be comprehensible. For the original audience Beran was a contemporary figure, while for today's younger generation he is an unfamiliar part of the past. This is a point to which we shall be returning, but we can take note of an important principle and fix it in our memory: that which has become a tradition over time through the selection process of social life is often more present, more contemporary, and more familiar than some individual facts of recent history.[21]

We can compare individual cases of intertextuality to shark's teeth. The shark's small teeth are bent backward, making it hard for whatever gets inside to get out of the shark's maw. Intertextuality also reminds us that individual pieces of tradition cannot be dropped (banished), because without them we would cease to understand the times that we wish to hold on to, and if we actually wanted to get rid of these too, we would cease to understand ourselves. There is another metaphor that expresses the function of intertextuality in an even wider context. Every text is a web of different connections, traditions, themes, and the modes of treating them, which we shall be considering later (Vernon K. Robbins). The word "text" is derived from the Latin "textum" — web/weft (the corresponding verb is *tego* — I weave). The connection with other texts is only a part of this texture, which can also be compared to a tapestry. If we tried to remove some kinds of weft, the whole picture would fall apart. The connection with older texts is inseparable from the whole comprehensively structured fab-

---

20. Today it is considered a non-Christian, probably even a pre-Christian, text.

21. On intertextuality, see T. R. Hatina, "Intertextuality and Historical Criticism in New Testament Studies: Is There a Relationship?" *Biblical Interpretation* 7 (1999): 28-43.

ric. Julia Kristeva argues that intertextuality in the wider sense of the word is an inherent property of every text, and that every text involves a link with tradition and brings its message against the background of tradition. Every text does indeed follow on from speech and the oral tradition arising from it. This means we should also define as intertextuality the historical, cultural, and social references (e.g., see 1 Cor. 9:7, "Who tends a flock and does not get any of its milk?") with which a text deliberately works as it uses its semantic means,[22] and that Kristeva's theory should be considered correct.

It is clear that intertextuality means the transformation and innovation of the older text — its use with a new intention, but one that we will not understand if we are unfamiliar with the intentions of the original text.

3.7.2. Historical Criticism (1)

We have mentioned the fact that language relates to a reality that we cannot grasp in any other way than through language, but one that itself transcends language. This is something expressed by language itself when it says that we are talking (with someone) about something. Speech is never a world just for itself.[23] Speech is thrown beyond itself with "ontological vehemence."[24] The text is not a nonreferential entity,[25] even though it contains literary tropes that have no existence outside the text in which we encounter them. Northrop Frye gives Carl Sandburg's poem about fog as an example:

> The fog comes
> on little cat feet.[26]

Even in this case (although Frye does not acknowledge this) the poetic metaphor has a real counterpart, but this is only a certain feeling that the metaphor evokes in the reader, which probably every reader knows.

---

22. Robbins, *The Tapestry of Early Christian Discourse*, 97ff.
23. Ricoeur, *Time and Narrative*, 1:122-26.
24. Ricoeur, *Time and Narrative*, 1:83.
25. Roger Lundin, Clarence Walhout, and Anthony C. Thiselton, *The Promise of Hermeneutics* (Grand Rapids: Eerdmans, 1999), 71ff.; cf. the review by Filip Čapek, "Neue hermeneutische Vorschläge für Interpretation im 21. Jahrhundert," *Communio viatorum* 43 (2001): 81-87, here 86.
26. N. Frye, *The Great Code: The Bible and Literature* (New York: Harcourt Brace Jovanovich, 1982), 84-85.

Hermeneutics as a Theory of Understanding

If we are trying to identify the function of the historical interpretation of the text, however, we cannot employ positivist arguments claiming that the truthful text is the one that most precisely reproduces reality. A text did not come into existence to return us to the past about which it speaks, but to show the world in a new light. It cannot just reproduce "reality" for the simple reason that it cannot mediate a direct relationship to it, and furthermore, it is always seeking to change it,[27] to set it in a certain framework and to look behind what is given on the direct stage of history. This is why not even the humanist cry *Ad fontes* (To the sources!) can provide motivation enough for our interest in the critical analysis of the relationship of texts to history. Texts are never pure descriptions of history, because they always concentrate on a particular segment of it; they make a choice, a selection of sources. They directly address the listener or reader, they turn their face directly toward the present.

Yet historical criticism of the text is still essential — not in order to understand the direct movement of the text, which, as we have just established, is directed not to the past but to the reader, but as a secondary movement. This movement is the feedback of interpretation of the text. It investigates whether the interpretation derives from that to which it appeals — whether the text is not in contradiction with itself. It checks the references. This applies in principle to every text, even if with fairy tales and poems the connection with history is indirect because they are oriented to universal phenomena and structures of history (§3.4). With texts that relate directly to particular events in history (i.e., texts that have a referential function), this feedback is essential. It is not a question of whether the texts precisely correspond to the facts but of whether interpretation of a text is right to appeal to the reference contained in the text. Interpretation is not a search for the one true reproduction of reality. We have seen that the past in its fullness remains other, hidden. We can react in different ways to a reference to it and can interpret individual reports and "draw out" the implications in different ways. Events in themselves conceal different possibilities of interpretation, continuation, and connection, even after centuries. What is even more important, however, is that no event is open to infinite possibilities of interpretation. An event always points at least in a certain direction and so excludes many more interpretations and connections than it allows. As with every critical assessment of a text, with historical criticism too **the exposure of inadmissible interpretations and unjustified connections** (which sooner or

---

27. See §2.2.2 above, excursus on the pragmatics of a text.

later turn against such nonauthentic interpretation) is the wide frame in which we need to identify its specific place. The pragmatics of the text allows several interpretations, but at the same time it defines a similar set of nonauthentic explanations. **From the point of view of the text, the history to which it relates is its prehistory, which it can neither shed not deny.**

In the early church this feedback developed gradually but, from a historical perspective, very fast. In the post-Easter period, the dominant mood among Jesus' followers was an enthusiasm that did not suppress the tradition of Jesus but nonetheless relativized it. The tradition was overlaid by new experience: "Even though we once knew Christ from a human point of view [*marg.* according to the flesh],[28] we know him no longer in that way. So if anyone is in Christ, there is a new creation: everything old has passed away; see, everything has become new!" (2 Cor. 5:16-17). Paul of Tarsus twice cites the emphatically expressed Aramaic invocation of God as Father (*abba* — Gal. 4:6; Rom. 8:15), which we know from the Lord's Prayer and from the Gethsemane story (Mark 14:36 and parallels). He does not draw his readers' attention to the fact that these are the words of Jesus. In both cases he reminds them that it was the Holy Spirit that inspired his readers to turn to God as to the Father and gave them the courage to do so. Against the enthusiasts who wished to continue in supposed direct communication with God and believed that they were already living in the kingdom of God (1 Cor. 4:1-13), however, he emphasizes Christ's death, his "cross," that is, the unknown, dark zone that the hope associated with faith must pass through: "we proclaim Christ crucified" (1 Cor. 1:23). While this kind of concentration on the death of Christ might not yet have provided a rationale for interest in the whole of Christ's story, it clearly already proclaims the need for feedback. This is clearly formulated in statements from the epistles of St. John, according to which "spirits" must be distinguished, depending on whether they acknowledge that Christ came "in the flesh" (*en sarki* — 1 John 4:1-3; 2 John 7). The culminating expression of this tendency is represented in the canonical gospels, which understand the story of Jesus as the foundation of all Christian teaching, and so the whole structure of the Christian canon.[29]

This is why biblical exegesis in its scholarly dimension has developed

---

28. In the Greek text we read *kata sarka*, "according to the flesh," which most probably relates to the (earthly) way of seeing, not to the person of Jesus himself.

29. Regarding canonization, see below, §3.8.1, and P. Ricoeur, "The Canon between the Text and the Community," in *Philosophical Hermeneutics and Biblical Exegesis*, ed. P. Pokorný and J. Roskovec (Tübingen: Mohr Siebeck, 2002), 7-26, here 16ff.

Hermeneutics as a Theory of Understanding

first and foremost as historical criticism. There was more than one reason for this, but **theologically historical criticism can be interpreted as an instrument of "memories" or "memory"** (Gr. *anamnēsis*) **corresponding to contemporary possibilities, which is the stabilizing agent of the fundamental biblical texts**[30] **and functions as the skeleton of the biblical canon,** even connecting the Christian Old and New Testaments.[31] Theologically, historical criticism can be understood as a means for the self-control of faith. Its role is thus similar to the role of repentance in spiritual life.

(We shall be considering individual methods of historical criticism in the next chapter, after we return again to the relationship between the text and past events).

EXCURSUS ON THE RELATIONSHIP BETWEEN AUTHOR AND TEXT

Not even the most orthodox structuralist denies the need to know about the time of writing of a text that has caught our interest and that we wish to interpret. One consequence of this approach is that we exploit information gained from other sources than the interpreted text alone. Naturally the interpretation must distinguish between the text and its author, but it is not admissible to separate and disconnect the two on principle. We cannot assume that the author (1) did not want to express his or her ideas in the text or (2) entirely failed to manage it. This can be accepted only if there are proofs of it, and the burden of proof *(onus probandi)* is on the interpreter who would wish to make a radical separation between author and text.

3.7.3. The Reader and the Text

BIBLIOGRAPHY

Croatto, J. Severino. *Biblical Hermeneutics: Toward a Theory of Reading as the Production of Meaning.* Maryknoll, N.Y.: Orbis Books, 1987.

30. In his monograph *La mémoire, l'historie, l'oubli*, Ricoeur stresses the role of memory for the meaning of the text (against the skepticism of postmodern philosophy). This is also valid as setting the limits of otherwise brilliant and useful postmodern monographs by S. Moore, *Literary Criticism and the Gospel* (New Haven: Yale University Press, 1989), and A. M. Jack, *Texts Reading Texts, Sacred and Secular* (Sheffield, Eng.: Sheffield Academic Press, 1999).

31. Bonnard, *Anamnesis*, opening paragraph.

Heidegger, Martin. *Sein und Zeit.* 1926; 4th ed., Halle: Niemeyer, 1935. ET *Being and Time* (London: SCM Press, 1962).
Iser, Wolfgang. *Der Akt des Lesens. Theorie ästhetischer Wirkung.* Munich: Fink, 1976. ET *The Act of Reading: A Theory of Aesthetic Response* (Baltimore: Johns Hopkins University Press, 1978).
Jauss, Hans R. *Ästhetische Erfahrung und literarische Hermeneutik.* 2d ed. Frankfurt: Suhrkamp, 1982.
Szondi, Peter. *Introduction to Literary Hermeneutics.* Cambridge: Cambridge University Press, 1995.
Thiselton, Anthony C. *New Horizons in Hermeneutics.* Grand Rapids: Zondervan, 1992.

The basic fact to bear in mind when working with a text is the motivation behind our interest in the particular text that we are interpreting. The term "provisional knowledge" or, more often, "**preunderstanding**" (taken from the German *Vorverständnis*) is the concept that we use for this kind of motivation. The new philosophy and theory of the text long failed to recognize the importance of preunderstanding because the notion was associated with prejudice and thus suspected of subjectivism. Then, however, phenomenology and the philosophy of existence launched a critique of the prejudices that thought hitherto had harbored against prejudices. Provisional knowledge is a part of our historicity. It reflects the fact that historical understanding is associated with decision making. If this takes the form of ingrained, unexamined "prejudices,"[32] we shall hardly get rid of them by refusing to talk about them, but only by defining them and trying to look at them with a degree of detachment.[33] In other words, identified "prejudices" cease to fetter interpretation and become preunderstanding. To get rid of them entirely would be impossible and in any case unhealthy (an entirely unprejudiced person would be an anomaly).

Preunderstanding grows out of tradition, which is what makes orientation in the natural world possible. It may be mediated by the function of the interpreted text in history or by other literature, but it is essentially extraliterary in origin. For example, if I want to keep bees and produce my own honey, I know (from the historical current of tradition) that for this I need knowledge and skills that can be acquired only by learning. If I have no one able to teach me everything and thus am unable to get my knowledge from direct speech and dialogue, I procure a handbook that initiates me into

---

32. "Prejudice" is not understood in a merely negative sense.
33. See R. Bultmann, "Ist voraussetzungslose Exegese möglich?" *Theologische Zeitschrift* 13 (1957): 409-17.

Hermeneutics as a Theory of Understanding

the mysteries of beekeeping. I do not know its content in advance. If I did, I would have no need to purchase it. But I know that I need it, and why I need it. I have an idea of its importance for me and for my life decisions. This is provisional knowledge. I shall have to read the text carefully, to interpret it and gradually get a grip of it, but I already know why I shall be doing that.

Provisional knowledge is thus both motivation and at the same time the starting point of work with a text. Even the first reading of a text usually has a corrective effect on some of the ideas associated with provisional knowledge, and this prompts the reader to start asking "better questions." The text then makes several more corrections to the reader's questions, and thus eventually all that remains of the original knowledge is the basic motivation — the relationship between the text and the interpreter. But we must be careful — what lies at the end of this process is not the text's correct answer to the reader's problem: it is decision and action on the part of the reader. Reading a text, then, is not a matter of passive reception. Nor is it active work only in the sense that the reader seeks by interpretation to obtain a correct answer. It is active work in the sense that the text engages the reader himself or herself in the process of the creation of meaning, for the meaning is not a prior given with ontological validity but relates to that which is not yet here but can be considered an "idea" of the text. This can apply on a very limited scale. With the study of a beekeeping manual, I embark on the realization of my bee colony. By reading nineteenth-century Russian literature, which I started to do out of interest in the culture of a great power with a major impact on Czech history, I came to realize, for example, the advantages I might have over the "useless people" — the literary heroes of that time.

EXCURSUS ON THE HERMENEUTIC CIRCLE

Our dialogue with a text is opened by the fact of our having a certain provisional knowledge, or preunderstanding, of the text, but one that is able to gain a degree of detachment from itself and to respect the internal autonomy of the text, so that after confrontation with the text it returns to itself, corrects its own question, returns again to the text in its broader context, and moves toward a new grasp of itself. From a part of the text we proceed to the "spirit" of the whole, and from the latter we can then understand the individual part; we are proceeding from questioning to the text and back again.[34]

34. Szondi, *Introduction to Literary Hermeneutics*, chap. 8, on Friedrich Ast.

Text

This a general and schematic description of what in hermeneutics is called the **hermeneutic circle**.[35] It will already be clear that this is not a vicious circle but actually a spiral[36] that allows us to gain a greater knowledge of ourselves as we gain a greater knowledge of the text. The problem, then, is not one of escaping from the circle but of stepping into it.[37] We can find a certain ancient analogue of the hermeneutic circle in the second statement of the Gospel of Thomas, which says, "He who searches, must search until he finds. When he finds, he will be disturbed. When he is disturbed, he will be astonished and will rule over all" (log. 2). The conclusion means that readers of Jesus' words will take seriously the prospect of the kingdom of God, the horizon beyond which they will no longer be ruled but will themselves rule because they will be capable of confronting and aligning their purposes with the will of God. From today's point of view the interesting analogy is the theme of astonishment, which has played an important role in philosophy from its origins (Plato, Aristotle)[38] to the present.

* * *

Understanding and elucidation of the time in which a text was produced is of course just the first step to "substitute" dialogue. It suggests what the author of the text had in common with the other people of his time. What was distinctive about the author's own point of view is something that must be identified above all from the text, but without a knowledge of the shared tradition — that is, the features common to our world and the world in which the text was produced — we would not be able to do so. We have already said (§2.4.2) that a good reconstruction and interpretation of a past world (remythologization) is the initial step to direct interpretation of the text for the present.

The unique character and otherness of the text as a partner of the dialogue must be respected unconditionally. If the text were open to any interpretation, than no dialogue would be possible. The silent text remains the counterpart and norm of all interpretations. A reader who fails to respect this and adjusts the text to his or her own views loses the possibility of authentic dialogue. Interpretation would not be interpretation and would bring us

---

35. Gadamer, *Wahrheit und Methode*, 275-76.

36. Manfred Oeming, *Biblische Hermeneutik* (Darmstadt: Wissenschaftliche Buchgesellschaft, 1998; ET *Contemporary Biblical Hermeneutics* [Hampshire, Eng.: Ashgate, 2006]), chap. 1.a.

37. Heidegger, *Being and Time*, §32.

38. Plato, *Theaetetus* 155d; Aristotle, *Metaphysics* 1.2.982b.

nothing essentially new.³⁹ If the Constance school (W. Iser, H. R. Jauss) strongly stresses the active role of the reader in the reception ("consumption") of the text (what is known as the functional model of the text-reader relationship), we for our part must emphasize even more clearly that this is a role subject to certain rules.⁴⁰ Otherwise, readers alienate themselves from the text. There is, for example, no humanist reading of Hitler's *Mein Kampf.*

In the light of what we have just said about the difference between the text and that to which the text relates, we must remind ourselves once again that any kind of attempt to look "behind" the text can offer only a view permitted by the text and cannot be considered a revelation of the "pure" past. It is, however, a way to what is "textualized," the picture of the past represented by the text; while this picture does not offer direct access to the past reality itself, it can show that the text wanted to relate to the past reality as a reality, and so to exclude false interpretations of its "textualized" world. A careful reading, which follows the individual functions of a text and its overall pragmatic, must almost always exclude a number of false interpretations. Possible understandings are not simply a matter of taste, nor are there an infinite number of them, and interpretation always means critical reduction of the number. This reduction is made possible by the structure of the text itself.⁴¹

In seeking to identify the specific orientation of a text, we need to start with its internal analysis, the determination of its pragmatics, the identification of its "matter," and its "referential horizon."

For example in Acts 8:26-40 we read a legendary story in which the author expresses his opinion through the dialogue that is the culmination of one of the stories narrated. It is the story of the deacon Philip, who met an Ethiopian high state official traveling by chariot in the desert. He was probably a supporter of Judaism (what was known as "God-fearing," Gr. *phoboumenos* or *sebomenos*), returning from Jerusalem, where he had bought a scroll (book) of the prophecy of Isaiah. He was reading it to himself aloud (only learned men could read a text silently, since the words and sentences were not separated),⁴² and so Philip heard what the affluent and influential man was reading. There followed a dialogue:

39. This is the sound argument made by J. Barton, "Thinking about Reader-Response Criticism," *Expository Times* 113 (2002): 147-51, here 148-49.

40. J. Frey, "Der implizite Leser und die biblischen Texte," *Theologische Beiträge* 23 (1992): 266-90, here 269-71.

41. See D. Tracy, *The Analogical Imagination* (New York: Crossroad, 1981).

42. A. K. Gavrilov, "Techniques of Reading in Classical Antiquity," *Classical Quarterly* 47 (1997): 56-73, showed that silent reading was not unknown among the ancient scholars.

PHILIP. Do you understand what you are reading?
COURTIER. How can I, unless someone guides me?

He immediately invites Philip to sit in the chariot; the deacon, as it were, hitches a ride and at the same time interprets the passage cited. It is from the prophecy of Isaiah (today we classify it as the so-called Deutero-Isaiah) on the Servant of the Lord, who is led to the slaughter like a lamb. The courtier asks, "About whom . . . does the prophet say this, about himself or about someone else?" Philip's interpretation on the basis of his own experience is that it is actually about Jesus, and in this way he brings the old text up to date. Regardless of whether and in what sense his interpretation corresponds to reality, Philip represents a new (in this case a Christian) view of the older tradition.

In the dialogue with an older written text, we can observe a principle that we spoke about at the beginning of this section, namely, that interpretation must include a dialogue with the world of a text that today may be just as unintelligible to us as the world of the prophecies of Isaiah was to the Ethiopian courtier. The author of Deutero-Isaiah certainly did not have Jesus in mind. What is certain, however, is that his statements related to a key (eschatological) stage of history with which the appearance of the Servant of the Lord is somehow integrally linked. And it was precisely the openness and mystery of the statements in the prophecy that allowed Philip to accord them a Christological interpretation. In this case we need to be familiar with the authority of the prophets, the historical horizon of their prophetic projects, and the practice of their reading and application in teaching in the synagogue.

The author of Acts summarized what Philip told the courtier with the words that Philip "proclaimed to him the good news about Jesus." The author could allow himself this kind of abbreviation because his book is full of testimony to the meaning of Jesus. His world (in this case, the world of the Jewish Bible) is the world against the background of which he was expressing himself and with the help of which he expressed the meaning of Jesus. His text is evidence of that dialogue. If today we wish to establish a dialogue with a text in which we are interested, we first need to reconstruct the dialogue between the text and its surroundings and to understand it. In this case the whole dialogue between the author and his world is part of a tradition that is also our past. Even though it concerns a geographic area distant from us (in the case of the Bible, the Near East, Egypt, Anatolia, Greece, and Italy), it already has to do with our past because the texts that were produced there are authoritative for us too and we keep coming back to them. They have become part of the past of our whole Western civilization, and Christians consciously identify with this choice.

3.7.4. Tradition and New Experiences

The beginning of the understanding of the past, the beginning of the interpretation of a text — the beginning of its confrontation with our present — is then the comprehension of the world in which its author lived and in which the text was produced.[43] We are linked with the author by a common current of tradition, one that we have entered at different places but that nevertheless connects us.

At the same time, however, we need to try to retain a certain distance from tradition and see it as an object of study in itself in order to be able to explore it, subject it to criticism, and understand its function. "The position between strangeness and familiarity, which is from our point of view distinctive for tradition, is a position between historically intended, distantiated objecthood and belonging to a certain tradition. This 'between' is the special space of hermeneutics."[44] Another way of putting it would be to say that the peculiar role of hermeneutics is to identify the direction in which an earlier tradition was innovated and changed so as to be able to express the experience of the author that can be read out of the text. Here, then, we have, on the one hand, the deepest accessible supra-individual side of tradition and, on the other, its most recent side, still directly functioning in the text and alive, in which new events and experiences are being processed. We experience the latter as personal address to us, that which is not tried and tested, that which is exposed to criticism and appears from the point of view of the older, more clearly sedimented tradition (e.g., myth) as the margin of experience.[45] It is something that may differ from tradition as given reality and is not determined by it but is nonetheless still connected with it, even if negatively. The text as creation is not a creation "out of nothing" (Lat. *ex nihilo*).[46] The familiar, sedimented tradition and the new, unique experience are the counter-

---

43. Gadamer, *Wahrheit und Methode*, 290.
44. Gadamer, *Wahrheit und Methode*, 279.
45. P. Ricoeur, "Le symbole et le mythe," *Le Semeur* 61, no 2 (1963): 47-53.
46. This is a specifically Christian category denoting the unique character of divine creation. Human activity always develops a given tradition; it is an innovation, although an inspired one.

parts that, on the level of the text, correspond to what we have discussed on the level of language as the difference and at the same time the mutual relatedness of the familiar repertoire of linguistic codes, on the one hand, and, on the other, the metaphorical attempt at expressing new experience.

On the level of the text, then, we are concerned with the identification of a new event in the framework of the tradition and against the background of its older layers. Even so banal a text as a sign on a door warning "No Entry" is understandable only against the background of tradition, that is, the background of the socially and culturally deeply ingrained knowledge that a door is a space of communication, a place where a private area opens into its surroundings. All this was assumed by the person who wrote "No Entry." By writing it, he or she was emphasizing that in this case the door functioned "against" tradition; it is not in this case a space of communication, but for the reader of the plate forbidding entry it is a barrier, a block.

In the incomparably more momentous early Christian statement that "Christ [the Messiah, the Anointed] died for our sins," cited by the apostle Paul (1 Cor. 15:3b), it is again assumed that the recipient of such a statement lives in a milieu in which the expectation of the "anointed" King (established by anointment with oil) and Savior played an important role. That the Anointed is a man degradingly executed on a cross is something new that cannot be read out of the tradition; it constitutes an innovation of tradition. It is an unexpected innovation, but intelligible against the background of tradition.

Similarly, Paul of Tarsus's own teaching that a person will pass the test (be "justified") at the last judgment of God by the love of God (by "grace") is intelligible only on the basis of the idea of the last judgment, the judgment at the end of history, that is (interpreting its function in our own contemporary terms), a judgment that will be able to take into consideration every circumstance of individual lives as they unfolded in the broad current of history. This is the judgment according to the Law of God traditionally associated with Moses as its human recipient. And so the statement about God's mercy (grace) is understandable only against the background of the law (Old Testament). It is a teaching that is hard for today's postmoderns to comprehend because, while they have a knowledge of law, including moral law, they have no certainty of its victory in history. Postmoderns do not live in the expectation of God's judgment.

The Israelite prophets were the institutionalized bearers of an orientation in life and in history that reckoned with new realities. These had not yet come into existence but nonetheless already had an effect on the present and showed the earlier tradition in a new light, in a new perspective. They based their positions on tradition and appealed to tradition, but they were showing the value of the new against its background. "See, the former things have come to pass, and new things I now declare; before they spring forth, I tell you of them" (Isa. 42:9, again Deutero-Isaiah).

This critical dialogue connecting with tradition is typical of the biblical canonical texts of Israel and early Christian literature.

A specific form of innovation of the traditional view of one's own history is to be found in what are known as the Deuteronomist texts (Deuteronomy 1 through 2 Kings 25) and in some of the prophets. This is a self-critical evaluation of the national concept of history that is designed to show the strength of the internal anchorage of Israel. The "new things" proclaimed by Deutero-Isaiah as an opening of the eyes and revelation of God's justice mean that Israel can recover from its transgressions because it has recognized and confessed them as sins. The historical crises of the past that had been experienced as injuries are interpreted by some of the prophets as if coming from the opposite side: "Who gave up Jacob to the spoiler? . . . Was it not the LORD, against whom we have sinned?" (Isa. 42:24). This is a concept of history linked to "repentance." By comparison, uncritical nationalism is an expression of internal weakness and inability to react in a new way to historical reality, to that which is truly applicable.

The way in which such critical innovation of tradition works is that the new experience is a "place" from which it is possible to see and recognize phenomena that have not previously come to the surface in the tradition but that from the point of view of the new experience appear to us as momentous in retrospect. Attention does not remain fixed on the new, attested unique phenomenon but goes back to tradition. Then, from the point of view of the new experience, tradition appears in an entirely different light. At the end of the nineteenth century T. G. Masaryk came out in support of the scholars who were arguing that the Králův Dvůr manuscripts were forgeries. (*Translator's note:* These manuscripts had been believed to contain ancient Czech epic poetry.) For the Czech public this was a shock, something entirely unexpected; it seemed to represent the willful abandonment of the tradition of a small nation that had been building its identity with reference to its glorious past. Yet eventually not only were the manuscripts conclusively exposed as forgeries, but it became clear at the same time that the future could not be built on self-delusion. It was a moment for realizing a truth that had not been self-evident in Czech society but that was undoubtedly valid. Without Masaryk's contribution, this realization would have come only later and with much more difficulty. It is an insight that we can use and develop to this day.

The innovations of tradition recorded in the Gospels, in Jesus' dialogues, are classic: when the Pharisees reproach him for the fact that his followers do things that are prohibited (according to the law of Moses), Jesus refers to King David himself, who even ate temple bread when he was hungry (Mark 2:23-26 and par., see 1 Sam. 21:1-6 — an example of intertextuality). To the rebuke that, by healing a cripple, he had broken the Ten Commandments (the commandment to rest on the Sabbath — Exod. 20:10), that is, what is permitted and what is forbidden, Jesus responded with a Socratic counterquestion, "Is it lawful to do good or to do harm on the sabbath, to save life or to kill?" (Mark 3:4 and par.). He was thus appealing to the deepest tradition on which the consecration of the Sabbath was founded: The Sabbath, the day of rest, was the day of celebration of liberation from slavery (Deut. 5:15), the day of celebration of God's good work (Exod. 20:11).

In the same way 1 Corinthians 15:12-56 can be read as an interpretation of the relatively fresh tradition of Christian testimony of faith, according to which "Christ is proclaimed as raised from the dead" (v. 12). The idea here is that, in the light of this testimony, Christ's resurrection can be understood as a sign of the end of the rule of death over all people. In the light of similar statements, 2 Corinthians 1:9 speaks simply of God as he who "raises the dead." What is happening here is the uncovering of a new feature on the face of the most recent reality (once again a metaphor for a metaphor! — this is a momentous piece of knowledge), something that we might call the "uncovering of the scope of the unique." Jesus' story thus becomes a revelation of that which "has a future."

Carrying on from tradition always assumes a knowledge of tradition and respect for its inheritance. From a certain point of view even deep innovation may be understood as a radically new, more authentic interpretation of an older tradition. "Do not think that I have come to abolish the law or the prophets; I have come not to abolish but to fulfill," says Jesus, according to the Collection of Sayings (Q — Matt. 5:17 and par.). This is the view of his teaching taken by adherents who likely still had ties with the synagogue, even in the second post-Easter generation, and it is probable that in certain contexts Jesus understood his own work in this way. But this is just one side. It is the second that predominates, that is, the view that tradition is not a smooth, unbroken current of ideas, customs, and attitudes to life. The new strata of tradition are often linked to the old by negation: *"You have heard that is was said to those of ancient times . . . But I say to you. . . ."* We read these as the words of Jesus several times in Matthew 5. Jesus is thus opening a new direction for the current of tradition — he is turning it into a new course. We need to investigate which side of Jesus' attitude came to the fore historically, but there is no doubt that both had a share in his unique impact.

We thus arrive in a roundabout way at a question that we have so far only hinted at. If the pragmatics of a text is always something that aims at changing the world, it is clear that the condition for the innovation of tradition is implicit in the character of the text as that which is being recorded for life, that is, for the future. **A good interpretation of a text is one that is able to determine, express, and evaluate its pragmatics.** The originality of the text is founded on its "point."[47]

3.7.5. Tradition and Story

If the new layers of texts were only variations on basic themes grounded in tradition, the narrative would never have any direction but would only move in a circle. Paul Ricoeur has shown in his analysis of Aristotle's *Poetics* that, although Aristotle understood art as "imitation" (Gr. *mimēsis*), which relates to tradition, that which creates a literary work is a story with a plot, which can unfold in a fictional environment. The fictional world suggests alternative (better or worse) worlds, and it is always inspiring to compare our world with them.

In describing history, this kind of fictional innovation cannot be carried out. Yet history itself is something so diverse and unexpected in its unrepeatability that no fiction can compare with it. The important thing is simply that we should respect this characteristic. History can be told and written precisely because in history new layers that cannot be interpreted simply by using the older layers of tradition are constantly being added to that tradition. History expressed purely as a structure, a history that could not be narrated, would lose all point. In his well-known monograph *Time and Narrative*, Paul Ricoeur offers a critique of such nomological models of history, that is, models that — to put it very roughly — understand history as the realization of certain fundamental definable laws and relationships. This is typical of all varieties of structuralism and of the Hegelian view of history (Georg W. F. Hegel, 1770-1831) and its Marxist materialist interpretation. The

---

47. P. Ricoeur, *Du texte à l'action* (Paris: du Seuil, 1986; ET *From Text to Action* [Evanston, Ill.: Northwestern University Press, 1991]), 124.

Hegelian concept seemingly depends on a careful analysis of history and takes time seriously, but by exploring history from the point of view of its assumed culmination, it produces a rather uninteresting picture. It sees history as the struggle between a number of principles or sides that through dialectical conflict overcome the alienation of absolute spirit, or of the exploited masses, and as thus heading toward a synthesis calculable in advance. This view of history strikingly resembles ancient myth with its closed horizon. Let us remember what thin gruel the Marxist concept of history has been, with everything turning into evidence for one philosophical theory! Such interpretations are to the real course of history much as ruling myths are to the real history of the ancient empires, whose rise and further life they were supposed to justify and shore up.

Ricoeur explores the function of the story using the literary model of *emplotment* (French *mise en intrigue*), which is essential to the depiction of a person according to ancient drama.[48] As conceived in literary terms, the plot is the substitute in drama for experiment in the exact sciences; its analysis allows one to identify the function of events that we encounter only in historically unique, unrepeatable form.

In drama and in the modern novel the plot is something unexpected, surprising, which forms the axis of the narrative; it is what makes the narrative interesting. It is an intervention in tradition and leaves its mark on the lives of all the actors. It manifests itself as accidental and fleeting, as something that will flow away into the past.

At the same time, however, although the plot is unpredictable in advance, it can be retrospectively set in the context of the society and traditions in which we live. We can gradually reconstruct its prehistory and "explain" it in causal terms. This is possible only retrospectively, because in advance any particular interpretation is just one of an infinite number of available possibilities, but retrospectively it is indeed possible,[49] for otherwise a plot would seem incredible, like a bad detective novel in which the murderer turns out to be a lunatic whose actions are essentially incalculable. Retrospective interpretation is thus the link between the contingency of the event and (1) human freedom and (2) the order of causation. We cannot apply a causal interpretation to the totality of reality because we ourselves are part of it and cannot step out of it.

The plot is thus an analogical model of history in its order and in its

---

48. Ricoeur, *Time and Narrative*, 1:205; cf. 1:246ff.
49. Ricoeur, *Time and Narrative*, 1:247-48.

freedom.⁵⁰ In history the individual makes decisions in a way that must respect certain general conditions we might compare to the rules of a game, but he or she must also react to the concrete situation and the pressures and opportunities it involves, which we might compare to the current situation on a chessboard. At the same time the person can and must act on the basis of a certain strategy (his or her own game plan), which includes the vision of a new set of circumstances. This strategy is goal orientated and gives action meaning.

Having brought up the analogy between concrete life experience and a game, it is worth mentioning what philosophy and theology have extracted from the analogy: absorption in a game can take a person to another world. This is something we often experience when reading a good novel. It is a personal experience that may lead to a goal but may also have a destructive effect. We can judge the character of what we have encountered by the results of such meetings and their evaluation (reflection). Experience of a good text can be a source of strength in life, whereas a bad text can be demoralizing. The symbolic world of some types of game may even lead to human disintegration (e.g., gambling).

Constructed narratives may be a means whereby some hitherto inaccessible level of tradition can be revealed and can be viewed from a new standpoint. Even the mere paraphrase of a well-known text may at the same time become part of an interpretation. In itself it does not interpret the story, but it may be an interpretation by appearing as another, oral version. Comparing it with the written text enables us to concentrate on the peculiar tension between the unexpected and the explicable side of events and to demonstrate the attempts of the author and narrator to set the story in the context of tradition, without which it would be hard to understand.

The analogy between emplotment and history is evident. Both in emplotment and in history something unexpected occurs, and in both cases it is possible to explain retrospectively what has happened as the result of particular causes (even history is retrospectively explicable in terms of causation), and in both areas one reason for the preservation and writing down of a story is the desire to set it within the horizon of the narrator's hope, whether as encouragement or warning.

If we must indicate the functions of the different levels of the text, it is clear that its surface results from its necessary "compression" into one dimension, its adaptation to human sensual perception, acoustic or visual.

---

50. Ricoeur, *Time and Narrative*, 1:318ff.

Text

Only under this surface do the levels of meaning appear that refer in grammatical structures to the past or the future, to various people and groups and their specific relationships. At this level we find most of the meaning that makes narration (and argumentation) attractive. This is what we want to remember. Further, deeper levels, in which structure comes to the fore and the concrete people and places fade away, are the "floors" on which the action or the argument takes place, but (for the reader) these have little importance in themselves. And at the very deepest level, in which we meet only fundamental relations expressed by elementary grammar (§4.2.1) — that is, meaning as European thought understands it (§5.3) — importance for the reader almost entirely disappears (see graph from §3.6).

The narrated story as a new reality inspires imitation (mimesis) at a third level, on which readers themselves become a part of the story — they become "involved" in it, doing so by understanding it as an open narrative, moving not in a circle but irreversibly onward toward a new horizon. On this journey the world of the text and the world of the reader (listener) meet. This means that the text is never written only "indicatively," that is, as an independent communication. In any case, this is something that follows from the hermeneutic circle (spiral) that we have introduced earlier. The specific dimension of this journey is what is known as the hermeneutic quadrilateral.

Excursus on the Hermeneutic Quadrilateral

One useful aid to understanding the factors involved in the process of interpretation of a text is the scheme called the "hermeneutic quadrilateral"[51] (see p. 102).

Each of the factors included in the scheme has its own linguistic world; different methods of interpretation may be distinguished, depending on which factor comes to the fore in them. It is a schema that has significance for the phenomenology of knowledge insofar as it characterizes the structure of the process of interpretation as a system.

We must bear in mind, however, that we cannot escape methodologically from the role of recipient and that our knowledge of the author and the "matter" comes to us only through the text. We must also be aware that the scheme necessarily simplifies a number of relationships. The true author is often different from the literary author. This is a problem that we meet in literature in many places, not only where an author writes under a pseudonym, but above all where

---

51. Oeming, *Biblische Hermeneutik*, chap. 1.a.

Hermeneutics as a Theory of Understanding

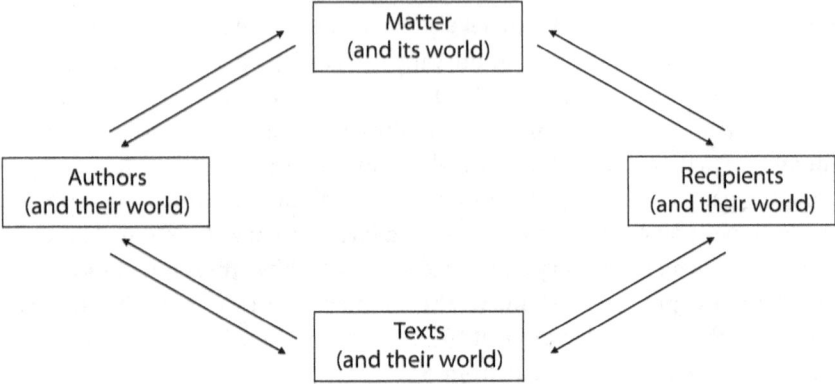

The hermeneutic quadrilateral, according to Oeming (chap. 1.a); it is one form of the hermeneutic circle.

appeal is made to the authority of a fictive author. This is the problem of pseudepigraphic texts, that is, texts written by an author under another name, not just to conceal and protect his or her identity, but in order to call on the authority of the alleged author. We meet such texts in the Bible too. In the Letters to the Colossians and the Ephesians the purpose is to appeal to the authority of the imprisoned apostle, who by his sufferings underlines what he preaches as an apostle, while as a prisoner he can no longer come in person: "For though I am absent in body, yet am I with you in spirit" (Col. 2:5).

The literary author may, however, be a construct created not simply by the real author but by the reader as he or she reads the text presenting the author. Similarly, a real author may have a certain idea of his or her readers that may not correspond to reality. Bernard Lategan summed up these relationships in the nice rule: "Author and reader stand in a 'chiastic' relationship to one another: the implied reader is a construct of the real author, and the implied author is a construct of the real reader."[52] A recipient must therefore be constantly aware that he or she is not the reader that the author had before his or her eyes. The reader must therefore think about the nature of the situation of the original recipient, the person whom the author had in mind (the *authorial reader*), even though it may sometimes be the case that even the original readers were not identical with the readers that the author had in mind. We do not know the extent to which the

---

52. B. C. Lategan and W. S. Voster, *Text and Reality* (Philadelphia: Fortress Press; Atlanta: Scholars Press, 1985), 67-68 (in the chapter "Reference, Reception, Redescription," Lategan).

Gospel of John was disseminated in the Johannine circle, which was undergoing internal crisis at the time when it was compiled, but we know that soon after its compilation it was included in the liturgical reading in the broader areas of the emerging Christian church.

In the section on rhetorical criticism in the next chapter, we shall therefore consider the more comprehensive model of relationships outlined by Vernon K. Robbins. Not even this comprehensive model can be regarded as exhaustive, however, because it does not include the relationship of the reader to the text — the provisional knowledge of its importance that arouses interest in the text interpreted. The analysis of the individual factors that (as we shall see) play a part in the process of understanding does not lead directly to its full comprehension. Their relationship needs to be considered philosophically or theologically.

3.8. The Effect of the Text

In the area of research into and interpretation of texts, the history of their effect (German *Wirkungsgeschichte* — "effective history," the history of a text's influences and effects) is a separate field in its own right. If in the historical conception of the task, earlier interpretation focused primarily on identifying the intention of the author and — in narrative texts — the real ("historical") course of events narrated, more recent literary interpretational approaches have respected the fact that a text has a certain autonomy and have shown interest in the history of its effects in other works, its effect in history. Western exegesis of the Bible has been showing a new interest in ancient, Byzantine, and modern interpretations and studying the concept of biblical tradition among early Christian authors — the so-called Church Fathers — and also the effect of biblical texts and motifs on literature and poetry from antiquity to the present, and on art and music. In biblical encyclopedias many entries now include information on the historical impact and development of the term, story, or theme concerned, and roughly from the 1980s academic biblical commentaries have started to include overviews of the history of the impact of the macrotext concerned, usually individual books of the Bible (e.g., the more recent Anchor Bible Commentary or the Theologischer Handkommentar zum Neuen Testament). In some commentaries (Evangelisch-katholischer Kommentar [EKK]) overviews of historical impact appear even at the end of the interpretation of individual pericopes.

Hermeneutics as a Theory of Understanding

Accounts of the history of impact are a striking feature of the new interpretational strategy and an important step forward. We shall be speaking about the fact that interpretation above all serves the cause of self-understanding, that it relates to the present, and that, without an interest in this part of its reality, we would not be interested in any particular text. In this context it is obviously very important to know how other people and other groups at other times and in other places have understood it. To gather and explore this material is completely essential for the contemporary interpreter, and any criticism of the current theoretical justifications for this activity must not and should not lead to any weakening of this line of research in practice.

If we have been speaking mainly of the history of the effect of biblical texts, this is only because the interpretation of these particular texts highlights all the problems and allows us to test out all the new methods that essentially apply to the interpretation of any text. The history of influence is a kind of reversed intertextuality. It does not seek to identify how a given text is anchored in the past and in older texts, but how it has influenced its future and our past — how our world is connected by its "intertextuality" with the text that we are interpreting. The effective history *(Wirkungsgeschichte)* of a particular text represents a cross-sectional picture of the internal interconnection of culture.

Even so, we must stress what we noted at the beginning of this section, namely, that **the history of effect is not the norm of interpretation and is subject to checking via the feedback mediated by the analysis of the interpreted text and its function** and by historical criticism (§3.7.3).

3.8.1. Canonization and Biblical Theology

BIBLIOGRAPHY

Childs, Brevard. *Biblical Theology of the Old and New Testaments.* Minneapolis: Fortress Press, 1992.

Hübner, Hans. *Biblische Theologie des Neuen Testaments.* 3 vols. Göttingen: Vandenhoeck & Ruprecht, 1990-95.

Pokorný, Petr. "The Problem of Biblical Theology." *Horizons in Biblical Theology* 15 (1993): 7-22.

Sanders, James A. *From Sacred Story to Sacred Text.* Philadelphia: Fortress Press, 1987.

Stuhlmacher, Peter. *Biblische Theologie des Neuen Testaments.* 2 vols. Göttingen: Vandenhoeck & Ruprecht, 1992-99.

We must be aware that the greatest success of the biblical texts was their canonization, that is, their inclusion by the church in its liturgical reading, in the Bible as Scripture. This is the culminating point of their effect — a fact that most studies of the history of their influence ignore. Obviously this fact was unknown when the individual biblical books were compiled. It is the best example illustrating the importance and limits of the history of effect. Canonization was and remains an extraordinary impulse generating interest in the individual biblical text and the Bible as a whole (canonical criticism). It would be irresponsible of Western culture to ignore this. Even the critical interest in the Bible expressed in a number of penetrating studies and works of lasting value in the nineteenth century and the early twentieth century was motivated by the fact that these were the cultic texts of the Christian church — its classics. The faith of Christians and the creed of the church has thus been the strongest motive for interest in the interpretation of Scripture, but an agnostic or even an atheist can be inspired by the faith of the church to an interest in the Bible, even though in this case it will be mainly an interest with a negative subtext, a polemic interest.

This observation shows how important a step canonization has been and still is. In the case of the biblical texts their church canonization had an institutional side as well. They were adopted by the church as its liturgical reading. It should be noted, however, that in ancient Alexandria people already spoke of a canon in the sense of an ideal set of texts of a certain type (of lyric poets, rhetors, authors of tragedy), which today we would call "classics." In a still more general sense "canon" is the designation for an authoritative tradition, which need not take the form of texts (e.g., the social canon).

Canonization itself as the high point of the effect of the canonized texts did not and does not imply that they should be interpreted in any one prescribed way. In the history of culture and in the history of the church and individual rival denominations, there have been different interpretations of the canonized writings. Canonization as an extreme evidence of effect is a way of indicating the fundamental importance of the canonized texts, but both the Christian, who is internally bound by the canonization to give priority to the interpretation of the biblical texts, and the non-Christian, for whom canonization is simply an indication of the historic importance of the Bible, must interpret its text in the expectation of many new meanings. Otherwise the approach would not be authentic: it would be closed and therefore one-sided. The basic objection to the project known as "canonical criticism," which means authenticating the common theological features of the canonized texts, is that by its very nature it tempts the scholar into one-sided interpretation and prioritizes the theme of canonization above the internal weight of the text itself in its synchronic and diachronic (reference, testimony) dimensions.

Christians naturally compare their understanding of a biblical text with church tradition and ask why these specific texts were canonized (this is the basic problem of canonical criticism). They are certainly also aware of their faith as the motivation for their interest in the biblical text, but new exploration of the text of the Bible is the feedback of their faith, and they are obliged to undertake it in line with all the rules of hermeneutics, even though proper Christians do so with a prayer on their lips. In any case, the interpreter must above all ask questions about the meaning of individual biblical texts and only secondarily questions about the theological intention behind canonization. In this sense canonization belongs to the history of dogmatics and not of Bible studies. Nonetheless, Bible scholars must concern themselves with canonization as a part of the effect of the text that they interpret, and above all as the total project of their interpretation, which they must critically test out, but cannot manage without. The question of the canon and with it the question of biblical theology belong to the history of the effect of the text. This is not primary work on the interpretation of the text, nor is it part of the "second movement" — feedback (see §3.7.2); it is a third procedural stage of interpretation, which makes an inventory of connections identified.

The fact that biblical exegesis did not shake the church[53] is not proof that some church regulations channeled or curtailed freedom of interpretation; rather, it above all demonstrates that the biblical texts themselves contain a number of convergent features that actually make ideas about biblical theology possible at all. To put it more precisely, the canonized set of texts and the theological themes and statements that they contain fulfill a dual function. On the one hand, they draw attention to the series of interpretations recorded in history that fail to correspond to them and should be regarded as misunderstandings or deliberate distortion of the text; on the other hand, they show in their vivid diversity that no single interpretation can capture their entire meaning and that different interpretations need not be mutually exclusive.

The tension between the plurality of meanings and the exclusion of certain illegitimate possibilities of meaning is manifest in the form of the

---

53. Pontifical Biblical Commission, "The Interpretation of the Bible in the Church" (April 23, 1993), *Origins* 23, no. 29 (January 6, 1994): 497-524.

biblical canon itself. On the one hand, it brings together and arranges in parallel various different testimonies to the same event: at the level of oral traditions these are the individual sets of Jesus' words (the collection of Jesus' sayings Q, quotations from the set of "words of the Lord" known to the apostle Paul, sayings known to Mark, sayings from Luke's special source [mostly parables], sayings put together in Matthew's own sources), the early Christian confessions of faith that we have already mentioned (the resurrection of Jesus, his death as sacrifice, Jesus as the immanent Son of Man, Jesus as Wisdom and such), and, on the level of literary texts, above all the four gospels. On the other hand, the canon is the result of choice, selection. Sets of the words of Jesus are rejected as a genre (Gospel of Thomas, Q, et al.), and Luke's collection of Jesus' parables was set in new contexts. Only a few stories (e.g., about the miraculous find of money *[statēr]* for temple tax in the mouth of a fish, Matt. 17:24-27) from the popular traditions about Jesus are included, as well as repeating motifs (Jesus walking on the water — overcoming the chaotic element), and from the popular apocalyptic tradition only one book and a few passages in other writings. The rules of Christian life as an independent literary genre (known primarily from the *Didache,* or Teaching of the Twelve Apostles) did not find a place in the canon either, even though individual sections of this type appear in many New Testament biblical texts. A major fundamental decision was to link the Christian set of liturgical texts with the Jewish Bible (the Christian Old Testament), including books that had not been accepted into the Hebrew Canon (known from the Septuagint, the Greek translation of the Bible, and from Latin translations). However, the Jewish literature of the Hellenistic and New Testament period that was popular among Christians was rejected. Also the Gnostic interpretation of Jesus' story as the way of liberation from fateful embodiment in matter and from the bondage of the creator of this world was very strongly rejected, for theological reasons. The canon is thus both a comprehensive text in which all kinds of different interpretations of the faith of Israel and the significance of Jesus may be recognized, and an interpretation of the preceding, founding Christian tradition and Jewish texts.

Canonical criticism, the pitfalls of which we have already mentioned, studies the reasons for the canonization of the different texts, their function in the framework of the canon, and at the same time it seeks the common features of the canonical texts, which can be interpreted as **biblical theology**. This discipline also includes the identification and comparison of quotations from the Tanach (the Jewish Bible, the Christian Old Testament) in

New Testament texts (see §3.7.1 — Excursus on Intertextuality).[54] The term "canonical criticism" was introduced by James A. Sanders in 1972.[55]

3.8.2. The Aesthetic Impact of the Text

BIBLIOGRAPHY

Lotman, Jurij M. *Struktura chudožestvennogo teksta*. Moscow: Iskusstvo, 1970. ET *The Structure of the Artistic Text* (Ann Arbor: University of Michigan, 1977).
Zima, Peter V. *Literarische Ästhetik*. Tübingen: Francke, 1991.

Many hermeneutic approaches make aesthetic judgment — that is, the function of the text defined from the point of view of "the impression of beauty" — the main object of consideration. This applies first and foremost to artistic texts, whether poetry, fiction, or belles lettres.

In our earlier account of metaphor we have ascertained that the border between the artistic and the so-called factual text is fluid. Metaphor is a means of artistic expression and may at the same time have an essential and irreplaceable cognitive function. And all art, which aims at the creation of a secondary language — an open symbolic (modeling) system — is at the same time a means whereby humankind communicates with itself.[56] This means that we must devote at least brief attention here to the aesthetic function of the text. The detachment of artistic expression from descriptively perceived reality, its "aesthetic distance," grows out of attempts to change the world and may become a direct element of the pragmatics of the text. There exists no text in which the aesthetic aspect is a matter of complete indifference, just as there exists no artistic text that does not require analysis of substance. For example, when we receive a circular, it seems that we in no way evaluate it aesthetically and do not even perceive it as an artistic text. Yet a circular written, for example, in today's decadent and dehumanized bureaucratic Czech can provoke such a feeling of disgust that it spoils our whole day.

The more important the factual text, the more clearly it is also an aes-

---

54. Typical instruments of such work are lists of New Testament quotations and allusions from the Jewish Bible (in Christian tradition, the so-called Old Testament), the best being by H. Hübner, *Vetus Testamentum in Novo*, 2 vols. (Göttingen: Vandenhoeck & Ruprecht, 1997-2003).

55. J. A. Sanders, *Torah and Canon* (Philadelphia: Fortress Press, 1972).

56. Lotman, *Struktura chudožestvennogo teksta*, 16, 20ff.

thetic object. This is a truth that is almost banal and can be demonstrated particularly vividly in interpretation of the Bible. When I and my colleagues were working on the Czech Ecumenical Translation of the Bible (CET), we took careful account of exegesis and textual issues but spent the most of our time working on the aesthetics of the text, with a view to our obligation to ensure that in this respect it corresponded as clearly as possible to the effect of the original on the reader that the author had in mind (i.e., the so-called authorial readers). Admittedly, the exegetical and textual analyses were for the most part dealt with in the commentaries and in the critical apparatus, and so only rarely was there a need for us to go over them again with research of our own; it was enough simply to summarize the various possibilities in a responsible way. The aesthetic aspect, however, had to be considered independently at every step. Yet this too is testimony to the inseparability of aesthetic considerations from the work of translation. For a long time Professor Souček wondered whether we ought not to give some hymnic passages to a poet for final stylization, but in the end he decided that the objective and aesthetic sides of a translation form so indivisible a unity that the Bible scholar is bound to take on the entire task and must master the aesthetic aspect, for otherwise he or she would not be a real biblical scholar. This does not mean that it would be wrong to entrust a poet with producing the final version from a rough translation, but such cases are more the exception than the rule, and useful experiments rather than the beginning of a new generally accepted practice.

The aesthetic function does not mean that the text should always have to find melodious and beautiful renderings in the common sense of the word. The important thing is that it should be emotionally effective. Consider the following examples, the first of which is spoken by the warning voice in the Revelation of St. John.

> Fallen, fallen is Babylon, the great!
>   It has become a dwelling place of demons,
> a haunt of every foul and hateful bird,
>   a haunt of every foul and hateful beast. (Rev. 18:2)

In contrast, we have the words of "a loud voice from the throne":

> See, the home [Greek: "tabernacle"] of God is among mortals.
> He will dwell with them as their God;
> they will be his peoples,

> and God himself will be with them;
> he will wipe every tear from their eyes. (Rev. 21:3-4)

Apart from such solemn proclamations, we also encounter stories that are simple but often have a second-level function:

> In the morning, while it was still very dark, he got up and went out to a deserted place, and there he prayed. And Simon and his companions hunted for him. When they found him, they said to him, "Everyone is searching for you." (Mark 1:35-37)

Through its narrative technique this simple but captivating narrative suggests the source of Jesus' magnetism and authority: it is his connection with God. If he had only taught, campaigned, and not been essentially connected with God, no one would have sought him out. In the context of Mark's gospel the reader cannot but interpret "Everyone is searching for you" as "Everyone needs you."

The simple style of the Gospel of Mark, and even more some of the noncanonical gospels that include folk narrative, is close to our own nonliterary form of speech in terms of the spectrum of registers in the Greek language. (*Translator's note:* Czech makes a very strong distinction between the written and the spoken forms of the language.) Petr Penáz conducted a useful experiment by trying to produce a translation that brought this home to the Czech reader, who could then compare its colloquial quality with the formal language of the Czech translation of Polybius's *History* or the letters of Pliny the Younger.

> A teacher, his name was Zacchaeus, was standing quite close and heard Jesus talking this way with his father and couldn't get over his amazement at how a small boy could be saying things like that. And a few days later he came up to Joseph and says, "You have a clever boy; he knows how to think." (Infancy Gospel of Thomas 6:1-2)

Yet this is not the only possible translation strategy. We need not look at a text only in the context of the surviving literature of the time but may also seek to identify its place in the whole society and culture of its time, in which readiness and ability to follow an uninterrupted text read out loud was less common than it is today in our culture. Everything suggests that the author of Mark was more educated than the mere idiom of the text indicates in comparison with the formal writings of his contemporaries. The gospel is evidently structured; it has a clear strategy in terms of presenting a picture of Jesus to readers and interpreting for them the older expressions of his meaning (i.e., verbally transmitted statements of his messianic function). Erich Auerbach has described the profundity of its view of Jesus' story (see below, §3.9.1), and to his comments we might add the well-thought-out yet masterfully simple way in which Mark interprets the concept of substitution in the death of Jesus Christ, which had originally been formulated using metaphors from the temple sacrificial cult, according to which he died for others and spilled his blood for them (the tradition of the Lord's Supper). For a milieu in which the function of the Jerusalem sacrificial cult was unknown, Mark describes how the high priests and scribes mocked Jesus hanging on the cross: "He saved others; he cannot save himself" (Mark 15:31). The listener, who has just heard the pericope on the Last Supper, knows that here Jesus' opponents are unwittingly telling the truth. From the point of view of post-Easter faith, Jesus indeed helped (all) others. He remained, however, entirely on the human side and throughout his life could only demonstrate the fact that a man cannot help himself. Indeed, if he had come down from the cross it would have been of no use to others, if for no other reason than that everyone would have seen that he had powers not shared by us, by other people. Right at the end of the original text of the gospel (according to the oldest manuscripts it ended after 16:8), we hear the message "He has been raised" (16:6). This is a devout periphrasis that omits the name of God but that clearly means that God has raised him. Jesus was linked to God only by the fact that he entrusted himself and his despair to God. Those who have recognized a divine revelation in him now realize that, even in death, they themselves are not matters of indifference to God. Thus in a new, noncultic way Mark expressed the basis of what the doctrinal tradition calls the substitutionary sacrifice of Christ. A gripping scene that, according to the pattern of ancient tragedy, should be perceived as a catastrophe that offers for the attentive listener a ray of hope and at the same time unmasks the limitations of Jesus' opponents. There is no need to add that it is an aesthetically thought-out and dramatically effective picture.

All this renders untenable the hypothesis that the evangelists were primitive collectors of traditions about Jesus. We can see that selection was more typical of them than mere collection and that they created the dramatic framework of the gospel — a structure that coincided with their material and theological intentions. From this it logically follows that, even if they did not have a professional education, they must have been capable of writing in a "higher" idiom and that the choice of the vernacular style (*sermo humilis,* or ordinary speech), or in some cases decision to leave it in the narratives included, was part of a literary strategy according to which addressing the most simple reader in a world language, at a literary level that was the highest consistent with that reader's comprehension, was the means for the global dissemination of Christian testimony. To translate such texts into our colloquial language means to obscure the fact that the authors had to set their prose at the highest level that their presumed readers would still be able to understand. And we have seen that, on the cultural side, this too was an extraordinary performance.

Let me repeat that I cannot offer an account of the aesthetics of the text but must leave that to the several major experts on the subject in our country. From the comments that I have made so far, the following points, which I have sought to illuminate through individual interpretations and examples from different sides, already stand out: (1) the aesthetic side of any text is integrally linked to its material intention (pragmatics), is part of its structure; and (2) because, when reading or being read to, we perceive the aesthetics of the text more immediately than its pragmatics, we need to ensure that we are not diverted by it from identifying the substantial purpose.

Point (2) of our conclusion requires further elucidation. The issue is not one of the reduction of the function of aesthetics but of methodological procedure. Some texts so captivate us by their aesthetics that we learn them by heart and they become a part of our world, but even so their substantial intention escapes us.

It is remarkable, for example, how many people are fascinated by the Christmas pericope in the Gospel of Luke (2:1-20), with its almost magical aesthetic. It has the peculiar contrast between the heavenly world with throngs of angels and the crib in the hay, as well as the newborn babe lying on that manger and the shepherds, who have just heard miraculous tidings of the birth, hastening to bow down to him. It is an unforgettable picture, and I am terribly sorry for children who have not had the chance to learn this text by heart so that it can stay with them all their lives.

Yet at the same time it is a text that has several levels of objective message, and so a one-sided emphasis on the aesthetic aspect may lead to neglect of these levels. Above all it is a *theologically* motivated harmonization of the beginning of Jesus' life story with world history, with the government of "Emperor Augustus" (Luke 2:1), which is supposed to indicate that what is about to be narrated is not a marginal episode but that precisely here we are reaching the core of world history, its central story and problem. It is indirectly connected with the biographical construct long ago discovered and described by *historical criticism:* the whole story depicts Jesus as the Davidic Messiah (Christ the Lord), and as such he has to be born in Bethlehem, "the city of David." Since it was generally known that Jesus grew up in Nazareth, "Luke" had to get him to Bethlehem and used the census — the official record-taking of people and property — to do so. Thus because of the census Jesus' parents (including the pregnant Mary!) had to travel to Bethlehem. In contrast to the first chapter, where the idea of conception from the Holy Spirit is taken literally and so Joseph is accorded only the role of foster parent, in this latter story Jesus' Davidic lineage is actually secured through Joseph (as is also the assumption in his edited traditional lineage given in Luke 3:23-38). According to Matthew, Joseph and Mary lived in Bethlehem, but after Jesus' birth they had to escape to Egypt and then moved to Nazareth, where Jesus grew up. This was because they rightly feared the cruel king Herod (the Great). In comparison with Luke's gospel, Jesus' birth was thus shifted back by almost ten years. The *ideological* function of these narratives is clear, but it would be positivistically naive to claim that this is proof that Jesus was not born in Bethlehem. Surprising things can and do happen in history. What is not in doubt, however, is that for the first two generations of Christians, Christian belief did not connect Jesus' messianic identity with birth in Bethlehem, and that the narratives of the two longer Synoptic narratives have — to use the language of literary criticism — an ideological function. It is *theologically,* however, that we must analyze what we might even go so far as to call the provocatively innovative, reinterpretive function of this narrative. The Davidic Messiah, from whom some groups expected the revival of the kingdom of David, was supposed to crush false rulers and, with the words of his mouth, destroy the nations committing iniquity (*Psalms of Solomon* 17:21-25). Instead of this, here the true Messiah is born under the sign of subjection to the emperor. The Jews considered censuses to be sacrilegious acts (2 Samuel 24), and they had been a cause of revolts (Acts 5:37). Nonetheless it is clear that this interpretation is not about compromise and diminishing the role of the Messiah but about deepening and broadening it. His army are throngs of heavenly angels. In the overall narrative strategy of Luke's gospel, a feature appears, moreover, that plays a key role in both the theology and the overall structure of the "Lukan" work: namely, the glory of Jesus as Christ is manifest precisely where he is condemned to passivity — in the crib and on the cross, at the beginning and at the end of the first work. Readers are led to understand that even there God is with them and that they will not be forsaken; indeed, it is precisely in such situations that the foundation of their hope becomes clear.

According to the Christmas pericope the authority of Jesus as Christ (the Messiah) transcends the borders of Israel and relates to all people: "Glory to God in the highest heaven, and on earth peace among those whom he favors" (Luke 2:14). Not people's moral qualifications but God's mercy is the basis of hope and ultimately also the motivation of ethics. *Philological* work is required if we are to translate and understand the word "angels" in this way.

We have not mentioned all the dimensions of Luke's Christmas pericope, but it is perhaps already clear that to notice only the surface aesthetics of the text and not to analyze its substantive message would be to flatten it out. Only when we recognize all its dimensions can we fully experience the depth of its aesthetic effect in a "second naïveté."

We have already noted that the methodological priority of content analysis takes precedence over the expression of the aesthetics of a text because, while the two form a unity, on a first reading it is the aesthetic side that comes more clearly to the surface and so there is a temptation for our attention to remain fixed on it.

Another reason for this priority is that, as we have argued at the beginning of this section, art is an open system, and thus an ambiguous system that is easily abused. In every period snobbish forms of expression, which are far from genuine experiment, present themselves as great art and sometimes survive for a time in an artificially created microclimate, even though their value in terms of meaning is low to the point of banality. Critical analysis can illuminate the true value, even in works primarily intended as art. How much more necessary, then, is a critical analysis of texts that even by their genre suggest that they are offering a factual message! The more open the system, the more thoroughly must we put to the test the realities and values to which it directly or indirectly refers.

This brings us to the final reason: the potential of the work of art to express the values and intentions of the creative subject (the human being) constitutes a great opportunity, for which the author carries personal responsibility, but also a great risk, because the artist is as much a sinful human being as anyone else and has a tendency to create false idols or to serve bad ideologies. It is therefore necessary to investigate the pragmatics of a work before succumbing to its charm. The artist cannot be excused by appeal to some kind of "artistic" morality different from the morality to which every other person is subject, that is, roughly that which is expressed in the second part of the Decalogue — the moral consciousness at the roots of the Western world. Josef B. Souček has analyzed this situation of the creative individual in his im-

Text

portant study *Slovo Boží a tvořící člověk* (The Word of God and the Creative Human Being) (1944). In his view, the evaluation of art, which is "in its deepest essence the expression of a positive but at the same time intrinsically dissatisfied attitude to the world," must start from criticism of specific expressions of art and explore the extent to which they are a form of play that can uncover sides of truth inaccessible to objective investigation, or whether they lead only to mere idols or to the self-deification of the author.

Given that in the interpretation of the text something is justified only in terms of methodology, we are now bound to emphasize the essential role of the aesthetic approach, which plays a bigger role than often appears to be the case. When we have verified the pragmatics of the text, we need to grasp the way in which what we have identified functioned at the same time aesthetically, so that we can once again go back to the text itself and read it with new eyes and double profit. We have mentioned the fact that the most important artistic expressions of the structure of the text are those that at the same time have their pragmatics. If we are able to identify the objective potential alternative answers, the rather modern-seeming open endings of some of the biblical books (Jonah, Acts, and Mark[57] in its original version),[58] which challenge the listening congregation of believers to a certain reaction, emerges as all the more effective.

For some texts, however, the pragmatics are entirely clear, but a relationship between them and the aesthetic effect cannot be discovered. This means we are dealing with a relationship of free cooperation between two relatively autonomous dimensions of the text. In such a case the Bible scholar is tempted to try rather too hard to find at least some sort of background of objective meaning for individual aesthetic phenomena. For example, Victor Fischl was criticized for carelessness in translation of the Psalms when he did not translate the Tetragrammaton (YHWH, read Yahweh) consistently as "Hospodin" or "Pán" (Lord), the two acknowledged Czech equivalents, or the word *Elohim* using the Czech equivalent "Bůh" (God).[59] In the

---

57. The open ending corresponds in this case to the title of the work: "The Beginning of the Gospel of Jesus Christ"; see P. Pokorný, "Zur Entstehung der Evangelien," *New Testament Studies* 32 (1986): 393-403. For the phenomenon of the open end, see J. Lee Magness, *Sense and Absence: Structure and Suspension in the Ending of Mark's Gospel* (Atlanta: Scholars Press, 1986).

58. P. Pokorný, *Theologie der lukanischen Schriften* (Göttingen: Vandenhoeck & Ruprecht, 1998), 17-18.

59. *Poezie Starého Zákona*, translated from Hebrew into Czech by Viktor Fischl (Heb. name: Avigdor Dagan) (Prague: Garamond, 2002).

five books of Moses, or Pentateuch, these variations had a semantic and historical meaning. In the Psalms, nobody has managed to identify a material function of this kind in the use of the alternatives, and so the reason for alternation is evidently aesthetic, and to translate them mechanically, when other expressions might work better in Czech in some places, would not be responsible vis-à-vis the text. The aesthetic side of the text must take its place, even in exegetical methodologies.

The Bible scholar, of course, cannot ignore poetry; in working with the Old Testament, he or she must know the rules of Jewish rhythmic poetry.

3.9. Genre

BIBLIOGRAPHY

Burridge, Richard A. *What Are the Gospels? A Comparison with the Graeco-Roman Biography.* Cambridge: Cambridge University Press, 1992.

Pearson, Brook W. R., and Stanley E. Porter. "The Genres of the New Testament." In *Handbook to Exegesis of the New Testament,* ed. S. E. Porter, 131-65. Leiden: Brill, 1997.

Voster, Willem S. "Der Ort der Gattung Evangelium in der Literaturgeschichte." *Verkündigung und Forschung* 29, no. 1 (1984): 2-25.

After all our observations and reflections on the text in general, we need now to look at the specific features of more extensive texts (macrotexts), which are formed according to particular traditional rules and can therefore be classified by means of the established marks of their individual groups into genres (varieties), and subgenres (modalities, etc.). Generally we speak of sorts of text (German *Textsorten*). These are concepts with which rhetorical analysis continues to work, but currently it is finding the categories of linguistic analysis inadequate for their interpretation.

Right at the beginning we must draw attention to the two basic methodological procedures of literary analysis, which also help in distinguishing between the individual genres. The first is **narrative**[60] analysis, which needs to be employed in the interpretation of narrated texts and those genres in which narration plays an important role (history, biography, epic, the novel, drama, the short story, the legend). The second is **discourse** analysis, which we cannot do without in the interpretation of texts involving argumentation (rhetorical genres, philosophical texts, epistles, sapiential literature [in part],

---

60. Narrative texts concentrate on action (plot, story).

etc.). Naturally this is a matter of method and not of the principle of the classification of genres. The latter are distinguished according to criteria given mainly historically and according to social function. In interpreting some of them, both methods must be used. For example, drama involves action but also dialogue with argumentation. In the field of biblical genres this applies to the literary subgenre of the gospel as well.

Genre (from French *genre* — gender, kind), or literary type, is the name given to a group of texts connected by a common repertoire of features of literary strategy (e.g., time, in which person they are told), content (the plot is different in each text but in a common genre refers to comparable problems), the typology of characters and dialogues (how the individual people communicate with each other), and stylistics and vocabulary (the level of language).

Genre is also related to similar social function (where it is disseminated, its effect on the reader). The definition of genre is achieved by comparing the structure and function of individual texts. Genres are partly established (we could say "sedimented") literary traditions, without a knowledge of which the meaning of the individual segments of a macrotext cannot be grasped. In comedy or in satire we cannot expect to find a guide to conduct in everyday life, and the misfortunes of the negative character (the villain) are not to be perceived ethically. If, for example, the villain falls into a canal, the spectators laugh, because comedy is written for their entertainment and recreation and at the same time is supposed, as if incidentally, to reassure them that evil can prosper only in the short term. Yet again, we cannot expect precise description from a poem. A poem can speak about the tone of a warped harp, it can celebrate a roof that cuts like a claw into the green of the surrounding landscape ("ah yes, it is that little pavilion. Its roof blushes like a bloodstain, like the claw of a leopard").[61] Metaphor on metaphor, but this is genuine verse. I am able to imagine a light modern building and the strong associations that it had for the poet. It is not an exact description, but it is an authentic expression.

Genre, then, already prefigures the understanding of the text; it is the channel into which ever new streams of water flow. It changes, sometimes it overflows and joins up with surrounding lakes, but the basic channel remains. Sometimes a torrent can create a new channel, but this is an exceptional event. In most cases the genre signals in advance the kind of area to which the text is orientated and how we need to understand it. It can do this

---

61. Quoted from memory by my sister.

because it connects literary production and readers in one cultural tradition. Awareness of certain basic genres is therefore not just an intellectual matter but also a rather indefinable matter of taste.[62] **The classification of individual texts in terms of genre is an obligatory part of their interpretation.** The as yet inconclusive discussion of the genre of the gospel is a proof of this. According to Ricoeur it is inconclusive because we normally understand the assignment of genre as the classification of a specific text, that is, in the taxonomic sense, and not as the means of production of a text.[63] Genre is a matter of the tradition into which an author places his or her text, but like every new creative act the text at the same time transcends the tradition. The text is defined by its genre only indirectly, because what is fundamental is often precisely that which transcends tradition. Genre is essential above all as the background of the individual features of the text.

There are strongly stabilized genres (drama, epic, love lyric, travelogue) and unstabilized genres (published film script). The essential tendency to structure human experience culminates in genre. Criticism of structuralism has already shown that this tendency has its limits. Genre must be sufficiently **open** to be able to "accommodate" various plots, various stories, various references to concrete events. This is why the gospels, for example, which for the most part concentrate on the story of Jesus, cannot be regarded as a genre in the full sense. They are more a subgenre of biography,[64] but above all they are concrete works determined by their plot (their narrative program) and their pragmatics.

At the same time, however, genre must be sufficiently **stabilized** for all the subclassified elements of coherence that would otherwise escape the reader's attention to find their place within its frame. On the level of grammar, these are the conjunctions and relative pronouns; on the level of stylistics, the common style of narrative, plot, and tradition (sometimes philosophy or theology) that unites the text in one whole; and at the level of pragmatics, it is argumentation (see §2.2.2). Genre raises expectations of an entirely definite kind in the reader.[65] It forms the basic framework, which

---

62. According to F. D. E. Schleiermacher, "Hermeneutik," in *Werke in Auswahl*, ed. F. Lücke, vol. 4 [1927-28, repr. Aalen, 1967], 204. Hermeneutic activity includes interest in history, philology, and religion, but also in style *(Geschmacksinteresse)*.

63. P. Ricoeur, *Essays on Biblical Interpretation* (London: SCM Press, 1981), 69.

64. This is the main thesis of the pioneering work of Richard A. Burridge, *What Are Gospels? A Comparison with Graeco-Roman Biography*, 2d ed. (Grand Rapids: Eerdmans, 2004); literary gospels are *bioi* — that is, biographies (243).

65. Gadamer, *Wahrheit und Methode*, 275.

the reader can understand as his or her possibility and thus become aware of the meaning of the text and at the same time perceive the unique narrative or argumentation as innovation that a particular text inserts into that framework, thus going beyond its conservatizing tendencies and creating its meaning *(significance)*. The character of genre as framework is fundamentally strengthened by the fact that we can distinguish it from the concrete plot or argument and can investigate it as an object, for the whole development of literary genre is, as it were, an unconscious exteriorization of linguistic structures on their different levels. These are the background of concrete statements embodying meaning: "The good writer partly conforms to the existing genre, and partly expands it."[66]

3.9.1. The Bible as Inspiration for Modern Literary Scholarship

BIBLIOGRAPHY

Auerbach, Erich. *Mimesis. Dargestellte Wirklichkeit in der abendländischen Literatur.* Bern: Francke, 1946. ET *Mimesis: The Representation of Reality in Western Literature* (Princeton: Princeton University Press, 1953).

Wilder, Amos N. *Early Christian Rhetoric.* 1964; 2d ed., Cambridge, Mass.: Harvard University Press, 1971.

As early as 1946, when studies of the history of Western literature by the Swiss literary scholar Erich Auerbach appeared under the title *Mimesis,* a move was evident in literary scholarship to interpret texts in the very wide context of tradition, essentially reaching right back to the beginnings of civilization. Anyone familiar with the theory of exegesis up to this point could have sensed that a time of major change was imminent. In Auerbach's study, the comparison of Old Testament narrative texts, the Homeric epics, and the Gospels with the novel *Satyricon* by the Roman writer Petronius and with Roman historiography exemplifies a kind of literary analysis that concentrates on the role of the individual characters, analyzes them from the point of view of the relevant genre, but above all establishes their specific features, including their innovation. These insights turned out to be an inspiration for theological exegesis as well, and one can only regret that it took so long for Auerbach's initial impulse to be exploited either in literary scholarship or in biblical study. The analysis of role, which later developed as a separate her-

---

[66]. Wellek and Warren, *Theory of Literature,* 336.

meneutic method, was subsequently to abandon the field of literature, with its proponents seeking to formalize it to the utmost. Diagrams of roles and functions can be a useful complement to prose exposition of argument, but the analyses offered in narrative prose by the first postwar classics of literary theory, by Erich Auerbach and the American Amos N. Wilder,[67] should remain our model for interpretation of texts.

Let us listen to a few sentences from Auerbach's comments on the Gospel of Mark.

> What is described in the long passages of the gospels and Acts of the Apostles and what is very often reflected in Paul's epistles as well is undoubtedly the birth of a movement in the depths, the development of historical forces. What is fundamental is that all kinds of random people appear in the story in great numbers. . . . In such a case, the ancient stylistic conventions fall away of themselves, however, for the reactions of the people carried along by the movement cannot be presented other than with the utmost seriousness . . . a random fisherman or tax gatherer or rich young man, a random Samaritan woman or adulteress, is confronted in his or her everyday situation with the reality of the existence of Jesus, and the way in which he or she acts at that moment has a deeply serious and often tragic meaning. The classical stylistic principle by which everyday reality could be imitated, described realistically only at the comic (or at the most the idyllic) level, thus completely ruled out the representation of a historical force in its concrete form.
>
> Given such a mode of looking at things, neither moralism not rhetoric in the classical sense can be employed. The story of how Peter denied Christ already eludes a judgment based on static categories by the sheer fact of being about the inner mental fluctuation of a single individual, and in the face of the idea that justification must be sought in faith and not in deeds, moralizing thinking has absolutely nothing to say. . . . Not a single classical genus is applicable to a scene like Peter's fall. It is too serious for comedy, too everyday and contemporary for tragedy, and too insignificant for history, and it is presented with an immediacy that has no parallel in classical literature.[68]

---

67. A. N. Wilder was the brother of the writer Thornton Wilder.
68. Auerbach, *Mimesis*, 44-46.

Excursus on the Style of Commentary

We should immediately exploit this digression to formulate another principle, one that is from our point of view momentous. **A good interpretation is itself a work of literature, since not only does it essentially follow the text in the latter's successive form, but it also uses every stylistic and aesthetic means to express shades of meaning that diagrams cannot identify.** If there have been attempts to turn literary analysis into an almost exact science,[69] a stress on the need for a literary frame is needed to set proper limits to this ambition. The literary aspect is not just a matter of embellishment, but of the very possibility of precise expression, which is achieved precisely by linguistic structure. Even the works of the great Bible scholars who formed their discipline as a critical science are written in a refined language, and we read them with excitement. In the introductory chapter to his commentary on the Book of Genesis,[70] Hermann Gunkel gives so captivating a picture of the oldest religious traditions of Israel, including an evocation of their psychological effects, that his interpretation itself becomes a work of art, and in its academic precision (corresponding of course to the state of research at the time), his interpretation culminates in a similarly painstaking and ambitious attempt to depict what he is speaking about in a metatext that is itself attractive in literary terms.

---

69. The Estonian literary scholar U. Masing, who under Communism was not allowed to publish in any international journals except the Czech Protestant quarterly *Communio viatorum*, called this the "biologization" of exegesis ("De hermeneutica," *Communio viatorum* 16 [1973]: 1-29).

70. Gunkel, *Genesis* (Göttingen: Vandenhoeck & Ruprecht, 1901; 8th ed., 1969), xv-xxvi.

4. Methods of Interpretation

BIBLIOGRAPHY

Egger, Wilhelm. *Methodenlehre zum Neuen Testament.* Freiburg: Herder, 1987; 3d ed., 1993.
Morgan, Robert, with John Barton. *Biblical Interpretation.* Oxford: Oxford University Press, 1988.
Oeming, Manfred. *Biblische Hermeneutik.* Darmstadt: Wissenschaftliche Buchgesellschaft, 1998. ET *Contemporary Biblical Hermeneutics* (Hampshire, Eng.: Ashgate, 2006).
Robbins, Vernon K. *The Tapestry of Early Christian Discourse.* London: Routledge, 1996.
Roloff, Jürgen. *Neues Testament.* Neukirchen: Neukirchener Verlag, 1977.
Strecker, Georg, and Udo Schnelle. *Einführung in die neutestamentliche Exegese.* 2d ed. Göttingen: Vandenhoeck & Ruprecht, 1985.
Tate, W. Randolph. *Biblical Interpretation: An Integrated Approach.* Peabody, Mass.: Hendrickson, 1991.

We have already noted that the very nature of hermeneutics as a discipline makes it impossible to create any single comprehensive methodology for it. Different individual methods have developed historically and have come to be applied through practice. The relationship between them is the subject of a mode of reflection that cannot be based on the individual methods themselves: it is of a higher order than they are, and it stands in much the same relationship to them as philosophy does to the individual sciences. This means that the methods cannot in practice be neatly separated out. Each of them goes beyond its theoretical starting point, because practice has shown that interpretation is impossible without a combination of several methods.

The otherwise understandable and essentially sympathetic way in which methods go beyond their own premises has a deceptive side, however, because especially in its beginnings almost every method, every approach, has a tendency to overvalue itself and present itself as absolute — a tendency exacerbated when the method is applied by incautious interpreters. This is why after several observations on the history of biblical exegesis and in part on the history of hermeneutics in general, we shall try to present the main methodological procedures in a way that seeks to identify not just their applications but their functions and their limits.

4.1. The Historical Background of Exegetical Methods and Hermeneutic Theories

BIBLIOGRAPHY

Brinkmann, Henning. *Mittelalterliche Hermeneutik.* Tübingen: Niemeyer, 1980.
Kosak, Herbert. *Leitfaden biblischer Hermeneutik.* Berlin: Evangelische Verlagsanstalt, 1970.
Lubac, Henri de. *Exégèse médiévale. Les quatre sens de l'Écriture.* 4 vols. Paris: Aubier, 1959-64. ET *Medieval Exegesis: The Four Senses of Scripture.* 2 vols. Grand Rapids: Eerdmans, 1998-2000.
Russell, Donald A. *Criticism in Antiquity.* Berkeley: University of California Press, 1981.

The most striking feature of all biblical books is their relationship to history. Often this is a relationship that is merely claimed, traditional, literary in conception, and thus unverifiable (Job 1:1: "There was once a man in the land of Uz whose name was Job"), but almost all the books of the Law and the Prophets have a relationship to specific events and places, present testimony about these events and places, and express their importance. These are texts with a pronounced referential aspect, which influences their narrative framework and which can usually be checked at least indirectly using contemporary historico-critical methods.

In the texts of other religious traditions — for example in the Babylonian epics or in the Vedas — one can find echoes of historical events, but these are references that conceal their own historicity and are worked into a mythical context. In the biblical canon relationship to history forms the skeleton of the texts, and even narratives that elude historical verification (such as the legend of the flood) are brought into relationship with the history in which the reader (listener) stands.

In some places of the books of the Law (Deuteronomy) and in the prophetic books (the "posterior prophets" of the Hebrew canon), we can see the author deliberately rejecting or criticizing the interpretation of the narrated events given by older tradition (see above, §3.7.4). This criticism is theological rather than historical in character, but it is clear that it is a matter of making a distinction vis-à-vis earlier texts and that it has its inner logic. It is an interpretation of history that put particular periods and individual events in history in new contexts, inserting them into a new paradigm. It is precisely in such texts, which were produced as interpretations of earlier events, that we can observe how **living interpretation itself becomes tradition, that is, a text that is the object of new interpretations.** The hermeneutic theme is thus established, with the methods coming into existence only subsequently.

A feature associated with this development is the conscious use of earlier texts (intertextuality — §3.7.1), especially clear in the books of the New Testament. Here we find quotations from ancient literature (e.g., as presented in Acts 17:28b, Paul quotes from Aratus's *Phaenomena*), from contemporary Jewish literature (the *Assumption of Moses* is cited in Jude 9), but particularly from Scripture (the Christian Old Testament) and from the entire range of the canonical Septuagint. A catalog of these citations and allusions (literal citations with source indicated, literal quotations without indication of source, and allusions) can be found in critical editions of the Greek text of the New Testament.

Both when interpreting older traditions, themes, and ideas and when referring to an earlier text, the biblical writers use various hermeneutic concepts, some of which (typology and allegory) are based on literary tropes — new, unusual designation of phenomena that show them in a different light. It is assumed that, between the tradition mentioned or text cited and the text in which the quotation or allusion appears, there is a direct (the history of salvation: promise and fulfillment) or indirect (antitype and type: allegory) connection. Here we shall mention at least the basic exegetical techniques of this kind that we encounter in the Bible and in the literature of its time. The definition and development of such techniques is part of patristics.

The history of salvation is a term that entered exegetical theory only in the nineteenth century, but the idea behind it was already familiar from the Old Testament. It concerns the way that some texts interpret events to which they relate as parts of a mutually interconnected line of action directed toward a certain goal connected with "salvation," that is, rescue from God's judgment and a fall into nothingness. It is assumed that these events constitute the hidden thread of meaning running through the great course of visible history with which they are sometimes synchronized (e.g., Luke 2:1; 3:1-2).

Hermeneutics as a Theory of Understanding

The basic theological sketch of these relations is provided by the apostle Paul, for example in Galatians 4:1-5, where he makes a distinction between two fundamental stages of history: the time in which pious people were guided from outside by the commandments and prohibitions of the law (as small children need to be taught), and then the time of the "fullness of time," when through Jesus Christ as his son, God entrusts people with responsibility and adopts them as his children, who then have direct access to him. This is an approach that inspired both authors and interpreters, and everything that we have said in the section on intertextuality (§3.7.1) applies to it.

We must respect contextualization of this kind and look for explanation in the later texts that quote the older texts. "Explanation" in this case seeks to identify what in the earlier testimony appeared so relevant at the time when the later text was produced. We cannot use such a later proclaimed connection to interpret the older texts but can present it only as an illustration of their effect *(Wirkungsgeschichte)* in commentary or homiletically (i.e., for purposes of preaching).

The relation **promise — fulfillment** is not based on a view of history as a whole but contextually connects that which we want to interpret and clarify with another concrete event (statement) in the past. It is a specific kind of intertextuality (§3.7.1). It therefore finds in the past, specifically in the past of Israel described in the biblical text, the places that are explicitly "open" to the future, that are God's "promises." Unlike the relations in the "history of salvation," here it is the mutual relation between two different events rather than their continuity that comes to the fore. Well-known instances include the statements about John the Baptist's appearance as fulfillment of the prophecy of Isaiah (Mark 1:2-4 and par.) or the so-called reflexive quotations from Scripture in Matthew's gospel, the first of which appears after the proclamation of Jesus' birth, which is commented on with the words, "All this took place to fulfill what had been spoken by the Lord through the prophet: 'Look, the virgin shall conceive and bear a son, and they shall name him Emmanuel'" Matt. 1:22-23). In promises that had been fulfilled in the past (the childless Abraham had become the father of the nation), Paul of Tarsus saw the guarantee of a new, more intense fulfillment that every one of his contemporaries could enter into through faith (Gal. 3:6-14; Rom. 4:13-24). What we have said about the relationship between the earlier and the later events in our account of the "history of salvation" also applies to the relationship between the older and later texts here: the proclaimed connection has validity only for the interpretation of the later text. In this case, however, we are concerned with a relationship that, from the

Methods of Interpretation

point of view of the reader of the newer text, that is, the text from Christian literature in which the Law or the Prophets is cited, has two sides. On first sight the earlier text guarantees the authority of the later one, but in fact the emphases are starting to shift: for some original readers such statements are a way of drawing attention to the momentousness of the past text, which their present religious experience should not be allowed to obscure or obliterate. When Paul quoted what in his time was already an old ecumenical "formula of faith" (1 Cor. 15:3b-5), which states said that Christ "died for our sins" and was "raised on the third day," both "according to the Scriptures," this was, for the listener from a pagan background, for the purpose of drawing attention to the continuing authority of the Jewish Bible (the Old Testament) in the Christian church. Here relations of intertextuality appear in particularly clear-cut form.

Unlike the other interpretational procedures, in the promise-fulfillment relationship it is evident that this is not a historically verifiable reality, and for today's reader the difference between the promise and the fulfillment is sometimes striking. For example, taken literally, Jesus' story was not the fulfillment of any of the promises mentioned by the apostle Paul and the Gospels: the covenant with God related to Abraham's descendants (Gen. 17:7) and not to Jesus, as Paul tried to prove on grammatical grounds (Gal. 3:16-19), and Jesus' entry into Jerusalem on a donkey could not be the fulfillment of the statement about the righteous Davidic king who would come on a donkey (Zech. 9:9) because the latter was supposed to establish eternal peace and rule over a great territory (v. 10). Yet the relationship between the promise and the fulfillment is not arbitrary but is mediated. Momentous stories and statements often begin to function in a way that to a certain extent means that they have emancipated themselves from their context. They cannot get rid of it entirely and their original, earlier context[1] continues to function as feedback in their interpretation, but they also appear outside this context because their listeners (these texts are mainly shared orally) sensed that precisely at this point the text broke through to a deeper level of expectation, its fulfillment lying not just in its literal context but in a wider register of hopes, the expressions of which refer to the vanishing point of life and history. Emancipated statements need not, of course, always relate to the ultimate goal, the highest values and reality. For example, the rule

---

1. In this case I would not like to speak of "author's intention" because we are speaking of texts that were recorded after a long period of being handed down and written down provisionally; therefore the actual authorial layer cannot be determined.

"Anyone unwilling to work should not eat" is recorded first in Pauline literature, in 2 Thessalonians 3:10, in a statement directed against enthusiastic expectation of the end of this age, just as we find many such emancipated statements taken from films or books in our ordinary language. Some of them lighten up our view of life (e.g., statements from the "works" of Jára Cimrman — an invented historical figure in a cult Czech comedy tradition), while others deepen it (e.g., sayings taken from the revered seventeenth-century minister and pedagogue Comenius), but these are always statements that have managed to go beyond their original context and acquire a new metaphorical meaning. This is the mediated (internal) justification of the promise-fulfillment relationship that we encounter in such sharply defined form in the New Testament. In the church environment it is so widespread that worshippers at religious services are not even aware that Jesus was not — literally speaking — a holy warrior who sat on the throne of David and killed the tyrant with the breath of his lips (Isaiah 9 and 11), but they are aware that what they experience and accept in their faith fulfills and transcends the extent of the hope expressed in the metaphors of promising.

Typological interpretation[2] was theoretically elaborated for interpretation of the Bible as early as the third century A.D. in Alexandria and in part in the school of Antioch, with which it is traditionally associated (Lucian of Antioch, d. 312; Ephraim of Syria, d. 373). Here too the issue is basically one of intertextuality,[3] but it is not assumed that there was a conscious relationship between the older event and that to which the text relates. The later event to which the text refers is evaluated as an episode or phenomenon that has its positive or negative analogue in the different, past event to which the earlier text refers. In this sense it is the distance of the time difference[4] that comes to the surface and not continuity, as in the project of the history of salvation. Jesus has his negative antitype in Adam (Rom. 5:14), John the Baptist has his positive antitype in the prophet Isaiah, Sarah has her antitype in Hagar, and the "new Jerusalem" in Mount Sinai (Gal. 4:21-31).[5]

Typological interpretation was employed in the Middle Ages to ex-

---

2. The word *typos* already appears in the New Testament (Rom. 5:14) to express this relationship, but it is not yet a technical term. In most places *typos* means "pattern" or "example."

3. See L. Goppelt, *Typos. Die typologische Deutung des Alten Testaments im Neuen* (1939; 3d ed., Darmstadt: Wissenschaftliche Buchgesellschaft, 1981).

4. E. Fuchs, *Hermeneutik* (Bad Cannstatt: Müllerschön, 1954), 200.

5. The last two examples are characterized in the Greek text as allegory, but from the point of view of later definitions, this was more a typological relationship. The terms that we employ emerged at least a century later.

Methods of Interpretation

press relationships between the Old and New Testament in pictures that were supposed to bring the Bible closer to the illiterate majority of the population *(Biblia pauperum)*. Typological techniques revealed the meaning of the analogy and in practice sought an analogical interpretation, even if without deeper reflection on its nature.

Allegory, a word derived from the Greek *allēgoreuō* (from *allos* + *agoreuō*, "speak other [in the agora/assembly]") is the oldest of all the techniques of interpretation that we are considering here. It was employed as an interpretation of particular events or older texts in ancient Greek literature (see above, §2.4), and we encounter it in the Bible in the Old Testament (Judg. 9:7-15, the trees choose the king; Eccl. 12:2-6, images of old age). The Stoic philosophers used allegory in interpreting Homer. In the Alexandrian school of exegesis (Origen, d. 254, Didymus the Blind, d. 398) in the third century A.D., it became the important exegetical procedure that it remained throughout the Middle Ages right up to the Reformation.[6] Allegory was the means whereby the meaning of a particular text could be expressed in a contemporary way. The text was taken out of its historical context, and its structure (plot, protagonists/actants) was set in a different historical or imaginary context that was intelligible to the listeners. The allegorical method was being criticized on these grounds as early as the fifth and sixth centuries (esp. by Theodore of Mopsuestia, ca. 350-428).

Allegory shares with the current structural analysis of text the basic principle of separation of the structure from the specific actors in the text and from relation to data external to the text. It does not, however, stop at the revealed structure; it is afraid of the naked body of the text and hurriedly dresses it in new clothes. The assumed structure stands out if we find the common denominator of the original text (phenomenon) and its allegorical interpretation.

The power of allegory as an exegetic method lies in the recognition that the text is not just a document of the past but functions in the present and that its interpretation must involve its transformation into a new linguistic world familiar to those for whom the interpretation is intended. This spiritual courage, combined with insight into one of the basic problems of interpretation, is something that can only be admired in the exegetes of the Middle Ages.

At the same time, however, there must be an emphatic "Beware!" — a

---

6. Augustine's allegorical interpretation of the first chapters of Genesis in book 13 of his *Confessions* is classic (e.g., the sky = Scripture).

caveat — against the danger to which this method is exposed and to which interpretations in which it is employed have very frequently succumbed. The validity of the transfer to a new bearer cannot in any way be checked within the framework of the method itself, and it is essentially (i.e., as far as the measure of allegorical method itself is concerned) entirely arbitrary. It depends only on the interpretational instinct of the exegete whether his or her allegorical interpretation functioned in the present in the same way as the original text functioned in its time. Instinct is not something to be relied on. Yet at the same time allegory is attractive. The reader correctly senses that the text possesses some hidden dimensions ("an excess of meaning") and may suppose that he or she will find them in the allegorical interpretation. In reality allegory is a beautiful trope, but as an exegetical method it is usually an escape from the true work of the interpreter. If it is not to be abused, the allegorical method must be combined with the search for the objective intention of the text.[7] **The hidden aspects of the text do not contain any extrahistorical secret. The text needs to be left with the advantage over our own ideas, and we should not attempt to reconstruct its hidden dimensions without indicating that this is only our supposition.**

Enumeration of the models that can be used to express the relationship between the text and the lived world of the exegete and the intended recipients of his or her account has suggested the multiple dimensions of this relationship. It is therefore understandable that in the Middle Ages scholars developed a theory of the fourfold meaning of Scripture, making a theologically based attempt to determine the function of the different methods.[8] A summarizing Latin verse runs:

Littera gesta docet,	The literal meaning teaches what happened;
quid credas allegoria,	allegory, what to believe;
moralis quid agas,	the moral, what to do;
quid speras anagogia.	the anagogical, in what to hope.

This is a carefully thought-out rule. The literal meaning *(littera)* relates to the past event described in the text. The allegorical interpretation referred

---

7. See the account of Origen in L. Karfíková, "Patristická exegeze. Órigenés a Augustin," part 2, chap. 2, in *Hermeneutika. Jako theorie porozumění* (Prague: Vyšehrad, 2005).

8. Traditionally it is associated with John Cassian (d. ca. 430); for an account, see J. Grondin, *Einführung in die philosophische Hermeneutik* (Darmstadt: Wissenschaftliche Buchgesellschaft, 1991), 50ff.

Methods of Interpretation

to in the second line transposes the function of the text from its past world to the world of the exegete and the exegete's contemporaries; this function is to convey (manifest) what may be relied upon and who may be believed; it is a matter of orientation in the world in the deepest sense of the word. As has been suggested, allegory was guided by dogmatic tradition, but it is not clear to what extent literal meaning can fulfill the function of feedback that we have sought to define in relation to historical criticism (§3.7.2). What we might call existential interpretation in the sense associated with Martin Heidegger or Rudolf Bultmann is summed up in the moral meaning. This is not a matter of stipulating moral norms, of moralism, but of the application in life of that which is ontologically presupposed by the text. The last line of the rule, which speaks of anagogical interpretation, was handed down in several versions. Its meaning is best defined as an allusion to the referential horizon of the text, which goes beyond our experience, such that the "matter" of the text will be fully revealed only in the future.

The fourfold meaning of the text is an expression of the comprehensive approach to the text adopted by rhetoric as the crowning element of the medieval trivium (grammar, logic, rhetoric).

In the Reformation, when Martin Luther insisted on the literal sense of Scripture, rejecting the theory of fourfold meaning and developing the theory of the single meaning of the text *(sensus unitas)*, this did not entail a rejection of the fields of meaning to which the other interpretations were directed. It was more that the text was supposed to fulfill the other functions as the norm of direct address *(fides ex auditu)* — that is, through preaching or personal testimony.

Although the rejection of the theory of fourfold meaning was theoretically a result of the rule of "Scripture alone" *(sola Scriptura)*, in practice it was above all a rejection of the influence of the dogmatic magisterium on the interpretation of Scripture wherever the results were at odds with the literary meaning of the biblical text. It was not the hermeneutic rules of Protestantism but the relaxation of the influence of the church authorities on the interpretation of Scripture that led to the development of biblical science in the Protestant world. Luther's *Scriptura sui ipsius interpres* (Scripture is its own interpreter)[9] is not a summary of exegetic methods (and we must not understand it in this way!) but an expression of the experience that, in the

---

9. WA 7.97.32; quoted with comment by O. Bayer, "Hermeneutical Theology," in *Philosophical Hermeneutics and Biblical Exegesis*, ed. P. Pokorný and J. Roskovec (Tübingen: Mohr Siebeck, 2002), 103-20, here 118.

process of interpretation, it is not a matter of our understanding of the text but of the text interpreting the life of the interpreter.

The work of the Croatian reformer Matthias Flacius Illyricus (1520-75), in his *Clavis Scripturae Sacrae,* adopts Luther's theory but in the interpretation of Scripture starts entirely from the basis of rhetoric as the discipline associated with practical interpretation *(Tropi et schemata Sacrarum Literarum).* His influence can also be traced in the work *Gnomon Novi Testamenti,* by the Lutheran Pietist exegete Johann Albrecht Bengel.

The theologically motivated rule of the Reformation according to which Scripture is its own interpreter meant in practice that we cannot prematurely introduce information from outside the text into our interpretation of Scripture. Of the heritage of the medieval trivium, it was now the turn of grammar to come to the fore.

As we have already shown, however, the tendency to entirely exclude information from outside the text is dangerous. The idea that any kind of text can be interpreted as a self-sustaining, autonomous structure is an illusion, as we have seen in our discussion of thoroughgoing structuralism (§2.2.1).

4.2. Philology

Because theology continued to engage with the biblical text as a testimony of divine revelation, as a science it came to be closely identified with grammar and with philology. Today we are aware of the further dimensions of language that we discussed in the first section. Philology developed into linguistics, which learned to go beyond its own frontiers and to open itself up to hermeneutic reflection. All the same, lexical and grammatical analysis is methodologically the beginning of the interpretation of any text. The semantics of the individual phrases, the definition of their grammatical types and forms, the analysis of their syntax — all these are basic operations that need not be described in detail but still require for their mastery a knowledge of the language in which the text is written, basic philological knowledge, and, in the case of interpretation of a text written in a language not generally familiar to the assumed addressees of the interpretation, a knowledge of the basic rules of translation.

Philological work is undervalued today, and modern students of hermeneutics could learn its principles from the old German Meyer Commentaries on the New Testament (the first versions appeared over 150 years ago) or the older interpretations in the classic International Critical Commentary

Methods of Interpretation

series from Edinburgh. These remain the basis for more recent commentaries. There is nothing wrong with that. Practically all exegetical work relies on older exegeses and only reexamines and checks its results in disputed passages. It is easy enough to identify such disputed places and open problems: we look for what we ourselves do not understand in the older interpretations. Sometimes, however, we may need to recheck what at first sight are comprehensible results of the modern German and English tradition and get over the barrier that they may represent.

4.2.1. Translation

BIBLIOGRAPHY

Buzetti, Carlo. *La Bibbia e la sua traduzione*. Turin: Leumann, 1993.
Dostálová, Růžena. "La traduzione nell'antichita classica." In *Comunicazione. Istituto papirologico "G. Vitelli,"* 19-42. Florence, 1995.
Klaudy, Kinga. "In Defence of Linguistic Theory of Translation." In *Hovory o překládání a tlumočení*, ed. M. Hrdlička and R. Redek, 136-55. Prague: Interlingue Servis, 1991.
Mounin, Georges. *Linguistique et traduction*. Brussels: Dessart & Mardaga, 1976.
Nida, Eugene A., and Charles R. Taber. *The Theory of Translation*. Brill: Leiden, 1969.
Pokorný, Petr. "Problém biblických překladů" [The Problem of Biblical Translations]. In *Tōn logōn asfaleia. Sborník Katolické teologické fakulty (FS F. Novák)*, ed. J. Brož, 210-15. Prague: Karolinum, 2000.
Porter, Stanley E., and Richard S. Hess. *Translating the Bible*. Sheffield, Eng.: Sheffield Academic Press, 1999.
Reiss, Katharina, and Hans J. Vermeer. *Grundlegung einer allgemeinen Translationstheorie*. Tübingen: Niemeyer, 1984.

Translation is a basic hermeneutic task without which we cannot interpret any text written in a language that is not understood by the majority of the anticipated receivers of the interpretation, either because it is a foreign language or because it is an older form of their mother tongue. The historical importance of translation as the first prerequisite of understanding is suggested by the legend of the Tower of Babel in Genesis 11, according to which the proliferation of human languages was a punishment for the pride of the builders in trying to construct a tower high enough to touch heaven. It is very likely that the description of the Pentecost miracle of mutual understanding between Jews who spoke different languages (Acts 2) was understood by "Luke," the author of the gospel and of Acts, as a new beginning.

Hermeneutics as a Theory of Understanding

What is certain is that Theodoret of Cyrrhus[10] understood this narrative as authorization for spreading the gospel in foreign (barbarian) languages: language can once again be regarded as an instrument of communication rather than division. This basic perspective, the "hopeful" dimension of communication, is actually the premise of any understanding at all, but it is in translation that we become particularly aware of its necessity.

If we look closer at the character of work on translation, we gain a better understanding of the whole hermeneutic process. The theory of translation is also important as a potential starting point of expositions of hermeneutics just because the necessity of translation is something understood even by people who believe that they can get by without hermeneutics as the theory of interpretation. When we are learning a foreign language, we become aware of phenomena that we had adopted automatically in using our own language and so had not noticed as a problem. When we learn individual "vocabulary," we realize that the semantic field of individual foreign expressions does not coincide neatly with all that is expressed by the words presented to us as their equivalents in our mother language. And all this even before we get to the structure of the sentence! When I was simultaneously translating lectures given by some of my German colleagues, I often had the urge to call out, "The verb, Hans, the verb!" I had to keep storing a growing amount of information translated into Czech in my short-term memory because the predicate was still missing. This is because in German the verb comes at the end of the sentence, but in Czech everything to which the verb relates usually comes after the verb. The Czech translator is left struggling to do this while the German speaker has already started on a new sentence!

At the same time, we have to try to observe other rules of translation that demand that the translated sentence should not be strikingly longer or shorter than the sentence in the original language.

This is already proof that a translation is no mere recoding of the initial text but a complicated communication operation. For translators to produce a good translation, they must have more than just a good knowledge of the two languages. They must also know the theory of translation. The basic impulse behind the development of this theory was provided by the Prague Circle between the world wars. As early as the years of the First World War, Vilém Mathesius wrote that the aim of a translation is to achieve the same artistic effect on the contemporary reader as the original had on the original reader. Later this statement was restated as a more general precept and we

---

10. *PG* 82.335.

therefore speak only of the rule of analogical effect. The theory of translation based on this rule is known as the *linguistic theory of translation* (LTT), which Eugene A. Nida elaborated after the Second World War for the practical needs of translation of the Bible.

As we have already seen, it is pretty well impossible to translate word for word, concordantly. This kind of translation is possible only in the case of a few expressions that have acquired the function of technical terms, in biblical texts sometimes substituting for entire brief professions of belief. In the New Testament these are Jesus' titles; in Johannine writings, for example, the terms "Word" *(logos)* or "glory" *(doxa)*; and in the Pauline epistles, the expression "justification" (i.e., at the judgment of God) or "gospel." The special function of such expressions needs to be explained in a note to the translation. In the first part of our account (§2) we noted more than once that it is the sentence that is the bearer of meaning. This is not a lexical but a grammatical form, which is structured differently in every language, and thus conversion from one language to another is possible only in a mediated way, via a metagrammar that includes elements of the transmitting and the receiving languages. In a good translation it is not necessary and often not even possible to translate a verb by a verb or a noun by a noun, or to use the same number of conjunctions as the original. The metagrammar identifies analogically functioning elements in the grammar of the two languages. Mostly it involves a reduction of the elements to indication or expression of (1) the subject — that which the action relates to, in practice a person or thing; (2) the action, usually expressed by a verb; and (3) the abstract, which expresses a valuation (positive-negative; characterizing, suggesting a perspective); and (4) relation — who, to whom, and so forth. The original text needs to be transformed twice — first into metagrammar and then into the second language. In its primary features the basic schema of translation therefore resembles the schema of interpretation:

> The author — the author's text in the original language (A) — the metagrammatical transformation — translation into the receiving language — reader of the translation.

The key role played in interpretation by the creation of a common linguistic world (§5.2), is in this case played by the transformation into metagrammar, which we have just described.

The result should not be strikingly longer than the original to the ear (phonetically).[11]

11. The length of the written record depends partially on orthography. Czech orthog-

Hermeneutics as a Theory of Understanding

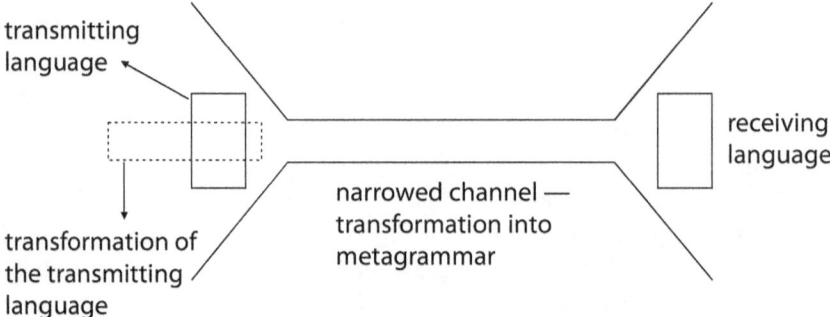

Adapted from Nida and Taber, pp. 164-65

The objection that some interpreters are not aware of these linguistic operations has no force. Certain procedures can be learned in practice and used unconsciously. But as soon as we encounter a new saying or turn of phrase, as is frequent in translating, the translator cannot manage without professional knowledge — without a theory of translation.

Translations of the Bible into national languages started in antiquity (Latin, Coptic, Syrian, Armenian, Georgian, Ethiopian), but the practice continued into the Middle Ages only rarely (Gothic and Old Slavonic as unofficial translations from the Latin, and some others, including the first fragmentary version of a Czech translation). It was the Reformation and humanism that gave the basic impulse for translations into modern vernacular languages. In their own cultural milieus the Reformation translations acquired such authority that they were later adjusted to the continuing development of the receiving language only by revisions, and when new translations were made at all, these were not used in the liturgy. Most such new translations were only of the New Testament. The signal of a new epoch was the New English Bible (complete Bible in 1970) — a new translation from the original languages.

Experts from the translation department of the *United Bible Societies* (UBS) then adapted the LTT to the need of creating translations of the Bible into the vernacular that would appeal to a wide range of potential readers. The translation was supposed to remove the ambiguities and obscurities of the original by opting for just one (the most likely) concept, and to convert terms bound up with biblical times into modern equivalents (e.g., the num-

---

raphy is unusually economical, while German takes up a lot of space. German-Czech decrees under the German Protectorate offer a telling illustration.

bering of night watches according to our modern clock). Later there was also a tendency, strong but in practice rather difficult to apply except by minor hints, to take the text of the original out of its patriarchal social framework (e.g., to replace the address to "brothers" with an address to the whole Christian community). This movement produced a whole cluster of translations of the *Common Language Translation* (CLT) type into many European languages (Gute Nachricht, Good News, Français courant, etc.). It brought the Bible closer to two generations of readers and sold millions in this form. It was a trend that eventually went beyond the bounds of translation proper and resulted in paraphrases of the *Living Bible* type, which appeared in several languages. Translation was supposed to replace interpretation.

Yet it was a trend that did not last. In 1973 a new English translation was produced in evangelical circles — the New International Version (NIV), which was closer to the original, rejected the peculiarities of CLT, but essentially held to the linguistic theory of translation and sold in hundreds of thousands. The New Revised Standard Version (1989), a translation supported by the UBS as an answer to the NIV, is today considered the belated but essential step by which the UBS at least partly preserved its important position as service provider of biblical texts for all denominations of the Christian church.

The equation that was inspired by the thought of Vilém Mathesius, and was the decisive step for the new conception of translation, applies only to the aesthetic effect of the translation.

We most often encounter this rule in an equation expressing ideal effect

$$\frac{\text{original} \to \text{original reader}}{\text{translation} \to \text{contemporary reader}}$$

The whole process of translation, however, has another side. We shall be discussing the fact that one of the reasons old texts interest us is precisely their age, their otherness, and that it is precisely as old texts that they continue to fascinate, even though they speak to us only indirectly (see §5.1). The function of the translation is therefore different from the function of the original. Readers cannot forget the distance in time; they are constantly aware of it, and the translation cannot hide it from them. Proper and geographic names are a clear accompanying sign of reference. They obstinately resist attempts at translation and so invite us into their own world. A translation that tries to obscure the difference would be dishonest. Jerusalem is Jerusalem and cannot be replaced by Prague. The stadion is an unfamiliar unit of length for today's reader but cannot be replaced with information in yards or miles, meters or kilometers. That would be an anachronism. The datum "sixty stadia" (Luke 24:13) can at best be translated as "three hour's journey" — that is, by a measure still used today.

Nor, where it is not essential, should a translation eliminate biblical metaphors by converting them into mere direct statements or replacing them with contemporary metaphors. On the contrary, it should strive to evoke the basic features of the past world, including the differences in style of different biblical texts, which the translation should at least suggest. This applies not only to the Bible but to all old texts.

A translation of the Bible is, moreover, a liturgical text, to be read out aloud on Sundays and feast days. There can and ought to be more than one translation in each language so as to allow the different aspects of the original to be highlighted, but the translations used in liturgy need to be clear and comprehensible to the ear, must reproduce the aesthetic dimension of the biblical text, and must be relatively easy to remember and learn by heart.

A good translation of a biblical text should also enable the reader to recognize which places require interpretation and which places require the use of a commentary. These are not just places that include period meanings and allusions, but also discursive texts (argument) that assume a certain level of philosophical or theological thought. A good translation does not therefore remove incomprehensible places and replace interpretation but should draw attention to places that require interpretation.

The basic means to test a translation is naturally to compare it with the original. A translation itself is a text that in principle, by its own character, is not designed for translation.

4.3. Synchronic Interpretation and Projects Based on It

BIBLIOGRAPHY

Amador, J. David Hester. *Academic Constraints in Rhetorical Criticism of the New Testament.* Sheffield, Eng.: Sheffield Academic Press, 1999.

Barthes, Roland, François Bovon, Franz J. Leenhardt, Robert Martin-Achard, and Jean Starobinski. *Analyse structurale et exégèse biblique. Essais d'interprétation.* Neuchâtel: Delachaux & Niestlé, 1971. ET *Structural Analysis and Biblical Exegesis: Interpretational Essays* (Pittsburgh: Pickwick Press, 1974).

Bovon, François, and Grégoire Rouiller, eds. *Exegesis. Problèmes de méthode et exercices de lecture (Genèse 22 et Luc 15).* Neuchâtel: Delachaux & Niestlé, 1975. ET *Exege-*

sis: Problems of Method and Exercises in Reading (Genesis 22 and Luke 15) (Pittsburgh: Pickwick Press, 1978).
Brooke, George J., and Jean-Daniel Kaestli. *Narrativity in Biblical and Related Texts.* Leuven: Leuven University Press, 2000.
Calloud, Jean. *L'analyse structurale du récit.* Lyons: Faculté de théologie de Lyon, 1973. ET *Structural Analysis of Narrative* (Philadelphia: Fortress Press, 1976).
Greenwood, David. *Structuralism and the Biblical Text.* Berlin: Mouton, 1985.
Greimas, Algirdas J. *Sémantique structurale.* 1986; 2d ed., Paris: Larousse, 1995.
Kennedy, George A. *New Testament Interpretation through Rhetorical Criticism.* Chapel Hill: University of North Carolina Press, 1984.
Lausberg, Heinrich. *Handbook of Literary Rhetoric.* Leiden: Brill, 1998.
Meynet, Roland. *L'analyse rhétorique.* Paris: du Cerf, 1989. ET *Rhetorical Analysis* (Sheffield, Eng.: Sheffield Academic Press, 1998).
Muilenburg, James. "Form Criticism and Beyond." *Journal of Biblical Literature* 88 (1969): 1-18.
Patte, Daniel. *Structural Exegesis for New Testament Critics.* Minneapolis: Fortress Press, 1990.
Pontifical Biblical Commission. "The Interpretation of the Bible in the Church" (April 23, 1993). *Origins* 23, no. 29 (January 6, 1994): 497-524.
Robbins, Vernon K. *The Tapestry of Early Christian Discourse.* London: Routledge, 1996.
Wilder, Amos N. *Early Christian Rhetoric.* 1964; 2d ed., Cambridge, Mass.: Harvard University Press, 1971.

Today literary interpretation for the most part starts from structural analysis of the text, as already described (§2.3). Yet it also involves a more comprehensive approach, one that, unlike structural analysis, respects and seriously explores the traditions that are the starting point of the text, which the text picks up and develops, becoming itself a new interpretation of those traditions.[12]

By the end of the 1960s it was clear that the diachronic approach to the text, which saw the text primarily as a historical source, was inadequate. The "school of the history of redaction" (see §4.4.4.2) sidelined the problem of the historical reconstruction of the events to which the texts related and turned to thorough mapping of the thinking of the author, who had worked all his or her material into the literary form of the text. If this school at least retained a diachronic element in understanding the literary form of the text as historically the last stage of its genesis, what is known as "rhetorical criticism" approaches the text in a thoroughly synchronic way — as a literary

---

12. P. Ricoeur, *Le conflit des interprétations* (Paris: du Seuil, 1989), cited from the German translation *Hermeneutik und Strukturalismus* (Munich: Kösel, 1973), 176-77. English translation: *Conflict of Interpretations* (Evanston, Ill.: Northwestern University Press, 1994).

whole that can be understood only when we know the rules of the formation of such a text in both its particular grammatical and its stylistic dimensions, as well as in the structuring of the whole literary genre.

Historical, diachronic interpretation focused above all on the creation of the text and its relation to what preceded its creation, while rhetorical analysis works synchronically — asking what connects a given text with the other texts of a similar type and from the same period. It seeks to understand form and content as mutually interconnected, to throw light on the unity of the text.

Terminologically, we need to draw attention to the fact that this is actually a thoroughly literary approach and that English-speaking scholars were the first to establish the term "rhetorical criticism," using "rhetorical" in this context in the broader sense of rhetoric as the crowning element of the medieval trivium, as mentioned above (§4.1). In this sense rhetoric is not (just) a matter of the verbal delivery of a text by an orator but relates to the overall literary treatment, which, as we can see from examples from Aristotle's *Poetics,* itself exploits the rules of rhetoric.

Like all movements and methodologies in literary criticism, rhetorical criticism necessarily seeks to understand the text from the inside, depending as little as possible on information gained from outside. A thorough synchronic approach is based on the text in its preserved form and does not even concern itself with the intention of the author. Either the author embodied it in the text and it can be read out of it, or, if it cannot, it cannot serve as a norm for interpretation of the text. We have already noted that the question "What did the author mean to say by this?" is definitely not in the foreground today. Furthermore, in some cases the author is hard or impossible to identify. To speak of the author's intentions is therefore, according to thorough proponents of structural analysis, an illusion (the term used is the *intentional fallacy*). But it is precisely here that a dispute currently going on between literary theoreticians starts: if the work expresses the intention of the author, it is clear that it can never express that intention in its entirety, but if great, classic works face every reader with the need to make a decision (see §5.5.2 on testimony), then knowledge of the author is an important contribution to understanding the function of the text[13] and so to making that decision. For this reason literary science is also interested in the lives of the great writers. The connection between an author's life and his or her work is entirely indirect, but it is impossible not to be interested in it. Earlier we

---

13. For a critique of the theory of the *intentional fallacy,* see, e.g., E. D. Hirsch Jr., *Validity in Interpretation* (New Haven: Yale University Press, 1967).

Methods of Interpretation

spoke of interpretation as a substitute for dialogue with the author (§3.3). In Plato's *Apology* (22B-C) we read that it is sometimes impossible to have a precise understanding of the intention of the author of a text, but in fact this remark relates only to the margins of the author's argumentation. Plato has no doubt that the author's basic intention is evident. This is usually comprehensible even where the author is unknown. We therefore cannot displace the author as subject from our ideas when we interpret a text. Yet, if we want to understand the issue from the point of view that interests supporters of a thoroughgoing synchronic interpretation, we are bound to note that only through the text can we get to know something of the author's inner world.

4.3.1. Rhetorical Criticism

"Rhetorical analysis" is the overall term for the synchronic analysis of texts as it has become established above all among English-speaking Bible scholars.[14] For this reason we shall take examples from the Bible. The term "rhetoric" in this context is used in a broad sense and includes philological and literary interpretation. Its elementary form is grammatico-stylistic analysis. This begins with individual sentences.

PSALM 90:7
For example, in Psalm 90:7 we read the sentence "For we are consumed by your anger; by your wrath we are overwhelmed." Stylistic analysis shows that this is a parallelism. Its two parallel parts can be identified by different arrangement on the page:

>   For your anger   consumes us;
>   by your wrath   we are overwhelmed.

The idea of being consumed is derived from the premise that a person's life is at odds with the will of God. The parallelism serves to drive the message home, expressing it aesthetically.

---

14. For a full presentation of the method of rhetorical criticism, see G. A. Kennedy, *New Testament Interpretation through Rhetorical Criticism* (Chapel Hill: University of North Carolina Press, 1984), 3-38; see also S. Porter and D. L. Stamps, eds., *Rhetorical Criticism and the Bible* (Sheffield, Eng.: Sheffield Academic Press, 2002). The term "rhetorical analysis" was proposed in 1968 by J. Muilenburg at the annual meeting of the Society of Biblical Literature, meeting in Berkeley, California.

Hermeneutics as a Theory of Understanding

More important than this kind of observation is the actual statement contained in the text, which thorough synchronic analysis can sometimes help us understand better. In this case it is a serious statement about the temporary, mortal character of human life. Unlike statements in which the finitude of human life is formulated as part of its nature as creation, here what is stressed is death not as culmination but as end, as a cutting off — that is, as a result of alienation from God. Connected with this is the small shift in the second part of the parallelism: fear of death arises here precisely from the fact that (alienated) human life calls forth God's wrath and is therefore something subject to judgment, not merely a matter of chance. But even the communication of a judgment of this kind (and Ps 90:7 is undoubtedly such a communication) implies and includes hope. We can find this hope in the context: "So teach us to count our days . . ." (mapping out life; v. 12) and "Turn, O Lord! . . . Satisfy us in the morning with your steadfast love" (vv. 13-14). Analysis of the structure of the verse is thus a springboard for actual interpretation.

JOHN 10:7-18
Using the technique of rhetorical analysis we can, for example, write out the section from the Gospel of John in which Jesus speaks of himself as "the good shepherd" in such a way that Jesus' "I am"s in verses 7 and 9 ("I am the gate") and in verses 11 and 14 ("I am the good shepherd") are arranged one above the other. Below them we then add "I came" from verse 10b and "I lay down my life" and "I lay it down" in verses 17 and 18. In terms of both grammar and style, each of these statements is a stimulus for and at the same time the founding statement of the following argumentation. In every case we read the Greek "I" *(egō)*; the pronoun is grammatically superfluous and serves simply to emphasize the role of the subject. Under verse 8 in a column set off to the right we then place the statements suggesting the consequences of the alternative possibility (allowing oneself to be led by other shepherds) and its limits (the sheep do not obey them, introduced by the conjunction "but" — to be entered on another offset righthand line). Expressed in Verse 9b is the positive meaning of "to go in through the door," which is Jesus. It means salvation and pasture (after use of the corresponding abstract the same reality is expressed metaphorically, in the frame of the linguistic field "shepherd"). The reader is already aware that here the door as a narrowed space of communication between two areas is an expression of the mediating role of Jesus. In Verse 10 the reverse possibility is expressed once again: to allow oneself to be guided by thieves and robbers. Its end is death (intro-

duced by the conjunction "but"; again a new statement). The following momentous new statement ("I came") is introduced by "in order": "in order that they should have life in abundance." Verses 12 and 13 ought to be set even further to the side, since they describe how destruction occurs under the guidance of the false shepherd. The latter is no longer characterized as a "thief" and "robber" but as hired labor. This is because in this extreme case he is no longer preying like a robber on the flock entrusted to him but running away from the wolf — a greater and common danger — failing to look after the sheep entrusted to him and giving them up to death. The second "I am the good shepherd" (v. 14) introduces the directly parallel, positively directed statement about the relationship between the good shepherd and the sheep (they know each other well — the statement needs once again to be broken down into two parts arranged one above the other) and follows a reference to the fundamental relationship of mutual knowledge, that is, the relationship between Jesus and "the Father" (God). This initiates a small section expressing the basis of the salvation that the good shepherd brings (vv. 15 and 16), in the same way as verses 12 and 13 spoke of destruction under the guidance of the false shepherd. The reason is that the relationship between Jesus and God is the ground of Jesus' actions to benefit the flock, for whose sake he is willing to give his life, which he has accepted as the gift of God. The point is that a new chance has been given (life). It exceeds the expectation of the readers (listeners): it relates not only to the sheep that feel addressed by the words about the flock but also to other "sheep" that will also be saved. Verse 17 expresses the pragmatics of Jesus' sacrifice: Jesus knows to whom his life belongs, and so he must give it up "in order to take it up again," and must give it up voluntarily (another "I lay down" in verse 18). Verse 18b should be set off to the left. It is a summary of what has been said. As a separate line in the stylistic articulation, it will form the final part of the complex sentence.

7	I am the gate (very truly).	× 8	thieves and bandits
9	I am the gate.		the sheep did not listen to them.
	Whoever enters by me will be saved.		
10b	I came into the world	× 10a	The thief comes only to steal.
11	I am the good shepherd.	× 12	The hired hand, who is not the
	The good shepherd lays down his life		shepherd, leaves the sheep and
	for the sheep		runs away.
14	I am the good shepherd.	× 13	The hired hand
	I know my own and my own know me.		does not care for the sheep.

Hermeneutics as a Theory of Understanding

15 The Father knows me and I know the Father.
And I lay down my life for the sheep.
16 I have other sheep . . . one flock, one shepherd.
17a For this reason the Father loves me,
17b I lay down my life
in order to take it up again.
18a No one takes it from me, but
18b I lay it down of my own accord.
I have power to lay it down,
and I have power to take it up again.
I have received this command from my Father.

The arrangement of verses that we have presented to readers here is in fact an attempt to highlight, as the successive "surface" of the text is traced from left to right and also downward, places that reach into the deeper structure of the metaphorical language. In the 1970s there was a fashion for this kind of exercise in arrangement of text, but it soon passed, and some textbooks of rhetorical analysis make rather tedious reading today. It is not that they were not useful, but they were less useful than biblical scholars believed at the time, and the technique often leads to the accumulation of superfluous information that distracts from the real issues. It would be the foundation of interpretation if we were to insist on a structuralist approach to the text (C-matrix),[15] but if we are interested in concrete statements and meaning, we must recognize that the findings yielded by the exercise are on the border between what the author was consciously expressing and what can be identified in the subconscious or unconscious structure of any serious communication. Interpretation itself must concentrate on the author's testimony — his or her conscious interpretation of tradition. Grammatical-stylistic subdivision is an essential warm-up exercise, and an interpreter should not embark on genuine interpretation of the text without it, but these preliminary exercises need not always be conducted in front of the reader. Contemporary commentaries offer only a small sample of material of this kind. To bring out the meaning of rhetorical analysis, I have chosen a text in which the basic realities appear in relatively simple grammatical and stylistic structures.

Analysis must in this case start from an overview of the whole text of John's gospel and its role in the framework of Christian literature. Only on this

---

15. This is different from the P-paradigm; see above §2.2.2.

Methods of Interpretation

basis can we understand the Johannine speech with the statements "I am," which have a "revelatory" function and draw the reader's attention to the fact that his or her own relatively egocentric world (see §2.1.2.2) has a counterpart to which it must relate. The explicit "I" is underlined. The semantics of the metaphor touches on the foundations of Christian faith: life "abundantly" (v. 10b) is "eternal life," life in the presence of God, the fulfillment and goal of earthly life. This may be deduced from the final statements, but the basic key to this level of the text has been given in the Johannine prologue in chapter 1. In the final statement there again appears the theme of the deliberate "descent" of Jesus to earth and his "incarnation" as the mode of God's journey to humankind — that is, the basic framework of Christian witness according to these currents within it that were to become the mainstream of the later church of the pagans, from which most of the canonized texts came. By contrast, the concrete identification of false leaders depends on knowledge of the period. From the text we can determine only their internal characteristics.

ROMANS 7:7-25

Let us take another example, this time a piece of argument (a discursive passage), and use Paul's reasoning in Romans 7:7-25, where the apostle analyzes the inner conflict of a person under the control of sin.[16]

> 7   Should we say that the law is sin? By no means!
>   Yet, if it had not been for the law, I would not have known sin.
>   I would not have known what it is to covet if the law had not said,
>   "You shall not covet."
>> 8 But sin, seizing an opportunity in the commandment,
>> produced in me all kinds of covetousness. (repeated in v. 11)
>> Apart from the law sin lies dead.
>> 9 I was once alive apart from the law,
>> but when the commandment came,
>> sin revived (10) and I died. . . .
> 13 Did what is good, then, bring death to me? By no means!
>   It was sin, working death in me through what is good, in order
>   that sin might be shown to be sin, and through the
>   commandment might become sinful beyond measure.
>   14 For we know that the law is spiritual;

---

16. N. Aletti, "Rhetorical Criticism and Its Usefulness," *Svensk exegetisk årsbok* 61 (1996): 77-95.

> (repeated statement from v. 12)
> but I am of flesh,
> sold into slavery under sin.
> 15 I do not understand my own actions.
> For I do not do what I want, but I do the very thing I hate.

The whole passage is divided into two sections by the two rhetorical questions, in verses 7 and 13. In both cases the apostle replies with an emphatic negative (Gr. *mē genoito*). The expositions that follow the questions consist of reasons for the negative position that at the same time develop into a positive thesis. In both cases the argument starts with a parallel expressing the same claim in two ways. This drives the point home to readers and helps them realize the implications. In the first segment Paul shows that law itself brings the distinction between good and evil, and so readers realize that to speak of evil means at the same time to be able to recognize and know what is good. But the apostle then suggests the other side of the process: by coming to know the law, we also come to know sin. Sin (alienation from God) can be recognized only where justice is known. The argument then takes a further step: while the law itself is just, the knowledge of the clear boundary between good and evil arouses a desire to go beyond it (transgress it); the law "awakens" covetousness *(epithymia)*.

In the second segment the author continues to speak consistently in the first person (let us underline the emphasized "I" — *ego*) and demonstrates his claims on the example of his own life and self-understanding.

> 16 Now if I do what I do not want,
> I agree that the law is good.
> 17 But in fact it is no longer I that do it,
> but sin that dwells within me.
> 18 For I know that nothing good dwells within me, that is, in my flesh [*sarx*]. I can will what is right, but I cannot do it.
> 19 For I do not do the good I want, but the evil I do not want is what I do.

The contradiction spoken of by the apostle is described as a splitting of the self ("it is no longer I . . .").

> 20 Now if I do what I do not want, it is no longer I that do it,
> but sin that dwells within me.

Methods of Interpretation

Sin appears here as a subject, as a power of a personal nature over a human being.

> 21 So I find it to be a law that
> when I want to do right, evil lies close at hand.
> 22 For I delight in the law of God in my inmost self,
> 23 but I see in my members another law
> at war with the law of my mind,
> making me captive to the law of sin
> that dwells in my members.

Starting from verse 21, we encounter the expression "law" *(nomos)* in new meanings.[17] Until now (vv. 14 and 16, and again 22 and 23), it has been entirely clear that what is meant is the law of Moses. Now in verse 21 the same expression appears in the sense of "rule," "inevitability" (natural principle), or "tendency" (to abandon the law), and in verse 23 there is a reference to the "law of sin." Law as the tendency to abandon the Mosaic law is not identical with the "law of sin" but may be the expression of the latter. "I"[18] is the place of the conflict, in which the influences of sin and the divine mercy manifest in Jesus meet and struggle.

> 24 Wretched man that I am!
>   Who will rescue me from this body of death?
> 25 Thanks be to God through Jesus Christ our Lord!
>   So then, with my mind I am a slave to the law of God,
>   but with my flesh I am a slave to the law of sin.

Verse 25 is an answer that is valid, provided that the preceding description is conceived as a matter of the Christian's past, that is, his or her life before coming to believe. The term "law" appears here in the first meaning, but its meaning has expanded. It is now only indirectly the law of Moses, for the context indicates that it is above all the will of God manifest in the person of Jesus and in his actions. Yet the peculiar interweaving of the statements, with the words about inner conflict appearing even after the solemn expression of gratitude in verse 25a, suggests that life in slavery to sin is not simply re-

---

17. See Aletti, "Rhetorical Criticism," 85-88.
18. In verses 18 and 25 (translated "flesh" in the NRSV), the expression used in Greek is *sarx*, by which Paul denotes the ontological alienation of humankind.

placed on conversion by the life of faith. Sin is manifest as a pressure even in this present age. Sin is something still to be reckoned with, and it is still necessary "by the Spirit" to "put to death the deeds of the body" (Rom 8:13). This is a conclusion that already goes slightly beyond the possibilities of rhetorical analysis, but we would not have reached it if we had failed to be aware of the individual steps in Paul's argumentation.

In this case an analysis of the agents (actants) involved in Paul's argumentation is particularly useful. Here the apostle himself appears as the model of a believing adherent of Jesus Christ who has retrospectively recognized that he is not an entirely autonomous being as "I." Through knowledge of the law of Moses, which he gained as a Jew, he has come to know "sin" (straying, revolt against God), which is described here as a subject. Sin influences a person's entire character and also abuses his or her knowledge of the law. Thus human beings become alienated not only from God but from their own selves, their humanity ("But in fact it is no longer I that do it," v. 17; "If I do what I do not want, it is no longer I that do it . . . ," v. 20 and so on). In describing this situation in a way that allows every reader to identify with his role and his argumentation, Paul is therefore a "mediating player." He even has in mind the human being as a historical being, because he uses his own case (in order to demonstrate the role of the human "I"), not only to describe the danger of sin, but also to present life without the law as his own experience, although as a born Jew he had not experienced this state unless he was referring to his transition from childhood to adulthood. Man stands as a mediating player between the law and sin, each of which — for these are personified subjects — tries to draw him to its side. It looks as if cunning (bifurcating) sin must inevitably win. Its victory is the death of the human being (vv. 10-11). It is only in verse 25 that it turns out that, behind the law, stands God himself, who intervenes on behalf of humankind, not only through the law, which teaches what is bad, but also through Jesus Christ. In the following section (Rom. 8:1-17), Paul shows how God, by validating the crucified Jesus, has revealed the limits of the power of sin: death is not the final reality; beyond and above it is the territory of the action of the Holy Spirit. Here Spirit does not appear as the opposite of matter; it is the place where the good will of God is spontaneously fulfilled, "in the Spirit." By appealing to Christ as the Lord (Gr. *kyrios*, v. 25), Paul does not cease to be exposed to the pressure of sin, but he conveys to his readers that the possibility of overcoming the internal conflict opens up only on God's side.

The examples given here suggest the potential of approaches rediscovered by rhetorical criticism, but there are also various inconsistencies in the theory of rhetorical criticism.

Methods of Interpretation

It is natural that the questions left open by rhetorical criticism have prompted, and are still prompting, attempts to create an integrated method for the interpretation of text. Only a minority of monographs and textbooks have consistently confined themselves to rhetorical analysis, the extreme example being Roland Meynet's *Rhetorical Analysis*. In the last section we based our discussion primarily on biblical texts because Bible study is the largest field in which scholars work intensively with ancient texts with the explicit intention of testing methods of literary hermeneutics in their interpretation. We have seen that the rule that findings must be based only on the text and there should be no initial use of any other sources apart from comparison with analogical structures in other texts cannot be respected to the letter. Although it was intended as the starting point for further work, it is impossible to apply consistently, even in the initial stage. One reason that a text becomes the object of interest is its age, which testifies to its power to find an audience. Without a preliminary determination of its age, we would be unable to tackle the elements of intertextuality that we find in it. Are passages in the text that we find we already know taken from older sources, or are our other sources later and dependent on the text before us? It is not usually hard to answer such questions, and we generally take such information more or less for granted in interpretation. But by doing so, we are already augmenting the "pure" rules of rhetorical analysis with other procedures.

To say this is obviously not to solve the problem and provide a comprehensive interpretative approach. It is therefore understandable that most of the textbooks and fundamental monographs on hermeneutics cover a range of different theories of, and approaches to, interpretation. An overview and practical assessment of these theories and approaches for the field of biblical studies appears in Robert Morgan and John Barton's well-known university textbook *Biblical Interpretation*.[19] W. Randolph Tate went a step further in his American textbook, which has an identical title and similar orientation.[20] As the subtitle, "An Integrated Approach," suggests, the author tried here to provide a methodologically rounded-off guide to the use of the various individual methods. He divides them into what is "behind" the text (questions of language), what is "inside" the world of the text, and what is "in front" of the text, that is, what readers bring from their side to dialogue with

---

19. Morgan and Barton, *Biblical Interpretation* (Oxford: Oxford University Press, 1988, and subsequent editions).

20. Tate, *Biblical Interpretation* (Peabody, Mass.: Hendrickson, 1991; 3d ed., 2008).

the text (this is above all a question of their preliminary knowledge). The book is an important attempt to create an integrated methodology, and at least from the point of view of didactics, this is in itself a success, but it still is no more than a compilation of methods that derive from different premises and traditions. To integrate them requires more than just combination. It is necessary to create a more comprehensive, thought-out hermeneutic theory.

We are compelled to create a more complex theory by the structure of some texts. Because structure is not just form but is a matter of the combination of statement and form that we meet even in the most elementary elements of speech (the phoneme and meaning cannot be separated from each other in the linguistic context), we need to express how the views or attitudes of the actants are reflected in the structure of the text. Using the example in Paul's Epistle to the Romans, we have already indicated how this can work in the case of a discursive text. It can be demonstrated, however, even more clearly in a narrative text:

Mark 3:1-6

The story of the healing of the man with the withered hand, for example, has a clear chiastic structure (graphically analogous to the Greek letter chi = X). A detailed analysis of the story reveals the dramatic plot, individual roles, and hidden argumentation.

Jesus as the positive character has his negative counterpart in the Pharisees and Herodians (the opponents). The reader is made aware of their attitude right at the beginning: "They watched him to see whether he would cure him on the sabbath" (v. 2), and also at the end: "[they conspired] against him, how to destroy him" (v. 6). Jesus is characterized by the fact that he heals and essentially saves life (soul, v. 4). The people in the synagogue and with them the reader (listener to the reading) are mediating actors, for it is they who have to decide. Clearly the crippled man himself, who is asked to "come forward" (v. 3), represents these people. They are faced with a question — "Is it lawful to do good or to do harm on the sabbath, to save life or to kill?" (v. 4; note the parallelism) — that the opponents cannot or do not want to answer. This question in itself involves a norm. And by their silence the opponents give the initiative into Jesus' hands (the positive character, the literary "hero"), and the reader recognizes that their attitude is in fact only a reaction to Jesus' action and words. This is confirmed by the fact that the opponents themselves breach the norm that they were unable to reject but did not wish to accept ("conspired . . . how to destroy him," v. 6).

(situation) "Again he entered the synagogue, and a man was there who had a withered hand."
A (opponents — Jesus) "They watched him to see whether he would cure him on the sabbath, so that they might accuse him."
  B (Jesus — sick man) "And he said to the man who had the withered hand, 'Come forward.'"
    C (Jesus — opponents) "Then he said to them, 'Is it lawful to do good or to do harm on the sabbath, to save life or to kill?'" (key question)
      D (confirmation of validity of key statement) "But they were silent."
    C' (Jesus — opponents) "He looked around at them with anger, he was grieved at their hardness of heart"
  B' (Jesus — sick man) "and said to the man, 'Stretch out your hand.' He stretched it out, and his hand was restored."
(confirmation of validity of key statement)
A' (opponents — Jesus) "The Pharisees went out and immediately conspired with the Herodians against him, how to destroy him."

By analyzing a pericope of this kind, we uncover not only its stylistics and aesthetic effect, but also the argumentation contained in it and the role of the different people — the bearers of the action (actants) — which we have tried to indicate here. Closer lexical and phraseological exploration would also reveal the "second level" of the story: in New Testament times "to save life" *(psychēn sōsai)* was already understood as having a double meaning. It related both to saving physical life and to "eternal salvation" (see "Do not fear those who kill the body but cannot kill the soul [*psychē*]," Matt. 10:28). At that time "soul" meant "life" and was an expression for the inner identity of the human being as a person. As soon as the reader sets this pericope in the context of the Gospel of Mark as a whole, it is evident that this second level of the story is, as it were, an overlap in the direction of the Easter gospel of Jesus' resurrection (Mark 16:6) and concerned with the substitutive and saving (soteriological) meaning of his life (e.g., Mark 10:45).

Is the striking symmetrical structure the conscious work of the author, or is it just a matter of the unconscious logic of speech? And is the second level his conscious work, or is it just a reflection of the polysemic character of the speech of early Christian groups — their idiolect? A consistently synchronic approach asks only about the function of the text, not the way that it was created. The trouble is that the overall intention of the text, which can be read out of its macrostructure (in this case it is a question of theological direction), is so momentous (this is about the gospel and the role of Jesus as the Son of God) that it is important to know how deeply it affects the structure of the individual pericopes. That is, how far are we able to connect — and how justified are we in connecting — what can be read out of it with the theology of the whole macrotext evidently formulated by the author? A wide-angle synchronic view makes it practically impossible to distinguish between the function of the text and the intention of the author. These are problems that continue to bedevil the synchronic method and suggest that it cannot be developed in isolation.

Nor have the problems of synchronic interpretation been solved even by some entirely newly conceived monographs. *Methodenlehre zum Neuen Testament,* a late-twentieth-century exegetic handbook written by Wilhelm Egger, introduces itself in the subtitle as "An Introduction to Linguistic and Historico-Critical Methods," which are classified into a number of didactically organized but differing categories. The handbook user is thus made well aware of their mutual connectedness, but this is something that the author neither explores nor explains.

The American Vernon K. Robbins pioneered attempts to create a holistic (integral) hermeneutics covering the rhetorical, social, and "ideological" (in the case of biblical texts, theological) sides of the text by investigating the "integrated strategies" of narrative.[21]

Initially Robbins worked with Burton Mack and published useful comparisons between Gospel pericopes and the Greek school exercises *(chreia/chria),* which set the statements of the wise in the framework of a particular story.[22] His major works, however, concentrate on comprehensive analysis of the text, conceived as the study of its texture. He took an important step forward from the usual structuralist approach with his model of the text as something that does not create a closed world (it is not a matter of constructs) but is linked up by its intertextuality not only with other texts but with the social reality of its time and also — on the basis of analogy in the social situations of different periods — with the time of potential readers. He shows that New Testament authors referred to the social criticism voiced by the prophets in ancient Israel, and they express the significance of Jesus by using a number of basic elements of Greek biographies (the genre

---

21. Robbins, *The Tapestry of Early Christian Discourse,* 3.

22. B. L. Mack and V. K. Robbins, *Patterns of Persuasion in the Gospels* (Sonoma, Calif.: Polebridge Press, 1989).

Methods of Interpretation

vita [Latin] or *bios* [Greek]) of the time, concurrently setting them in the framework of a great "myth."²³ The "ideological" aspect of a text is not a marginal aspect of that text but is the key to its other layers, including its social function — the expression of the view of a minority that differs from majority society and proclaims its different scale of values.

In his most extensive monograph of the same year (1996), Robbins remolded his previous research into a comprehensive model of the texture of the text, giving us insights into how the text functioned in its milieu and which of its aspects we highlight when using different methods of interpretation.²⁴

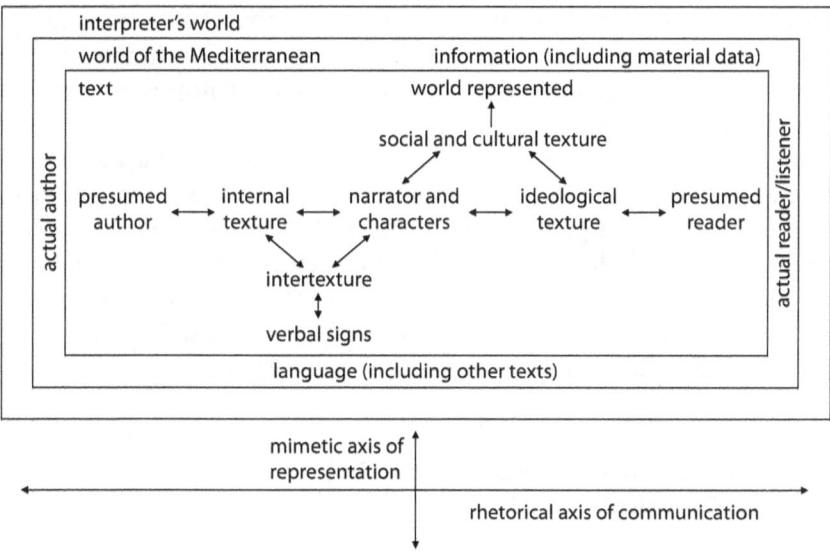

Robbins brought to contemporary discussion an awareness of contexts and sought to define the functions of the different methodological approaches. He also drew attention to the role of reference, which we shall be considering later. His scheme usefully maps relationships internal to the text and the relationships of the text to its surroundings, but it fails to express the role of the interpreter's reflexivity or the relationship of the reader to the text, the reader's "preliminary knowledge."²⁵ This is not in it-

---

23. V. K. Robbins, *Exploring the Texture of the Texts: A Guide to Socio-rhetorical Interpretation* (Valley Forge, Pa.: Trinity Press International, 1996), 106-10.

24. Robbins, *The Tapestry of Early Christian Discourse*, 37.

25. Robbins does not cite R. Bultmann, Ernst Fuchs, Eberhard Jüngel, or even Martin

153

self a fault, so long as the work is not taken for a comprehensive method of interpretation.

The difficulties with a consistently synchronic analysis of the text are implicit in the fact that such an analysis is based on investigation of the unconscious logic of speech, whereas in the case of narrative texts with a proclaimed reference to history, analysis of text structures can be fully productive only when combined with reflection on their conscious pragmatics and their historical role. The message of the text therefore needs to be constantly evaluated in relation to the situation for which it was intended, and the direction in which it sought to influence that situation. In such a case the historical and literary levels are intermingled, and interpretation is essentially connected with theological or philosophical reflection. Synchronic analysis can be the beginning but not the "be-all and end-all" of the process of the interpretation of the text.

Interpretation proper will always have to connect the analysis of structure with investigation of the relationship of the text to traditions, knowledge of which may be presupposed among its first readers and innovation of which is the means by which the text expresses its specific orientation, its pragmatics and — in the Bible — its witness. This does not mean that in terms of method we should not begin our interpretation with tasks that are part of synchronic analysis.

4.3.2. The Synchronic Dimension of the Text in Initial Exegetical Operations

To locate the synchronic elements of interpretation within a practical outline of the procedure of interpreting the text (exegesis), we need to start with the demarcation of the segment of the text to be commented upon. Even in the interpretation of larger wholes (books), the basic element remains the smaller segment that can be commented upon in such a way that the reader or listener is capable of keeping the basic information in mind until the end of the interpretation.

Commentary has to proceed segment by segment because the surface of the text, which is the starting point for all the other relations, is formed successively (see §3.6). We have noted that, at the start of interpretation of

---

Heidegger in this context. He persuasively criticizes Bultmann as the father of the "school of the history of form" (*Patterns of Persuasion*, 6ff.).

Methods of Interpretation

larger wholes and before separate interpretation of a particular segment, we need to try to determine the literary genre of the work that we are interpreting a part of, or are interpreting part by part. We need to uncover its structure and familiarize the reader with it, and we need to be familiar with existing reconstruction of the thought (philosophical or theological) of the whole work (esp. with discursive texts) — its "world" (in the case of narrative texts) — but the interpretation itself proceeds by smaller units. In the Bible we call these units pericopes, literally the "segments," in which individual parts of the Bible are read during religious service. The reading of such a segment takes two to five minutes, and the principles behind the demarcation of the individual pericopes go back to the Middle Ages. As with the segment and the whole, interpretation of the individual statement (in the Bible this is the verse[26] or part thereof) needs to be set in the context of the segment. The pericope usually consists of smaller text segments connected by theme (one story, a group of statements linked by the same problem or phenomenon to which they relate), literary framework (events or statements associated with one place, with a certain time), or by a single argument or by shared literary function (admonishment, greetings, the conclusion of a letter).

Determining the beginning and end of a pericope is not as a rule a problem, because usually it coincides with a paragraph in most editions of the printed text of the original and translations, but there are places where different editors and translators have divided the text in different ways. In these cases the interpreter must make a decision on the basis of his or her own idea of the structure of the text. For example, does the second part of 1 Corinthians 12:31 belong to the preceding pericope, as Roger Stephanus believed when he divided the Bible chapters into verses in 1551 and as most translations agree? The end of the pericope on the gifts of the spirit would then read, "But strive for the greater gifts. And I will show you a still more excellent way." Or do we have the beginning of a new pericope in verse 31b, as understood by the new edition of the Greek text and some translations, including the Czech Ecumenical Translation ("And I shall show you a still more excellent way: . . .")? Or finally, is all of verse 31 the introduction to the hymn to love in chapter 13, as it is understood by the Jerusalem Bible ("Be

---

26. In the Bible the smallest unit of its modern subdivision is known as the "verse," even though these verses are not metrical forms. The medieval division into chapters and the modern division into verses is, with a few minor exceptions, standardized in all editions of the Bible of all denominations. The older systems of subdivision are indicated only in critical editions of the text in original languages.

Hermeneutics as a Theory of Understanding

ambitious for the higher gifts. And I am going to show you ...")? In the first case the disputed sentence becomes the positive culmination of statements warning against the overestimation of the individual charismata (gifts of the Spirit); in the second it introduces the hymn to love, and in the third, verse 31 as a whole argues for the claim that what is to come will be the description of a gift that is greater than everything spoken about before.

If we read the first verse of chapter 14 ("Pursue love and strive for the spiritual gifts, and especially that you may prophesy"), however, we can see that the division adopted, among others, by the Czech Ecumenical Translation is the most suitable. The "greater gifts," spoken of in the first part of verse 31, are represented by prophetic speech, that is, a comprehensible actualized expression of the "gospel," while love (Gr. *agapē*) is set even higher than the greater gifts; it is the "more excellent way" (*kath' hyperbolēn hodon*, 12:31b), the element common to all the gifts. Thus we must make love our aim, even when "striving" (the verb *zēloō*, in 1 Cor. 12:31a and 14:1) for higher gifts. To simplify, we could say that, while Paul speaks of the equality of all gifts of the Spirit (note the metaphor of the body and its members in 1 Cor. 12:12-26), he nonetheless presupposes a certain categorization of the charismata, or gifts of the Spirit: prophetic speech is a "greater gift" (12:31a), which needs to be striven for *the most* (14:1b), and finally love as the most excellent way (12:31b), to which even the gift of prophecy must be subordinated (13:8-9).

The preliminary analysis of the structure of the relevant text segment, which sometimes needs to be made when we are determining where the interpreted passage starts and ends, is of fundamental importance for the strategy of interpretation as well. In most discursive texts we need to start from its wider frame and proceed, as it were, centripetally, to the statements we wish to interpret. As we have seen, this was the approach that needed to be taken in the interpretation of 1 Corinthians 13 and its separate parts. It is because the author usually conceived a letter as a whole.

With narrative texts it is more economical to start from the fundamental statement with which the whole story culminates. For example, in the pericope about the prayer in Gethsemane (Mark 14:32-42 and par.), this will be the words of Jesus' prayer; the whole scene is clearly a means of setting them vividly in Jesus' life — a technique common in treatment of individual important statements and one documented in rhetorical exercises of the period *(chreia)*. The process of basic observation leading to such a conclusion is, however, purely literary in character: the address to God as Father expresses a fundamental relationship, and the words about the cup are in this context a reference to something pernicious that endangers the relationship (see Mark 10:38-39), as is suggested by the parallel statement about the soul sick unto death in 14:34. This conclusion can be supported by similar statements in the same text and clear instances of intertextuality (see §3.7.1): the mention of the cup is evidently a reference to the cup of bitterness that we read about in a prophecy of Deutero-Isaiah (51:17). The address to God as Father, familiar from the Lord's Prayer (Matt. 6:9b-13 and par. [Q]), is typical of the Jesus tradition (esp. Luke 10:21-22 [Q])), and its Aramaic version "Abba" is used in the letters of Paul (Gal. 4:6; Rom. 8:15). That the center of the pericope is indeed a contrast between Jesus' relationship to God and his mortal anxiety is something that can be read from the references to a tradition in Mark's gospel set in Gethsemane, as well as in other parts of the New Testament, such as Hebrews 5:8-9 and John 12:27. This clear center provides the starting point for exploration of the functions of other parts of the pericope. Thus, for example, the theme of Jesus' disciples sleeping is not just the opposite of vigilance (Mark 14:34) but at the same time expresses the idea that Jesus bears the burden of doubt as a substitute for other people, whose sleep may therefore be transformed into rest (v. 41a; the understanding of the statement as a question [in the Czech Ecumenical Translation] evidently does not correspond to its function in the frame of the text).

Going from the narrated framework to the key statements cannot be ruled out, but it would clearly take us longer than starting with the key, fundamental point and using it to illumine the framework. In the case of discursive texts, however, the framework refers directly to the basic statements.

In each case **it is useful to start the interpretation of a text with an analysis in which the synchronic approach** predominates. The choice of centripetal or centrifugal strategy, however, is already a matter of considerations that have their historical side and are not purely structural.

4.4. Historical Methods

BIBLIOGRAPHY

Barbour, Robert S. *Traditio-historical Criticism of the Gospels.* London: SPCK, 1972.
Kaiser, Otto, Werner G. Kümmel, and Gottfried Adam. *Einführung in die exegetischen Methoden.* 4th ed. Munich: Kaiser, 1969.
Morgan, Robert, with John Barton. *Biblical Interpretation.* Oxford: Oxford University Press, 1988, 167ff.

Hermeneutics as a Theory of Understanding

Historical methods of interpretation start where synchronic methods end. We know, however, that the two sides cannot in fact be entirely separated methodologically and that, even in the description of historical (diachronic) methods, we encounter elements of structural analysis.

4.4.1. Reconstruction of the Text

In literary science we understand the term "reconstruction of the text" to mean the authentication of the text's manuscript basis. If working with a printed text we have to check whether this was a faithful reproduction of the author's manuscript (typescript), whether alterations are for example simply adaptation to contemporary orthography, whether it is an abridged version and if so what the reasons were for abridgement. For example the Czech communist Julius Fučík's "Reportage Written from the Gallows" was for years published in altered form, some passages being left out. In the case of relatively recent important texts an edition usually provides a note describing the relationship of the published text or translation to the autograph (the author's original manuscript) and sometimes an appended list of alterations. If a text exists in several versions all produced by the same author, who has added or reworked parts of it, one version has to be taken as starting point and attention must be drawn to differences to be found in other versions in the interpretation.

In the case of ancient texts a surviving autograph is very rare, however, and so the original text must be reconstructed. This is the task of textual criticism. Textual criticism is the oldest field of critical analysis of manuscripts and was developed as far back as the Hellenistic period in the Alexandrian Museion.

As far as the methods of textual criticism are concerned, we need only state a necessary minimum here because most of the important information is contained in the critical editions of ancient texts, with the greatest attention devoted to the Christian Bible — that is, the Greek original of the New Testament; the Septuagint, the Greek translation of the Jewish Bible (i.e., the Christian Old Testament); the Hebrew original of the principal writings of the Old Testament; and also the Latin translation of these (*Vetus Latina* and *Vulgata*). Textual criticism evolved into a separate field of literary science and biblical exegesis, and the elements of it learned by today's biblical scholars as part of their studies are simply what they need in order to understand critical editions, just as they need to understand archaeological reports — in

Methods of Interpretation

much the same way as a physician has to be able to understand a surgical diagnosis without himself needing to know how to operate. In practice, then, they need to have a basic orientation in the note apparatus of critical editions of the basic text (in our context, mainly the biblical text) and need to know how to interpret this apparatus. Currently, commentaries on the critical apparatus are being published,[27] and in an edition for translators of the Bible (*The Greek New Testament*, ed. Barbara Aland, 5th ed., 1993), evaluation is indicated by a classification of variant readings on a scale from A down to D (the D rating classifying a reading as almost equally valid as the text presented in the reconstruction).

Work on the reconstruction of a text involves a combination of two procedures.[28] The first involves assembling the records of the text contained in different documents (manuscripts, transcriptions, quotations, translations), dating them (in most cases paleographically, by type of script), identifying mutual dependencies, and then excluding deviations that have appeared at identifiably later dates. Yet while "genealogies" of manuscripts *(stemma codicorum)* serve as a synopsis of manuscript findings, they do not entirely solve the problem of reconstruction. There will still remain a few types of text that display a great many common deviations, the origins of which we cannot explain, which may go back as far as the assumed autograph. The fact that we have almost no autographs for ancient texts is largely because writings that later became acknowledged spiritual assets went through an initial stage of gradual emergence into the public realm, followed by gradual acceptance by a wider public. This process preceded their full recognition (reception), and only after reception were the transcriptions of such writings subjected to more rigorous authentication. In the case of biblical texts this reception took the form of canonization (acceptance into the set [canon] of liturgical readings).

The chronological method of looking for the oldest deviations without documented origin must therefore be combined with a second procedure — consideration of possible reasons for deviations. Sometimes a very old deviation can be explained as a scribe's accidental omission of a word before a word with the same ending (homeoteleuton). Elsewhere a variation can be

---

27. The best known is the commentary by Bruce M. Metzger on the critical apparatus in the basic edition of the Greek New Testament: *A Textual Commentary on the Greek New Testament* (Stuttgart: United Bible Societies, 1971 [and further editions]).

28. I have written on this subject in P. Pokorný and U. Heckel, *Einleitung in das Neue Testament* (Tübingen: Mohr Siebeck, 2007), §4.

explained by the fact that the scribe had in his memory the text of another of the Synoptic Gospels and carried it over into a parallel section in the gospel that he was transcribing. In the textual apparatus this kind of deviation is sometimes designated by a small *p* (i.e., the influence of a parallel).

To find explanations for some other variations, however, we have to think in theological terms. In Luke's gospel there are two important variations that look like insertions. Both are documented in a group of similar witnesses genealogically headed by the Sinai Codex (no. 01, designated ℵ) — Luke 22:43-44 and 23:34. According to the first variation Jesus, while praying in Gethsemane, is strengthened by an angel; according to the second Jesus asks God to forgive his executioners, "for they do not know what they are doing." The problem cannot be resolved by the genealogical method because the other group of manuscripts (where the variations do not appear) is headed by the Bodmer Codex ($\mathfrak{P}$75). While the Bodmer Codex is older, the Sinai Codex is not dependent on it, which means that the two must have had some common precursor unknown to us. The omission of the relevant passages in the second group can nonetheless be explained theologically. The idea that Jesus needed to be strengthened by an angel was scandalous at the time when Jesus was beginning to be regarded as a person of the Holy Trinity. Jesus' words on the forgiveness of those who had come to execute him, in contrast, were for some decades following the writing of Luke's gospel scandalous for those Christians who tied human hope to personal profession of faith in Jesus. Furthermore, the idea of the crucifixion of Jesus as the result of unwitting sin can be found in Luke's other book, in Acts 3:17. All this means that the longer text here is very probably closer to the original.

It is true that a reconstructed text is an artificial creation, and so it is not surprising that there have always been voices calling for editions based on a single manuscript tradition. Editions of this kind would make the other different traditions, which would be presented in the critical apparatus, more visible. The existing critical edition of the Hebrew text of the Old Testament was essentially conceived in this way, although the new one will be changing over to the system of reconstruction. Another criticism of the reconstructive approach is that all the methods used hitherto are premised on the idea that there actually existed a single autograph, even though it cannot be excluded that in some cases the author himself reworked his own text subsequently. Yet despite these objections, attempts to reconstruct the text cannot be stopped. First and foremost, because they are quite successful. Today our starting points are versions known in the third century, while Luther (whose translation of the whole Bible appeared in 1534) and the Czech

Methods of Interpretation

Kralice translators (the whole Bible in six volumes, 1579-93) were still translating from manuscripts of the High Middle Ages. Critical reconstruction also has the advantage of being able to include treatment of small surviving fragments of texts, which is very important because most text records are quite fragmentary. Finally, reconstructions have great ecumenical potential, just like the Latin Vulgate of Jerome (this was also a critical reconstruction) at the beginning of the fifth century. Critical reconstructions based on the work of the Institute for New Testament Textual Research, at the University of Münster, today provide the basis for most new translations of the Bible into a great many different languages. This of course does not of course rule out publication of critical editions based on a single manuscript, but such projects would be extremely expensive.

4.4.2. Paraphrase, Remythologization, Pragmatics

We have already established that a translation cannot of itself substitute for interpretation proper (§3.2). Even so, translation is an eminently hermeneutic affair, and not only in the case of "small" hermeneutics, such as relying on immediate communication to the speaker of a different language (e.g., the simultaneous translation of a lecture, where translation is a complete hermeneutic operation in itself). What I am thinking of now is translation of an ancient text, in our case most often a Hebrew or Greek text. Here it is quite obvious that translation is not interpretation. Usually what happens is that a good translation only emphasizes the distance of the text from our world. When we read in the Book of Joshua, for example, of how "the sun stood still" over Gibeon so that a charismatic Israelite general could be victorious in battle (Josh. 10:12-13), or when we read of the massacres of the civilian population commanded by the Lord (e.g., 1 Samuel 15),[29] we are chilled by

---

29. At the time when the narratives of the holy wars were produced, the commandment not to take booty or captives that was associated with holy war was supposed to be a warning against plunder, considered to be the motive for most wars. Making the opening of battle conditional on the verdict of the priest or prophet had a similar function. In the biblical period the institution of holy wars was not actual practice (in 1 Kings 3:11 Solomon praises God for not desiring the death of his enemies) but was projected into the past and was a rather unfortunate form of warning against the temptation of pagan religions. See M. Prudký, "Tzv. Svaté války ve starověkém Orientu a ve zvěstování Bible" (The So-Called Holy War in the Ancient Orient and in Biblical Proclamation), *Zprávy Společnosti křesťanů a židů* 50 (2004): 8-15.

Hermeneutics as a Theory of Understanding

the otherness of the Old Testament world, which disturbs us more in a new translation than in the Kralice Bible or the King James Version. In old translations the difference of language has become a kind of veil of archaism that tends to obscure and relativize the contradictions. A good new translation lets them come to the foreground. Yet precisely this is an important prerequisite for interpretation.

Identifying what puzzles us in an ancient text is already the first step in interpretation. It is only the first step, but it is essential. Our deficiencies in knowledge of the period background (i.e., the referential dimension of the text) appear at first sight. Indirectly linked to this are differences in the picture of the world, which can be reconstructed to a considerable extent synchronically, and only then, after thorough consideration of the wider contexts, can the scale of values offered or assumed by the interpreted text be reconstructed as well.

Deconstruction, as the term is used in postmodern literary theory, is the methodological side of this process. By breaking down the text into the individual elements of its structure and the individual pieces of information included in its references, we can investigate which elements are constitutive and which are secondary. The constitutive are those without which the literary structure would lose its inner cohesion and logic and without which the communication would lose its pragmatics, while the secondary are those that are essentially dispensable.

A judgment of this kind can be verifiable to the extent that we know how to judge whether the structure of a sentence or the effectiveness of a literary figure is vitiated by the removal of certain elements. We need to ascertain systematically, however, what information can be read out from the text and what part of this information was the reason for writing the text.

It is methodologically useful for us to try to paraphrase the text. This exercise shows in practice which statements and which aspects of the structure of the text are replaceable. On a first paraphrase we need to proceed very carefully and to reproduce literally every expression for which we have no precise substitute. In renarrating the content of the works of the classics, this is particularly important. Initially we only shorten the text, leaving distinctive vocabulary in place. In Johannine texts, for example, we must retain the expression *doxa* = "glory," which means the culmination of life and the proximity of God. This is an iron rule in the reproduction of classical texts.

Only when it is clear to us which expressions, links, ideas, and themes are distinctive for a given text can we embark on deeper paraphrase and replace selected terms and phenomena by a similarly consistent (adequate and

Methods of Interpretation

corresponding) alternative, closer to today's reader in its mode (e.g., "alienation" [from God] instead of "sin"). It is only with phenomena that have a primarily aesthetic function that we can strive for a similar effect using a different method, different variations (e.g., by a different order in the alternating use of the words "God" and "Lord" in places where no theological intention can be identified in the employment of one or the other, as for example in the majority of the psalms). What is important, however, is for us to be aware that even prose texts have their aesthetic side, which is an inseparable part of these texts and cannot be separated from their pragmatics.

In order to make sure that our interpretation is not altering the text to fit in with our own ideas, we need to be familiar with the world in which the text came into existence. Often we have to reconstruct it. In the case of ancient texts this means setting it in the framework of the relevant mythical archetypes (see §2.4.2, first treatment of myth). In practice this means remythologization of the text. We can take most of the inventory and repertoire of earlier pictures of the world from other sources and compare them with the world of the text that we are interpreting, but we must use information gained from the text itself to fill out or indeed adjust the picture given from other sources.

For example, to interpret a beautiful third-century tomb inscription published by G. Quispel, we need to know the world of Gnostic, specifically Valentinian, philosophico-theological speculations. The first part of the inscription is as follows, in translation from the Greek:

> Thou, filled with longing for the paternal light, sister and spouse, my Sophe, anointed in the baths of Christ with immortal sacred salve, hasten to glimpse the divine features of the Aeons, the great angel of the great council, the true Son; thou camest into the bridal chamber and deathless climbed into the bosom of the Father.[30]

According to Valentinus, the Son of God is the first emanation of the light of God the Father (see John 1:4-5). "The paternal light" is "heaven," and "the baths of Christ" are baptism understood as the means to obtain immortality. Anointing with holy oil was a Valentinian sacrament higher than baptism and clearly associated with the imparting of the "Holy Spirit" (see 1 John 2:20). Sophe, the wife of the man who had the monument erected, is also called his sister — that is, his sister in Christ. The aeons are personified

---

30. First published by A. Ferrua in *Rivista di archeologia cristiana* 21 (1945): 165-221, where the text is reconstructed and annotated.

astral spaces dividing earth from heaven ("glory"). Meeting them is the sign that Sophe is ascending into the divine realm (the direction "above"; "climbed" is the direction toward the key position). Because the aeons guard the entrance to "heaven" itself, the brief suggestion that they allow the deceased woman passage through their space in an almost friendly fashion is an expression of the hope that she is approaching the divine world. In Valentinian Gnosis, "the bridal chamber," a phrase expressing a range of ideas about spiritual marriage, was the term for the highest sacrament of initiation — coming close to Christ (Irenaeus, *Adv. haer.* 1.21.3; HNC II.3, *Gospel of Philip* 74). After taking into account and reflecting on all this information leading to the remythologization of the interpreted text, we find that, while the emotional charge and aesthetic effect of the inscription are extraordinarily immediate (i.e., it speaks a contemporary language), the underlying "second schema," the encoded path to immortality and belief that it involves the divine basis of shared baptism and special initiation, emerges only with the remythologization of the text. Remythologization, then, seeks other contemporary texts that characterize the spiritual world of the time.

It often becomes evident that the interpreted text is itself an important part of a movement that is reinterpreting older pictures of the world, sometimes very radically. Let us compare, for example, the theme of the wanderings of Odysseus, influenced by the gods, with the later treatment of the same motif and similar arrangement of history in Virgil's *Aeneid,* or the biblical myth of the beginning of the world (Gen. 1:1–2:4a, Priestly source; 2:4b–4:26, Yahwist source) with the legends known from Sumeria and Babylon, for example, the Babylonian epic *Enuma Elish.*

It is clear that the environment in which a text was produced can be understood only if we are aware that it is not self-evident, and only if we appreciate the necessity of comparing information on the ideas of the relevant period with what can be read from the text itself. This principle also applies to the usefulness of comparison with analogical texts (texts with analogical themes or function) that cannot be identified as having had any influence on the text in question or as having influenced it, and thus the only connection is similar phenomena (i.e., a phenomenological connection). Thus we can reach interesting conclusions when comparing the motif of the wanderings of the Israelites in the desert with the wanderings of the warriors after the Trojan War, whether returning home (Gr. *nostoi* — Greeks, Achaeans) or escaping (Trojans).

The unfortunate consequences of potentially misunderstanding a text (e.g., subjectively assessing what is essential and what is secondary) can be reduced if, when faced with individual innovation in the interpretation of a tradition, we try to identify what new terms and structures are replacing it. This begins with grammar and stylistics. When we find a prosody based on syllabic quantity substituted for accentual verse or syllabo-tonic hexameter, we need to know what the original hexameter in the prose text was meant to evoke. Did it have a mainly aesthetic function? Was it supposed to aid memorization? Was it supposed to give an impression of great age (e.g., the Sibylline Oracles)? Was it supposed to have a comic effect (like some Homeric hymns)?

When, for example, we consider Jesus' healing of the sick, this is not so much a precise analogy to healing as we understand it today as a description of Jesus' combat with forces in opposition to God. This is obvious in the case of the exorcisms (e.g., Mark 5:1-20 and par.), but if we have a knowledge of the Greek text, we see that even a fever, for example, can have certain personal features (Mark 1:29-31). The communicative urge involved in interpretation creates a pressure on us to bring the whole story closer to the contemporary reader by stressing the result of the action (i.e., healing, and comparing Jesus to a doctor), but in the context of the world of the New Testament texts, the concerns that come to the fore are different: above all, in the framework of Jesus' teaching on the kingdom of God, his healings are a vivid expression of the priorities in the alternative project of the world that his "kingdom of God" undoubtedly constitutes, namely, that to help the sick, as well as the poor, women, and children, is more important than all the rest — than the heroism of the conqueror and soldier, than wealth and power. Second, it is clear that in the post-Easter tradition the healings are understood as prefiguration of the resurrection to eternal life (theologically elaborated in the story of the raising of Lazarus in John 11).[31] In contrast to Gnostic and Docetic ideas, in the early Christian tradition this is not a question of the mortification of the body and escape into eternity, but of a full earthly life and firm hope in death as a connecting vessel with life. This is an understanding that is manifest in the view of the apostle Paul. Although he states explicitly that death is the better way out, he is nonetheless aware that he has a mission in his life and so wants to recover from illness and defend himself in a trial (Phil. 1:21-26), and he writes to the Christians in Corinth that their disputes (social differences in the celebration of the Lord's Supper as the prefigurations of the kingdom of God) are affecting their health: "For this reason many of you are weak and ill, and some have died" (1 Cor. 11:30; see 11:27-34).

---

31. The fundamental hermeneutic problems have been demonstrated, using the example of this story, by J. Kremer, *Lazarus* (Stuttgart: Verlag Katholisches Bibelwerk, 1985).

When we identify the oldest stratum of tradition about Jesus' healings using historical methods, we find two stories that do not quite fit into the framework suggested above and that the later evangelists (Matthew and Luke) leave out: Mark 7:32-36, the healing of a deaf and dumb man, and 8:22-26, the healing of a blind man. In both cases we find a description of healing practices that, despite resembling what we today call shamanism, are still definitely forms of treatment. The prospect of the kingdom of God was evidently an impulse for efforts to overcome sickness by all available methods, and legitimized them. It rejected the concept of illness as personal punishment or as fate.

At this point in our account we are already getting close to the basic problem of hermeneutics: *remythologization,* or the reconstruction of the referential horizon of the time (see §2.4.2), which makes it possible for us to investigate the original pragmatic of the text, that is, how it functioned in its time. Then we can look for the modern function that seeks to change both the situation of a person and the historical process in a similar direction. For example, it is evident that modern scientific medicine is an analogy of biblical shamanism and that the responsible surgeon is closer to the biblical model in his or her functioning than the pious man who decides to treat dental decay or blood poisoning by faith and prayer. Yet however justified such an analogy, it cannot be considered interpretation, because in the original text what plays the crucial role is the idea that illness is connected with human sin, and the fight against illness is part of a vivid demonstration of the meaning of the kingdom of God. Jesus refused to attribute disease to the sin of the sufferer (John 9:1-5), because sin is absurd and the innocent also suffer from its consequences, but for him illness was still the consequence of human sin. We can find an objective modern analogy to this awareness in the argument based on the observation that global spending on health services represents only a fraction of the amount spent on armaments; if expenditure on medical research and health services rose to even one-fifth of expenditure on arms, a cure could be found for most life-threatening diseases, and human life would be substantially prolonged. This is a contemporary observation corresponding to the theory of illness as the result of human sin but not the sin of the sufferer. Pragmatically, it leads to the requirement for a different but similarly functioning orientation of human activity. Yet even this extended analogy is still not a real interpretation of the project of the world represented by the concept "the kingdom of God." The reason is that it does not involve awareness that the kingdom of God is the proper future of people and of the whole world or

Methods of Interpretation

that there is a need to assure everyone of this prospect, which is the motivation of any kind of activity on the immediate level or the deeper and indirect level.

Here we have reached the very threshold of interpretation proper, to which the final section of this account will be devoted. We have established that every interpretation involves the meeting of two linguistic worlds separated from each other by space, by different experience, and especially by time. This encounter gives rise to problems in communication (lack of understanding, misunderstanding). To understand the earlier texts we need to investigate how they function (their pragmatics) and to look for contemporary analogies, but a direct "translation" is not possible; trying to identify meaning only via contemporary analogy produces a picture that leaves out and obscures important statements of the text. We thus have recommended as a first step that the interpreter retains his or her awareness of the world of the text and tries to reconstruct it.

Naturally we must keep in mind the risk that reconstruction may be one-sided, and we must be willing to revise our reconstruction at any time. We have already, however, got as far as identifying the four factors with which we must reckon in any interpretation: the reconstructed past world and the text that was produced in it on the one hand, and our world and our interpretation of the text on the other. We have established that none of these factors may be neglected. By comparing the text with its time, we grasp the direction of the text (its pragmatic), which must have an analogy in the relationship of our interpretation to the world of today. What is fundamental, however, is the mutual relationship between what we may define as two parallel movements, that is, the movement identified (the text and its world) and the movement anticipated, or provoked (the interpretation and our world). We have also established that the text is the feedback of interpretation, and that the authenticity and reliability of an interpretation are verified by return to the text. Finally, we have discovered the existence of analogical historical activities that can be developed in the present. Interpretation proper, however, must find the common denominator of the two worlds. This is the problem of hermeneutics.

4.4.3. *Historical Criticism (2)*

We have already talked about the indispensability of historical criticism and about its function (§3.7.2). It remains for us to characterize its methods.

Hermeneutics as a Theory of Understanding

As in the judgment of a court case, acceptance of evidence requires the existence of two independent testimonies (see also below, §5.5) that are in agreement. This rule, which is based on the referential function of the text (§3.7.2), substantiates the references included in the text by a method that corresponds to this side of the text.

Since the milieu of the text is tradition representing history, assessment of the information provided in a particular text requires that this information be confirmed by another, independent source on which a picture of history may also be based: eyewitnesses, tradition, picture, photograph, or, in the case of New Testament biblical texts, another text. For example, Jesus' words on blasphemy against the Holy Spirit appear in Mark's gospel (3:28-29), with a parallel in Matthew 12:31, and at the same time in the common source of Matthew's and Luke's gospels (Q: Matt. 12:32 and Luke 12:10). In Matthew's gospel the two versions are presented alongside each other in the same place. This double record, together with the fact that the same statement is understood differently in each source (in Q it is related to the post-Easter confession of belief in Jesus), clearly assigns the statement to the authenticated elements of Jesus' teaching.

For most of our information on Jesus' life and teaching, however, we are dependent on just one reliable record. Although a certain story may be repeated three times in all the Synoptic Gospels, this is not proof of its historical credibility (not even to speak of its spiritual authority). Some of these statements recorded only by a single independent witness can nonetheless be authenticated by a different method: *it may be considered valid as reliable information if it can be shown that the people who asserted it could not have had an interest in inventing it.* For example, Jesus' supporters would definitely not have fabricated the story that their master was baptized by John the Baptist (Mark 1:9-11 and par.), given that they ranked Jesus above John and that early Christian tradition was trying to shift John into the role of Jesus' predecessor. This tendency is already clearly visible in Matthew's version of the pericope on the baptism of Jesus, where John says, "I need to be baptized by you, and do you come to me?" and Jesus must persuade John to baptize him (Matt. 3:14-15). In John's gospel, he no longer even dares to baptize Jesus and merely declares that Jesus is "the Lamb of God" (1:29). The authenticity of the slanders against John and Jesus, which are recorded in the collection Q (Matt. 11:18-19; Luke 7:33-35), is self-evident on the criterion of the absence of interest in invention on the part of the witness. Using this criterion, the handful of reliable pieces of information about Jesus can be more than doubled, but even so, this represents only a fraction compared to all the texts of the Jesus tradition that were not demonstrably produced later, in the post-Easter period, but that cannot be verified.

In the 1960s and 1970s scholars adopted a new variant of the principle of replacement of the second independent witness as just described. This is known as the *Rule of (Double) Dissimilarity*, which states that information may be regarded as authentic if its origin can be identified neither in the thought of the Jewish world of the time nor in the needs of the emergent church.[32] It is on this basis, for example, that such well-known texts as the parable of the Good Samaritan (Luke 10:25-37) or the Prodigal Son (Luke 15:11-32) may be regarded as a record of Jesus' teaching (obviously retold by the evangelists). The rule of dissimilarity may also be used in investigating the peculiarities of vocabulary and rhetoric of the different strata of the Jesus tradition.[33]

In the last two decades, however, the rule of dissimilarity has been exposed to serious criticism from some American Bible scholars. It has been pointed out that, if applied as a criterion of exclusion, it would mean assuming that Jesus had done nothing but utter original ideas and radically distinguish himself from his milieu. In reality, his world was the world of a pious Jew living in the Hellenized environment of the eastern Mediterranean in the first century of the Roman Empire, and he also honored the tradition of human wisdom expressed by the prophets, and by such universally familiar metaphors as "to be lost" for a life without prospects, "heaven" for the key position, and so forth (these are what are known as anthropological universalia).

All this scarcely means, however, that we should abandon the principle of dissimilarity. It means only that the positive criteria of verification that operate directly or indirectly on the principle of two independent witnesses, and so inevitably cannot validate identification of more than a part of reality, need to be augmented by secondary criteria that are all essentially a matter of the elaboration of the criterion of coherence. Coherence is the deeper level of the unity of the text, based on more than just its stylistic unity (i.e., its cohesion). Coherence relates to the cognitive level of the text — the level at which its individual parts can be said to have a similar meaning or create a

---

32. The principle was first formulated by E. Käsemann, "Das Problem des historischen Jesus," in *Exegetische Versuche und Besinnungen*, vol. 1, 4th ed. (Göttingen: Vandenhoeck & Ruprecht, 1965), 187-214, here 205; and in the Anglo-Saxon world, by N. Perrin, *Rediscovering the Teaching of Jesus* (London: SCM Press, 1967; 2d ed., 1976), 43.

33. P. Pokorný, "Lexikalische und rhetorische Eigentumlichkeiten der ältesten Jesustradition," in *Der historische Jesus*, ed. J. Schröter and R. Brucker (Berlin: de Gruyter, 2002), 393-408.

meaning in their mutual relation.³⁴ This criterion can be extended from one text to a group of texts connected by a common theme. We can investigate the group according to this criterion by asking whether they mutually exclude each other, and whether they provide a coherent picture into which other data, not positively verifiable, can fit. Those data that do fit into the picture can then be used to reconstruct events or teaching mentioned in the text. Furthermore, where some data recorded only in one source support a certain interpretation of an obscure passage, we can insert such an interpretation into the reconstructed picture, at least on an experimental basis. This is known as *the criterion of accumulated indirect proofs*.

More controversial is the criterion of frequency of appearance of data as a method for legitimizing the credibility of a certain piece of information, or excluding it if its appearance is isolated. This is involved in the methods applied and promoted by the California Jesuit seminar — a working group of like-minded scholars who tried to create a general model of Jesus' activities. One result, for example, was that, in his book on Jesus, J. D. Crossan does not mention the parable of the Prodigal Son in Luke 15:11-32 on the grounds that it does not appear anywhere else, even though it is a text that has a significant theological parallel in the parable of the Laborers in the Vineyard (Matt. 20:1-16).

We are speaking here of criteria inspired by the rule applied by Ernst Troeltsch, according to which everything that does not correspond to contemporary human experience should be regarded as inauthentic.

By contrast, Gerd Theissen formulated *the criterion of contextual plausibility*, according to which authentic information must be comprehensible in the conditions of its assumed origin. At first sight this looks like a repudiation of the criterion of dissimilarity that had been adopted in Jesus scholarship. In fact it means that information that we verify using the rule of two witnesses, that we discover as new information, or that is inexplicable in terms of Judaism or the early church (the criterion of double dissimilarity) must at least be comprehensible in the conditions of its assumed origin — that is, it must also be evident that people at the time genuinely understood it as a provocation and did not just shrug their shoulders as at something irrelevant or incomprehensible to them.

Basically we must bear in mind that (1) every piece of information authenticated using positive criteria must be taken seriously, even if it deviates

---

34. Eve-Marie Becker, "Was ist 'Kohärenz?'" *Zeitschrift für die neutestamentlichen Wissenschaft* 94 (2003): 97-121, especially 103ff.

Methods of Interpretation

from information that we have established hitherto, but that (2) information accepted simply on the basis of the criterion of coherence and other secondary criteria obviously cannot be allowed to contradict the overall picture established hitherto. This inevitably means that gaps will appear in reconstructed realities, but in historical criticism, critical destruction is always better than noncritical reconstruction. In Jesus scholarship this means, for example, that the gaps in the picture of Jesus do not matter, but the false features that can appear there as a result of noncritical reconstruction do enormous damage.

4.4.4. "Cross-Cutting" Methods

I call certain methods "cross-cutting" because they combine the literary analysis of a text with consideration of its layering in time. The basic German textbooks (Egger, Oeming) categorize them as diachronic methods, but from the basis of the theory of the text as we have formulated it in preceding chapters, it follows that the referential function is the fundamental property of the text, to which its very structure refers (§3.7.2). Cross-cutting methods are therefore methods that correspond to the nature of the text, and division into a synchronic and a diachronic approach is just a necessary abstraction enabling us to highlight the dominant features of individual methods and making it possible to classify them for teaching purposes. The fact that in the two methods that we shall examine now the decisive roles are played by diachronic elements of analysis is the reason we place them in this part of our account.

4.4.4.1. The Critique of Tradition — the History of Form

BIBLIOGRAPHY

Berger, Klaus. *Formgeschichte des Neuen Testaments*. Heidelberg: Quelle & Meyer, 1984.
Bultmann, Rudolf. *Geschichte der synoptischen Tradition*. 1921; 10th ed., Göttingen: Vandenhoeck & Ruprecht, 1995. ET *The History of the Synoptic Tradition* (Oxford: Blackwell, 1972).
Dibelius, Martin. *Die Formgeschichte des Evangeliums*. Tübingen: Mohr, 1919; 6th ed., 1971. ET *From Tradition to Gospel* (trans. from rev. 2d ed.; Cambridge: J. Clarke, 1971).

At the beginning of the twentieth century the German Bible scholar Hermann Gunkel (1862-1932) adopted a new approach to the study of certain texts of the Old Testament Law and the Prophets. He looked in these texts for literary forms in which we encounter what are often repeated materials of oral tradition (epics, prayers, cultic texts, hymns). Such forms and modalities have a social function and, with religious texts, often a liturgical function. In the text of the Gospels we can sometimes quite clearly make out whole passages taken from the aural tradition, and so determine the kind of occasions on which they were used.

The German term "Sitz im Leben" has come to be used for this identification of oral character and context, with the corresponding school of scholarship known as the Formgeschichtliche Schule, or form-critical school. Its focus is not on the place of these texts in the life of Jesus but on their constantly repeated, returning role in the life of early Christian communities, which molded individual statements as pebbles are carved out and smoothed in the current of a river. It is clear that prayers (esp. the Lord's Prayer) had their place both in the liturgy and in personal daily piety *(praxis pietatis)*, and hymnic prayers (e.g., Luke 1:46-55, the Magnificat) were sung or recited (in the Orient there is no clear line of division) as part of religious service. It is not difficult to recognize the folk miracle narratives (novellas) that circulated among Jesus' simple followers and were repeated in the free part of the religious service. The novellas include a number of stories about Jesus' miracles. Most share a scheme that includes a statement about the seriousness of the illness, an enumeration of witnesses, the healing word or gesture, the demonstration of healing, and the amazement of those present (the chorus). This is a transformation of similar models familiar from other areas. In the novels the legendary and miraculous (miracle for the sake of the miraculous) features were elaborated, and novellas are also typically present in extracanonical texts such as the Gospel of Peter. The latter includes an actual description of the resurrection of Christ — the objectification of one interpretation of the Easter experience. Individual elements of these narratives found their way into texts that were later canonized (e.g., the story of the fish in whose mouth Jesus' pupils were supposed to have found a coin to pay the temple tax, Matt. 17:24-27), but in general the church squeezed them out of its services. The novellas do not provide any historically usable information, but they suggest the honor in which Jesus was held in the broad ranks of his adherents. Explaining this point to students in a lecture some years ago, I recalled how in 1946 a Swiss peasant told me that Churchill had invented radar. Obviously this was nonsense, but the man was expressing the honor that this soldier and politician enjoyed, even among simple people beyond the frontiers of his country.

Methods of Interpretation

Other basic forms include confessions of faith, narratives of witnesses (passion texts), Old Testament etiological narratives (explaining the origins of the name of a place or person), and legends (e.g., the stories of Joseph, of the creation of the world, etc.).

Even prior to the compilation of the Gospels, some sayings had been collected, producing clusters of sayings associated by a similar form and theme, for example the parables in Mark 4:1-34 or the apocalyptic statements in Mark 13.

The period of oral transmission also saw the emergence of smaller discrete groupings of material with a linking element: for example, the stories of Jesus' days in Capernaum formed Mark 1:21-34 and 2:1-12. The evangelist inserted these into his own work, splitting them up and placing a summary of Jesus' activities and another tale of healing in between them (1:35-45). Even before the writing of the gospel, the narrative of Jesus' betrayal, arrest, condemnation, and execution (the passion story) had been linked up with the tradition of Jesus' last supper and the institution of Holy Communion (Mark 14:22-25 and par.). This linkage is attested as early as the 50s in the writings of the apostle Paul (1 Cor. 11:23-25).

The most important advance made by the form-critical school, one that has its parallel in historical poetics, was the uncovering of units of narrative, their core being a saying framed by a narrative. Sometimes it is a narrative similar to a novella, but the saying invests the story with a new meaning. For example, in the story of the healing of the paralytic in Mark 2:1-12 and parallels, the emphasis is shifted from the healing to the forgiveness of sins (v. 5). The statement on faith (v. 36) plays a similar role in the context of Mark 5:21-43. Dibelius called such textual units paradigms (Gr. *paradeigmata*), and Bultmann called them apophthegms *(apophthegmata)*, because he found similar statements in ancient philosophical and sapiential tradition. The 1980s saw interest in the study of the rhetorical exercises *(chreia)*, which involved the framing of individual sayings of the philosophers with a situation appropriately illustrating their force (see also §4.3.1). Exercises of this kind have come down to us through the Alexandrian poet Machon or the Greek rhetor Theon. Because Jesus' sayings of this type have some peculiar features (often they clearly polemicize with the tradition from which their framework is taken; they assume a special authority [commission] rather than just the status of philosophical argument, and they are sayings attributed to one person), Vernon Robbins (see §4.3.1) invented a special term for them — "pronouncement stories" — which has been adopted by a number of American Bible scholars.

Hermeneutics as a Theory of Understanding

The form-critical school focused on the social and liturgical function of texts encountered primarily in the Synoptic Gospels, but the method was essentially historical. It was about the reconstruction and assessment of a layer of the text that had already gone through a certain period of aural tradition without being included in a literary whole. For this reason the school drew inspiration from research into the typical patterns of oral tradition in ethnography and folklore studies. It brought a fundamental demonstration of the original independence of individual pericopes from the literary framework (Karl Ludwig Schmidt, 1891-1956). The order of the pericopes and the overall literary and theological framework of the Gospels were the work of the evangelists and do not testify directly to the historical course of events, but only to the idea that the evangelists had formed of them — an idea marked above all by their theological intentions.

Like every new discovery, the findings of the form-critical school showed a tendency to emancipation from the initial critical premises of the movement. The works of a number of biblical scholars of the second generation tended to give readers the impression that the environment in which the approach was elaborated and polished was the milieu in which it had emerged in the first place. It also became evident that there were serious pitfalls when it came to applying a method that had originated in the interpretation of the Law and the later Prophets to the interpretation of the Gospels. Only forty years separated the life of Jesus from the writing of Mark's gospel, while there was sometimes half a millennium between the historical events mentioned in Old Testament texts and their literary fixation (record). Furthermore, the authors of the Gospels made a greater individual contribution to the formation of the last stage of development of the text than did the "tradents" in ancient Israel. Many forms that thirty years ago were attributed to aural tradition are today considered to be the work of the evangelists, who deliberately copied the cultic forms of tradition.

Yet the basic advance brought by the method, which later merged with the criticism of tradition, remains unchallengeable. One attempt to recast it as a general stylistic theory of New Testament texts (Klaus Berger) produced many individual interesting observations, but overall it has become clear that such catalogs of stylistic and rhetorical modalities are redundant from the point of view of the economy of scholarly work. The method of the form-critical school is an original combination of the literary and the sociological approaches to texts that has specific use in relation to texts that require such an approach because of their stratigraphy (i.e., historical layering).

4.4.4.2. Redaction Criticism

BIBLIOGRAPHY

Conzelmann, Hans. *Die Mitte der Zeit. Studien zur Theologie des Lukas*. Tübingen: Mohr, 1954; 4th ed., 1962. ET *The Theology of St. Luke* (London: SCM Press, 1982).
Marxsen, Willi. *Der Evangelist Markus*. Göttingen: Vandenhoeck & Ruprecht, 1956. ET *Mark the Evangelist* (Nashville: Abingdon Press, 1969).
Rohde, Joachim. *Die redaktionsgeschichtliche Methode*. Berlin: EVA, 1965. ET *Rediscovering the Teaching of the Evangelists* (London: SCM Press, 1968).

Just before the Second World War a number of scholars (esp. George D. Kilpatrick and Krister Stendahl) began to study the literary and theological intentions behind the ways in which the evangelists combined the separate elements of tradition into a larger whole. This is essentially the method of redaction criticism consistently applied by Hans Conzelmann in his 1954 monograph *Die Mitte der Zeit* (The Center of Time). Here Conzelmann demonstrated the strategies by which the author of Luke's gospel and the Acts of the Apostles coped with the postponement of the coming of the kingdom of heaven expected by Jesus. Jesus' appearance became the center of what was essentially a two-part work, so that an event linked to the expected end of history became the "center of history." The concept was later to influence the Christian (and today virtually global) orientation in history, based on the distinction between dates "before Christ" and "after Christ" (B.C. and A.D.). With Jesus' appearance, the kingdom of God as a goal and also as a reality started to "break in" to history. "The kingdom of God is among you," declares Jesus, according to Luke 17:21.

The new method acquired its name in Willy Marxsen's *Der Evangelist Markus* of 1956. We see that the evangelists, as creative redactors and witnesses of faith, retold the earlier traditions by selecting, arranging, linking, and interpreting.

The basic connecting technique was to move Jesus (the literary "hero") from one place to another, depending on the specific association of each location with the tradition from which the narrative was taken (e.g., "From there he set out and went away to the region of Tyre," Mark 7:24; or "They came to Bethsaida," Mark 8:22), or moving Jesus in time ("Immediately thereafter," "For six days," and so forth). An overall theological desire to create a literary structure corresponding to this purpose, however, was the basic condition for the writing of the Gospels as a whole. To discover it is the aim of redaction criticism.

Hermeneutics as a Theory of Understanding

In the oldest gospel, Mark, the fundamental aim is to interpret traditions from the life of Jesus in the light of the gospel (Gr. *euangelion*) — that is, as the news of Jesus' new presence ("resurrection"), as we know it primarily from the so-called formula of faith in 1 Corinthians 15:1-5. The whole tradition about the life of Jesus is integrated under the heading "the beginning of good news" (Mark 1:1), while the gospel itself contained in 1 Corinthians 15:3b-5 takes center stage in the passion story and is summarized in Mark 16:6-7. Mark 16:9-20 is an addition that does not appear in the oldest manuscripts. Mark's gospel is additionally unified by the theme of Jesus as the Son of God in accordance with another version of the gospel on Christ's resurrection, in Romans 1:3-4.[35]

The basic methods of redaction criticism therefore consist of comparison of related or parallel texts, stratigraphy of the text interpreted, and word statistics that allow us to identify the key terms in the author's (redactor's) vocabulary. For example, in Mark's gospel the expression *euthys* ("immediately") appears forty-two times, but in Matthew's gospel, only seven times, even though it is double the length. Since we encounter it mainly in Mark's linking passages, it is clearly one of Mark's favorite words, and its frequent appearance is a marker enabling us to distinguish with quite a high level of probability between the editor's part of the text and the older tradition.

Redaction criticism could develop only after the methods of tradition criticism propounded by the school of form criticism had been accepted and absorbed. It is akin to synchronic approaches because it is concerned with the final, literary stage of the development of the text and investigates its structure. At root, however, it is a diachronic, historical approach because it is interested in the whole text as the final stage of the development of the text, which it interprets on the basis of methodological discrimination of the whole text from the orientation of the older layers, especially the layer of stabilized aural tradition that the school of form criticism had begun to uncover. To point this out is to complicate the classification of exegetical methods and approaches presented by some practical textbooks of hermeneutics (the best of these was written by M. Oeming; see the literature for §1). The fundamental lesson is that **exegetical methods are constituted by practice; the analysis of their function in connection with the theory of the text is a matter for hermeneutic reflection. This function can be precisely determined, but only rarely can it be revealed by just one kind of exegetic practice.**

---

35. For more detail, see Pokorný and Heckel, *Einleitung in das Neue Testament*, 363ff.

5. Interpretation

BIBLIOGRAPHY

Charlesworth, James H. "Polanyi, Merleau-Ponty, Arendt, and the Foundation of Biblical Hermeneutics." In *Interpretation of the Bible*, ed. J. Krašovec, 1531-56. Sheffield, Eng.: Sheffield Academic Press, 1998.
Heidegger, Martin. *Sein und Zeit*. 1926; 4th ed., Halle: Niemeyer, 1935. ET *Being and Time* (London: SCM Press, 1962).
Hejdánek, Ladislav. "Hermeneutik und die Zeit." In *Philosophical Hermeneutics and Biblical Exegesis*, ed. Petr Pokorný and Jan Roskovec, 42-48. Tübingen: Mohr Siebeck, 2002.
Jeanrond, Werner G. *Text und Interpretation als Kategorien theologischen Denkens*. Tübingen: Mohr, 1986.
Kouba, Pavel. "Kritérium interpretace" [The Criterion of Interpretation]. In *Logos a Svět* (FS L. Hejdánek and J. S. Trojan), 129-33. Prague: OIKOYMENH, 1997.
Lundin, Roger, Clarence Walhout, and Anthony C. Thiselton, *The Promise of Hermeneutics*. Grand Rapids: Eerdmans, 1999.
Mathauser, Zdeněk. "Verständnis und Gültigkeit. Zu kunstlerischen und biblischen Texten." In *Philosophical Hermeneutics and Biblical Exegesis*, ed. Petr Pokorný and Jan Roskovec, 29-41. Tübingen: Mohr Siebeck, 2002.
Ricoeur, Paul. *De l'interprétation. Essai sur Freud*. Paris: du Seuil, 1965.
———. *Essays on Biblical Interpretation*. London: SCM Press, 1981.
Tracy, David. *The Analogical Imagination: Christian Theology and the Culture of Pluralism*. New York: Crossroad, 1981.

5.1. The Otherness and Attraction of Ancient Texts

Hermeneutics has developed as **the interpretation of ancient texts that have acquired a certain authority. We have a peculiarly ambivalent atti-**

tude to such texts. On the one hand, we sense the importance of such texts for our life and our orientation in the world. Sometimes we are even convinced of this from the very start. On the other hand, however, we do not understand them, or we understand them only in part. Viewed from a certain angle, therefore, interpretation is the methodological and critical confrontation of these two sides of our experience with an interpreted text. **What makes such texts attractive, namely, their venerable quality of being "tried, tested, and authoritative," is also their handicap — their distance in time, together with difference of culture, is a barrier that hinders us from understanding them more fully.** Thus on the one hand they repel us, and on the other they attract us. The discord between "repulsion" and "attraction" is the polarity that indicates the way to the goal.[1] **The elements of otherness resist us by being noncontemporary, but they attract us precisely because they have retained their weight for so long a time, because they can be a path to understanding the past, but above all because it is precisely their authority and durability that lead us to associate with them an expectation more important to us, namely, that they may even open a path "ahead," to the future** (they may be a "memory of the future").

5.2. The Meeting of Worlds

We have talked about the fact that interpretation is actually a substitute for the direct dialogue that we cannot have with the text. We have also seen that the text can emancipate itself from its author, with whom it would be possible to have a dialogue, and lead its own life. Interpretation bridges the gap (sometimes the real abyss) between the world of the text and the lived world of the reader. It takes the form of a text itself, a metatext that consciously mediates between the reader and the text, thematizes the differences between their worlds, and reflects on them philosophically or theologically.

The confrontation of the world of the text and the world of the reader is complicated because what we actually have here is, on one hand, the reconstructed world in which the text originated and the text itself, and, on the other hand, our own world and our interpretation of the text. These are the

---

1. Here for the sake of diversity I have used the terminology employed by František Palacký in his account of historical movement in his *Dějiny národu českého v Čechách a v Moravě* [History of the Czech People in Bohemia and Moravia] (Prague: Kočí, 1907), 11:4470.

Interpretation

four factors with which we must reckon in interpretation. None may be neglected. By comparing the text with its environment, we understand the purpose of the text (its pragmatics), which, if we want to understand the text, must have an analogy in the relationship of our interpretation of the text to today's world. What is fundamental, however, is the mutual relationship of this double movement: the movement identified (the text in relation to its world) and the movement expected, provoked (our understanding of the text in relation to our world).

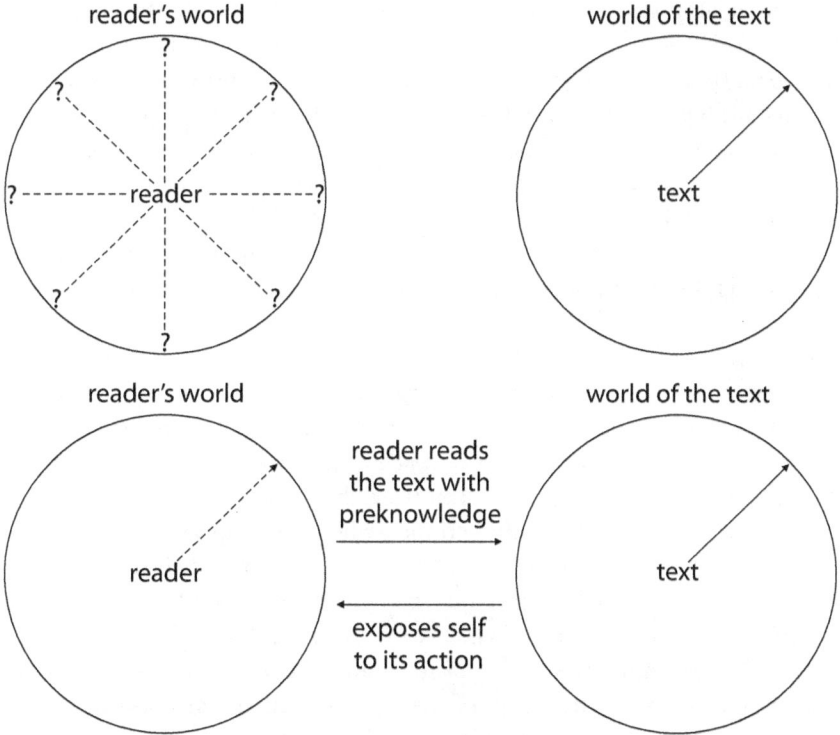

It follows from what we have just said that the text is the norm of (and gives feedback to) interpretation; the authenticity and reliability of an interpretation are verified by return to the text. We have also established that historical activities can be developed in the present that are analogous to those in the text. Interpretation proper, however, must find the common denominator of the two worlds. That is the problem of hermeneutics.

In seeking common features that would make it possible to establish

Hermeneutics as a Theory of Understanding

an integral connection between the two worlds, we can start from the most basic relationship that exists between them, which is represented by the reader's **question.** This is an expression of his or her preunderstanding, the fact that the reader has a certain provisional knowledge of and interest in the text. What he or she expects from the text must be confronted with what the text offers, that is, with what we discover as its pragmatics, or function in the world for which it was originally intended, the basic features of which can be read from the text itself. The tension between the movement of the text toward itself, inward into its own world, and its action on the outside — the fact that it suggests even to the modern reader a solution to his or her questions and that it offers some momentous testimonies — is the basis of the hermeneutic circle, which, as we have said (§3.7.3), leads to a new self-understanding on the part of the interpreter. We shall have to consider this personal side of interpretation later. Now we must suggest the actual nature of this connecting up of two worlds, one of which is the immediate environment in which we live and act.

One way that we can imagine the process of connection between the two worlds is to think of readers entering into the world of the text so fully that they move in it just as they do in the world of their own experience. They become a kind of amphibian. They will have a double scale of measurement, always temporarily adopting the world of the text (the alternative project of the world that the text offers readers) as their own. This is quite a familiar phenomenon: the readers get to know the world of the text, accept its values, and can jump from their own world into the imagined world in a single moment, and then when the telephone rings, for example, jump back into the world of their own lives. But this is not interpretation. It might be the beginning of interpretation, but in the case of such shifting from world to world, which we experience, for example, when engrossed in a good novel, one can observe an opposite tendency. This is the tendency to separate the world of the text from the present world and to escape into the former as a refuge in which we are protected from the stress of our present worries. It is a compensatory activity that can be healthy and useful in small doses but is the undertow of our activity and desire for self-understanding; it is re-creation. We have already said that the interpretation of the text requires conscious thought on the relationship between the two worlds. This can be achieved only with the use of particular methods.

According to Gadamer, a prerequisite for interpretation and an integral part of our understanding of the text is the "fusion of horizons"

(Horizontverschmelzung).[2] This means the fusion, or coalescence, of the horizon of the text and that of its reader.

This is a very complicated issue, but the gist of the idea will already be clear: to create a world that could become a homeland for the modern readers of the text (not the reader of the interpretation; the interpretation creates such a world) and for the authorial readers, that is, for the readers assumed by the text. The latter need not be identical with the first actual readers, but their world ought not to differ fundamentally from the world of the first real readers, for otherwise the authority of the text would be challenged because we would have to regard the text as a literary creation unable to communicate effectively with the people of its time.

So far we have described the first part of the actual event that is the essence of interpretation. Old texts, the modern relevance of which the reader senses, cannot be related directly to our present because their world is different from ours. But now we can make the first step toward linking the worlds: in some situations they intersect, and at least in a certain segment of our experience, we can grasp what such a text means in our contemporary world. Jesus' statements about the Son of Man are today unintelligible and require interpretation. In contrast, the story of the customs officer Zacchaeus (Luke 19:1-10), in which Jesus sits down at a table with a man who as a tax collector is (understandably) not accepted by the surrounding society and who has decided to compensate for his isolation and short stature by gaining a high position (supreme customs officer), is so effective and intelligible that it can retrospectively become the key to understanding the appeals to love your enemy or Paul's interpretation of these appeals, "Overcome evil with good" (Rom. 12:21). This immediate intelligibility applies not only to texts that concern overall orientation in life but also to those that express in brief some basic human feelings and experiences, and do so in a way that at the same time can express the second level of the text. The scene from book 6 of Homer's *Iliad* in which Hector bids farewell to his wife and little son before battle is a moving example of this. Hector wants to take his son in his arms, but the boy burst out crying, scared by Hector's metal helmet and horsehair crest. Hector immediately takes off the helmet and "now kissed and rocked [his beloved son] in his arms" (6.474). Despite Hector's fighting words, the whole scene is infused with a feeling of fatefulness and parting in the deepest sense of the word. The helplessness of the child and the sorrow of the parents are feelings

---

2. H.-G. Gadamer, *Wahrheit und Methode* (1960; 2d ed., Tübingen: Mohr Siebeck, 1965; ET *Truth and Method*, 2d Eng. ed. [London: Sheed & Ward, 1989]), 286-89.

that almost any human being can share, including contemporary people, who are separated from the writing of the *Iliad* by more than two and a half millennia. In the literary strategy of the ancient epic, this scene is the background against which the tragedy of Hector's imminent death stands out.

Fundamentally, then, modern readers can, at least for a moment, put themselves in the position of the people for whom a classical text was intended. **What we have in common is our humanity, which is the distinctive mark of the human race, at the very least since it started to leave intelligible written records.** In this sense what are known as **anthropological universals** are a common denominator. They are what are shared by the human race, or to express it in a theological metaphor, they are the traces of the Creator's work.

The problem is, however, that what we perceive best across the centuries is precisely that which is part of the elementary, universal expression of human life. **Even at the dawn of civilizations these expressions have become sedimented as universal social consciousness. But that which is oriented to change, which is "an event," is usually less intelligible.**

When Gadamer spoke of the fusion of horizons, he was not thinking of anthropological universals, or at least not directly. He was not concerned just with universally intelligible individual situations that might attract our attention in the past world. In relation to human beings in history, the issue is not just one of situation but one of the whole scheme of our *Dasein* ("being-there"). Gadamer's image of the horizon is an expression of the search for a place from which communication between the two worlds might be possible. We might compare it to the search for a place in the mountains from which one can see two cities that lie on either side of the range and thus are not visible to each other. Gadamer's premise is not that we should climb the mountain and so create a total, comprehensive and universal picture of mutual connections. His concern is only that, as they meet, the horizons can be the mediator of communication between the two worlds.

Those seeking after the common horizon are the readers of today, who enlarge their world to include the past world, because they (you and I) ask the question of the relationship between our own world and the world of the text and become aware of some of the basic difficulties that mean that the world of the text is not entirely intelligible to us. This is a momentous step, but not even this step yet constitutes a complete solution, because the past world will never be wholly accessible to us; there will always be the "différance," which has been particularly emphasized by some postmodern philosophical movements (J. Derrida). The active role of the reader in dialogue with the text, a dialogue that we have defined as the hermeneutic circle (§3.7.3), can also be

Interpretation

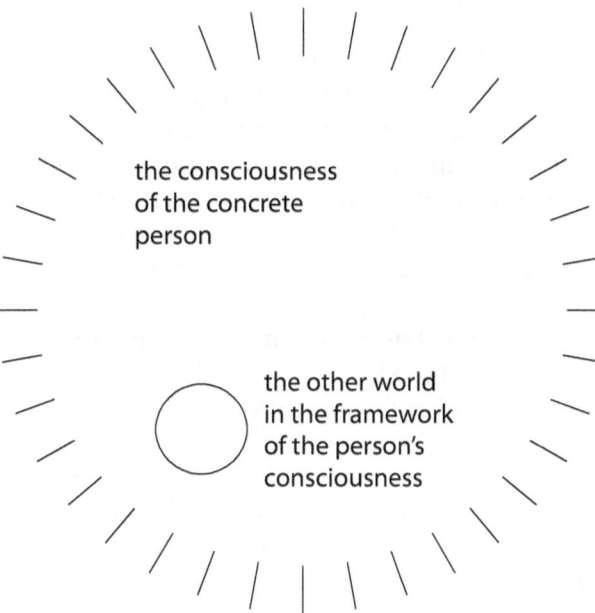

The initial position in work on linking the world of the text with the world of the reader: the reader knows that the "other world" exists; it is a part of his or her consciousness. This has been enriched by knowledge of the concrete other world. The other world is smaller, because even the greatest expert knows fundamentally less about it than he or she knows about the world of personal experience. Above all, however, the other world is encapsulated in our mind. We may learn more about it, but it is a past, a world that is closed. The fact that we know of it does not mean that we know how to interpret it.

understood in terms of the reader cutting a circle that will never lead to full understanding. He or she thus steps out of the apparently vicious circular movement by adapting the text to his or her world. This is how the participation of the reader in the process of reading and interpretation was understood by members of the Constance school. It is a correct answer only in the sense that the common world is genuinely our problem, our question, and our construct — something that we use to orientate ourselves in life. Our projects of the world must nonetheless be fundamentally open, just as our thinking and critique of our own thinking must be open.[3]

---

3. The open social character of the interpretation of the literary work has been pointed out by David Tracy in his study *The Analogical Imagination*, 64ff.

It is not, then, just a matter of the enlargement of the reader's world to include the world of the text or texts that he or she reads and seeks to understand — an enlargement that would fill in the gaps with the reader's imagination. **It is a matter of the reconstruction of the reader's thinking, in which confrontation with the text and its world has led to the "opening up" of the reader's life world** (his life project, the project of his "Dasein"), to the discovery of the reader's own situatedness,[4] to the de-ideologization of our pictures of the world, and to insight into the historicity of our pictures of the world.

The shared horizon is therefore ahead of us. It is that which we have not yet reached. It is that to which the internal movement (the pragmatics, function) **of the text and of the understanding** of the (open) reader **is directed**. It is the direction of the gaze of both toward that which is beyond our horizon.[5]

The opening of the text to the future, in which the text will reach its application and its fulfillment, is clearly also the rationale of Gadamer's explications of the "inner word" *(logos, verbum interius)*; this concept expresses a certain orientation that does not fully fit into the text and is less the result of reflection than its inspiration. In his exposition of the "inner word," Gadamer starts from Augustine's treatise *De doctrina christiana* and draws on the doctrine of the Holy Trinity up to the period of Scholastic philosophy. The uttered or written word is always concrete, but precisely in its concreteness it refers to a basis that transcends, outruns its own concreteness (e.g., the fact that it is a Hebrew or an English or a Czech word). According to the fundamental theological statements of the church, this also applies to Christ as the incarnation of God — as a unique, concrete word. Thus the text points to its source precisely in its historic concreteness and the limitations that this inevitably entails, and so God's being cannot be exhausted in the text.[6]

That this is not an abstract consideration becomes clear when we compare various different texts that may become the subject of our interpretation. We already know that in each case our interest in the text involves a certain preunderstanding; that is, we have an idea of how what we learn

---

4. Kouba, "Kritérium interpretace," 132-33.

5. O. Bayer, "Hermeneutical Theology," in *Philosophical Hermeneutics and Biblical Exegesis*, ed. P. Pokorný and J. Roskovec (Tübingen: Mohr Siebeck, 2002), 103-20, here 116 (with a reminder of the fact that this reality played a part in the philosophy of G. W. F. Hegel). Orientation to the future, to that which (so far) does not exist, has been emphasized by L. Hejdánek, "Hermeneutik und die Zeit."

6. Gadamer, *Wahrheit und Methode*, 398ff.

from the text will enter into our life and leave a trace on it. This does not mean that we are making arbitrary use of the text, because a reading and interpretation of the text must respect how it functioned in its own world, must respect its "point." Thus the text will lead us in a certain direction, but its full test is a matter of the future. This applies to the reading of a beekeeping manual, a novel, or a penciled message. With texts relating to history or life as a whole, their "point" is a reality that goes beyond our horizon; their "not yet" relates to our whole historical situatedness.

Once again we must remind ourselves of something that seems to be a marginal issue, namely, that openness of interpretation does not mean indeterminacy — that any interpretation is possible. A text can lead us to its application in different ways, but the direction is evident and verifiable and can be read from an analysis of its pragmatics if we adopt a sufficiently thorough methodological distance from it. Our preunderstanding on the one hand and openness of interpretation on the other mean that some data about the text will remain outside our field of observation. For example, in interpretation of biblical narrative texts we need not pay attention to the grammatical analysis of every word or investigate the structure of every segment of the text, as long as we know its genre and if the context does not suggest that precisely in this case some structural peculiarity is semantically important. The situation is similar if we think of the example of a letter written by a mother from a spa, one full of instructions about the household and messages to neighbors. Her daughter will not be looking for corrections, transcriptions, or grammatical errors but will read from the letter primarily that her mother loves her and trusts her. Then she will concentrate on fulfilling her mother's wishes. Obviously the border between what is a part of pragmatics and what is inessential work on interpretation is not clear-cut. Hebrew scholars devote greater attention to the structural analysis of the text than is required in the analysis of the Greek text of early Christian writings because the very punctuation of the Hebrew text (the writing in of vowels) is a secondary layer which allows the text to be newly reconstructed. Indeed, even in a letter from a spa the layout of the text on the page can sometimes indirectly suggest the kind of attitude the mother has toward her daughter.

5.3. Understanding the Text as Part of Self-Understanding

We have already suggested several times that the interpretation of a text is actually a path to the better self-understanding of the interpreter and those for whom the interpretation is intended. The roots of this concept of interpretation can be traced in the modern period as far back as F. D. Schleiermacher, but it is inseparably associated with Martin Heidegger, who recognized the full implications of the hermeneutic question and hermeneutic procedures and began to understand hermeneutics as the theory of understanding and comprehension in general,[7] as a universal hermeneutics of facticity.[8] **To understand something means to understand oneself.**[9] To "adopt" (Lundin) a word (to "make it one's own") means that, by using it, I am discovering a (new) possibility of action and self-understanding, and thereby understanding of my *Dasein* as well. If I did not know that I could use the word in some way, that it could in some way "fill" my life, make it authentic, I would not consider it. The possibilities for the sake of which I notice the word might be just a matter of grasping small, momentary, and marginal possibilities, but they also could concern the whole plan and disposition of my life.[10] **Understanding is the acceptance of an interpretation through which a statement manifests itself intelligibly as a discovery, clarification, or enrichment of the meaning of life.** Ricoeur's hermeneutics is premised on the idea that **man understands himself by a detour. This is at the least a double detour: through the text that interests the man, and through the interpretation of his own world that the text offers him. Man thus keeps returning to the text with understanding and by understanding the text starts to (better) understand himself.**[11] Heidegger speaks more of the word than the text, since he sees the text as something impersonal just because it can emancipate itself from its author, but we have just indicated the circumstances in which we can speak even in this context of text. In any case, on the basis of our previous observations we can say of a text too, and not only a word, that we approach it with a certain preunderstanding.

The understanding of the text is actually preunderstanding that has been processed and cultivated. Not in the sense of the reader investing the text with his or her own ideas, but because (1) the reader is required to de-

---

7. M. Heidegger, "Ontologie. Hermeneutik der Faktizität," in *Gesamtausgabe*, vol. 63 (Frankfurt: Klostermann, 1988), 80.

8. H.-G. Gadamer, "Die Universalität des hermeneutischen Problems" (1966), recently in *Gadamer Lesebuch* (Tübingen: Mohr Siebeck, 1997), 58-70.

9. A. C. Thiselton, *New Horizons in Hermeneutics* (Grand Rapids: Zondervan, 1992), 272ff.

10. Heidegger, *Being and Time*, §32.

11. P. Ricoeur, "Existence et herméneutique," in *Interpretation der Welt*, FS R. Guardini (Würzburg: Echter Verlag, 1965), 32-51.

Interpretation

velop a better awareness of his or her hermeneutic situation and so (2) a better grasp of the otherness of the text.

Difficulties with some of the stages in the interpretation of ancient texts in which there is an initial need to get a conscious distance from the interpreted text led Rudolf Bultmann to propose a more direct route, or interpretational "short cut." He declared the world of the text to be something secondary to its actual proclamation (Gr. *kērygma*), in the same sense that circumcision as a ritual procedure was secondary in the eyes of the apostle Paul. In other words, he fundamentally relativized the "world of the text." He applied this principle not just, for example, to the notion of the three-tiered cosmos shared by the Bible (heaven, earth as a floating flat surface, and the underworld as its basement), but also to ideas such as the liturgical statements about Christ's death as substitute victim, which originated before Paul of Tarsus wrote his first surviving letters. These were statements that assumed a knowledge of cult sacrifice, whether sacrifices of reconciliation (Leviticus 16) or sacrifice in the sense of the lamb slaughtered at the Feast of Passover to commemorate the death of the lambs in the old legend (Exodus 12) of the sacrifice of the lambs saving the life of the firstborn sons of Israel. According to Bultmann, all this is a "secular" *(weltlich)* expression of that which transcends the world[12] and so can be "made one's own" precisely by looking away from the structures of the historical world of the Bible and from the specifics of their individual features. It suffices for us to know that this is a picture of a world that is different from ours, for according to Bultmann we ought not to concentrate on the individual ideas that we meet in the interpreted texts but on the self-understanding *(Selbstverständnis)* that the text offers the human being. The biblical "proclamatory," kerygmatic texts offer the human being a self-comprehension that is open, that takes on an awareness of what had previously seemed an "impossible possibility."

The discovery of the role of the subject at a time when exegesis was dominated by positivistically conceived historical criticism was a breakthrough with irreversible consequences. For all its radicalism, Bultmann's approach cannot be branded as something alien to texts, including biblical texts. Yet it is an approach that is clearly incomplete, partial. The reason is that human beings do not form their self-understanding in a vacuum, and the question is always one of the plan and disposition of their concrete, particular life, in which biblical projects can be sources of inspiration. We can-

---

12. R. Bultmann, "Neues Testament und Mythologie" (1941), in *Kerygma und Mythus*, vol. 1, 5th ed., ed. Hans W. Bartsch (Hamburg-Bergstedt: Reich, 1967), 15-48, here 22.

not of course transfer the texts into our present directly, because they belong to another world, but we can explore their functions in their world and create our own, contemporary, analogically functioning models. Our journey does not end by discovering a new and vital experience to date, an "impossible possibility," but with our attempt to bring it to life, with our search for a new orientation in history. We search for a meaning that must be supposed if that what we encounter is presented as proclamation *(kērygma)*. Bultmann rejects the idea that we can take up and follow directly the tradition that the biblical texts represent, claiming that all that we can read out of past texts (in this case, specifically the texts of the New Testament) is simply *that* we have a new possibility, *that* our world is not a world imprisoned in the ideas in which we live, and that our decision making in life, with which orientation in the contemporary world is necessarily linked, ought to be *responsible*.

The weakness of this conception becomes apparent in Bultmann's interpretation of concrete texts, where exegesis of each segment can be summarized in terms of statements about new or "impossible" possibilities. This interpretation is interesting and truly brilliant in places where it reconstructs the world of the text, where the author for a moment takes the position of a religious theorist and leaves readers room to do their own hermeneutic work for themselves. It reckons with the communicability of the new self-understanding and rightly emphasizes the role of the subject, but the problem is that it does not take into account the reader's social dimension, the fact that **the understanding of the text is also,** as we have noted **(admittedly, via the individual human subjects), a social matter and is also handed down by tradition.** In this respect Bultmann has been rightly criticized.

5.4. Historicity and Revelation

If we can speak of the world of the text, in which the text itself functions and, in our interpretative detachment, we can uncover certain analogies with our own situation and use these to start to understand ourselves better, this does not mean that the confrontation of our life world and the world of the text is the goal of interpretation. The "world of the text" is an abstraction, a matter of basic direction markers that can be placed over the text like the signs on transparent paper that we place on a map or on a picture in order to bring out the unrepeatable contours of reality. We have spoken of how interpretation must arrive at a point where it starts to follow the text in its successive form — the text as action or as argumentation (§3.6) — and where the reader starts to return progressively from interpretation to the text itself.

Interpretation does not therefore end in a general proposition but goes back to the concrete text. This is because the text shares with us our historicity, the unrepeatability of our lives, and thus individual events and decisions within it can relate to our present only indirectly. Sometimes they relate by generalization, more often by analogy. The historical unrepeatability of revelation makes its direct verification impossible. We must look for concrete contents, meanings that engage us despite their strangeness, their distance, or perhaps just because of that distance. In the third chapter (§3.7.2) we spoke about the referential side of the text, its relationship to its "milieu," a world that is also preserved in texts but that the texts indicate is not exhausted in them. Proper names are like claws with which they cling to their period and to a time running into the past — their world. Yet such a text attracts us, and sometimes it is precisely in such a text that we encounter something that changes our outlook. Why is it that under certain circumstances we may find support in a revelation bound up with concrete events?

5.5. Revelation and Witness

BIBLIOGRAPHY

Griesch, Jean. "Témoignage et l'attestation." In *L'herméneutique à l'école de la phénoménologie*, ed. P. Ricoeur, 305-26. Paris, 1995.
Nabert, Jean. "Métaphysique du témoignage et herméneutique de l'absolu." In *Le désir de Dieu*, 261-380, here 276ff. Paris: du Cerf, 1955.
Ricoeur, Paul. "The Hermeneutics of Testimony" (1972). In *Essays on Biblical Interpretation*, 119-54. London: SCM Press, 1981.
———. "Towards a Hermeneutic of the Idea of Revelation" (1976). In *Essays on Biblical Interpretation*, 73-118.

5.5.1. Revelation

In the Hebrew Bible the text often declares that God revealed himself at a certain place. A "revelation" is something distinct from a miraculous, objective disclosure of a divine reality. The latter is what is known as epiphany. In theological terminology a revelation, unlike an epiphany, is an encounter with God in history in the world of human life. It is not an intervention breaking through the order of life but a revelation of deeper connection, an insight into the deep level, or more precisely a vista toward the *eschaton,* the absolute future. Revelation need not be a psychologically intense experience — often it is recognizable only after the event, in the assessment of what has happened. It may be the result of thought or long-term experience — for example, when the Israelite tribes discovered in the narrative of the exodus from Egypt a revelation of the nature of the Lord (Yahweh) and, by their testimony, confirmed that the revelation of this aspect of God had been a support to them in many hardships and provided them with a compass on their path through history.

> A wandering Aramean was my ancestor; and he went down into Egypt and lived there as an alien, few in number, and there he became a great nation, mighty and populous. When the Egyptians treated us harshly and afflicted us, by imposing hard labor on us, we cried to the LORD, the God of our ancestors; the LORD heard our voice and saw our affliction, our toil, and our oppression. The LORD brought us out of Egypt with a mighty hand and an outstretched arm, with a terrifying display of power, and with signs and wonders; and he brought us into this place and gave us this land, a land flowing with milk and honey. So now I bring the first of the fruit of the ground that you, O LORD, have given me. (Deut. 26:5b-10a)

This is a narrative about a certain segment of history that thus becomes a revelation in the witness of Israel. It is a tradition handed down in different forms: from the narrative in Joshua 24:2-13, to the witness in liturgically compact form in the passage cited from Deuteronomy 26 (what is known as the "small historical creed"), to the hymn (e.g., Psalm 105) or the hymn with liturgical responses, like Psalm 136.

As time went by, the function of revelation was also attributed to the activities of individual prophets. This was most clearly reflected in the canonization of their speeches or the traditions from which their speeches came. We also encounter revelation in discursive texts. The psychological aspect of the call to become a prophet can be described only in very general terms. It was certainly associated with an intense experience in most cases, but this itself never played a decisive role in the public pronouncements of the prophets. What these stressed as decisive was the divine commission with which they stood forward (see Jer. 2:1) and the reception and response.

It might have been a response only in a minority of their listeners, but it was always a response that had an effect on the lives of other people. Christians adopted this tradition as their own past, and from the middle of the second century they started to interpret Jesus' words and his whole life against its background — as divine revelation (Heb. 1:1ff).[13] The preceding revelations spoken of in the Law and Prophets (i.e., in Scripture, the Christian Old Testament) thus became partial revelations, with Jesus' story as the final and sufficient revelation of the nature of God — "revelation" here in the concrete event, in the historical story.[14] This Christian tradition was the source of the concept of revelation, which has had a major effect on the whole hermeneutic discussion.

The concept of revelation (Gr. *apokalypsis,* Lat. *revelatio*) was taken from apocalyptics, where it meant the prefiguration of the last events — namely, that which will come at the end of history, which transcends it and is its goal. When the Christians termed a certain event theologically a revelation,[15] it meant that they recognized in it something relating to the decisive, eschatological future. By this they implied that there can be events that, from our point of view, are unique and unrepeatable but that nonetheless reveal the reality to which our existence is directed, and thus they reveal a part of our future or its key feature.

From the hermeneutic point of view, **revelation** can then be understood as a kind of "emplotment" (§3.7.5) that, when retrospectively assessed, opens up a new view on life as a whole.[16] It is not a wonder in the sense of the miraculous, something that God might perform or some trap that "fate" might set us with a view to interfering in the course of history to our benefit or loss. **It is an event that, considered in retrospect, makes possible a congruent interpretation of a certain stage in history or life and, in the case of a biblical revelation, of life and history as a whole.** Retrospective insight reveals that we cannot see the revelation as something alien with regard to what is self-evident, but that we grasp its "revelatory" function only when we

---

13. The oldest recorded instances of the use of the term "revelation" in theological thought are Ignatius, *Letter to the Magnesians* 8.2, and Irenaeus, *Adversus omnes haereses* 4.20.5.

14. From the point of view of systematic theology, see E. Jüngel, *Gott als Geheimnis der Welt* (Tübingen: Mohr Siebeck, 1977), 299.

15. At the same time, the term is used in literary contexts as the designation of a literary genre.

16. This is not a matter of an analogy of metaphor, as it is regarded by N. Frye, *The Great Code: The Bible and Literature* (New York: Harcourt Brace Jovanovich, 1982), 52.

understand the revelation as something more self-evident than what normally seems to us self-evident[17] — as something that reveals the hidden inner structure of our whole lives and world. This does not, then, involve something that would represent a higher degree of the self-evident, but something that shows itself as evident through its own persuasiveness, and thus it is only in comparison with the revelation that the self-evident appears less self-evident (and less human). Of course, I am already reflecting now on the ideas that led to the definition of the concept of revelation in the theological and philosophical sense (in contrast to the narrower concept of revelation in religious studies, which is derived from the function of revelation [*apokalypsis*] in apocalyptics; the broader concept is one more like ultrareflection — a term that points to pondering the tradition that expresses the logic of Christian experience).

In 1 Corinthians 15:12 we read an interpretation of a relatively fresh tradition of Christian witness of faith, according to which Christ was "raised from the dead." This is the basic Christian testimony. The function of revelation is assigned to the reality to which these words testify because it can be understood as a sign of the limits of the rule of death over all people. The apostle Paul says that God "gives life to the dead and calls into existence the things that do not exist" (Rom 4:17; see also 2 Cor. 1:9), and in 1 Cor. 15:35-50 he interprets eschatological resurrection by analogy with the sprouting of sown grain. In Acts Jesus' resurrection becomes the basis for the idea that God is he who "raises the dead" (26:8). The issue here is the revelation of a new feature on the face of the last reality — something that we might call the "disclosure of the reach of the unique." It is not a matter of generalization because it is about an unrepeatable event, but it is an event that has a deeper context. At the beginning of the Letter to the Hebrews, the divine revelation is characterized as the decisive word of God, in which the partial messages of the prophets culminate (1:1-2). It is the "generalization" (a term I am now using as a provocative metaphor) of something that we encounter only once in history but that by its nature transcends its own time. The very fact that the Christians could classify such an event into a certain category testifies to its internal and, retrospectively, its outwardly verifiable gravity. In this way the story of Jesus becomes a revelation of that which "has a future." In his *Principles of Christian Theology* John Macquarrie offered a definition: "It is not that God at a certain moment added another act of reconciliation to his pre-

---

17. E. Jüngel, "Extra Christum nulla salus — als Grundsatz natürlicher Theologie?" (1977), in *Entsprechung: Gott — Wahrheit — Mensch* (Munich: Kaiser, 1980), 178-92, here 187ff.

vious activities or that we might determine the time when this reconciliation began. It is more that at a given moment there emerged a new and crucial interpretation of an act that was still going on, an activity that has the same origin as creation itself."[18] Macquarrie pinpoints the way in which revelation opens up to the human being something that is not bound to the moment at which it became evident to some people. His definition gives the impression of a kind of ongoing train of events. In fact, while what is involved is a movement that precedes its revelation, the goal of that movement is ahead, and so through revelation a fundamental feature of the unrealized future intervenes in the present.

The term "revelation" came into general usage only from the second century, but the verb *apokalyptō* had already been used by the apostle Paul as an expression for the communication of God's will (1 Cor. 2:10), and as we have noted, the experience of revelation had already been expressed in the Law and the Prophets. In early Christian literature it was expressed with captivating precision by "Luke," the author of a two-part work about Jesus. Jesus' coming is, on the one hand, described using the techniques of ancient religious experience (visions, messengers of the heavenly world, miraculous events), but the evaluative metaphorical level that intersects with the historical testimony is theologically precise and convincing. Jesus' arrival in the world is the fulfillment of ancient promises but is still concerned with something that does not yet exist here. Revelation is the revelation of the reality that people are children of God's promise (*eudokia*, Luke 2:14), but this is something that is not yet valid on earth. There is no place (*ouk . . . topos*, v. 7) for Jesus under the roof. The reader of the Greek text would necessarily have understood the clear reference here to utopia (from *ou* + *topos*), to that which (as yet!) has no place in the world. Jesus comes, as it were, against the will of the world, but the reader recognizes that a divine matter is being revealed here (Luke 10:21-22) and that, retrospectively, Jesus' "coming" (incarnation) is the beginning of a movement that will have an impact in the very metropolis of the empire where Paul of Tarsus, although a prisoner, taught about the Lord Jesus Christ quite openly and unhindered (Acts 28:31). Jesus' words and works suddenly start to appear to readers as something familiar, proclaimed from the beginning by the prophets and yet relating to "the time of universal restoration" (*chronoi apokatastaseōs pantōn*, Acts 3:21a). We

---

18. Macquarrie, *Principles of Christian Theology* (New York: Scribner, 1977), quotation taken from A. E. McGrath, *The Blackwell Encyclopaedia of Modern Christian Thought* (Oxford: Basil Blackwell, 1995), s.v. "Soteriology."

have noted that revelation has no direct feedback, which means that the claims of revelation cannot be verified rationally. The attempt to construct a logically rational theology is at best a useful way of eroding Enlightenment ideas about rationality, but such attempts do not elucidate what theology is about. Among the many phenomena that can be expressed only by metaphor or by some other poetic (i.e., creative) technique (see §2.4.1), we must put revelation at the top of the list.[19]

5.5.2. Witness

Revelation cannot be verified in a truly direct way, and so we are dependent on the witness of those who had a special experience of particular events (or a tradition about them) that helped them in their lives. At this point the hermeneutics that works with the term "revelation" would seem to have abandoned the field of critical scholarly praxis.

Yet Paul Ricoeur points out that **witness** has always had a recognized social role and has been associated with a certain ritual. Furthermore — and in scholarly discussion this should be taken extremely seriously — it is **the basis of an academic discipline as important as law.**[20] We may add that **history, another scholarly discipline** cultivated in universities and enjoying general trust, is also **based on testimony.** Witness, or testimony, then, is not an "unscientific" term.

If we apply the age-old rule of law (jurisprudence) to the biblical testimony that refers to certain events that are considered to be crucial (revelations), we are bound to realize that the interpreter, like the interpreter of historical testimony, is taking on the role of judge. A man who is a judge cannot decide cases on the basis of his own ideas, moods, sympathies, or antipathies but only according to the rules of law and, of course, according to the seriousness of the testimony submitted. However much he distances himself from his own emotions, though, he cannot remain indifferent to the testimony as such, or more precisely to the case to which the testimony relates. No testimony can relieve him of this duty, because every testimony combines information with evaluation of that information.

What, then, are the legal rules for judgment on the kind of testimony that we know from the Hebraic-Christian tradition and its texts? Legal sys-

---

19. Ricoeur, "Towards a Hermeneutic of the Idea of Revelation," 101.
20. Ricoeur, "The Hermeneutics of Testimony," 124.

tems may vary, and the very function of testimony in judicial systems is different from testimony in the assessment of historical evidence. In all areas in which testimony plays a part, the key question is the authenticity of the testimony. And the authenticity of testimony can in all these areas be measured by a number of common criteria.

First is *the defenselessness of the witness before the judge.* In practice this means that the acceptance of the authenticity of testimony, its reception, may not be something forced on the judge by manifest power or threat or indirect extortion. On the contrary, authentic witnesses regard their testimony as so momentous that they are ready to sacrifice something for it — in extreme cases, even their own life. The name "martyr" given to Christians who died for their faith is derived from the Greek expression for witness — *martys.* The apostle Paul added weight to his testimony precisely by its defenselessness (e.g., 2 Cor. 11:30).

Second, there is general recognition (see above, §4.4.3) of the second rule of authentic testimony, namely, that *the claim contained in the testimony must by supported by at least two independent witnesses.* It is not easy to fulfill this condition when studying individual pieces of information about the life and teaching of Jesus because most are derived from a single source, most often the Gospel according to Mark or the Q collection. Only in a minority of cases do data from these two main sources overlap or enjoy other independent support (in the data contained in Paul's epistles, in the Gospel of Thomas, in other noncanonical texts). If, however, we are talking about the crucial role of the story of Jesus for human hope, the testimony of the early Christian texts is unambiguous and convincing. It is supported by the sheer diversity of formulations of Jesus' crucial role (different supreme terms for Jesus, different projects of his significance such as resurrection from the dead, elevation [ascension], his death as substitutive sacrifice, his functional identification with the apocalyptic Son of Man, or the collection of his sayings motivated by belief in their permanent validity and "vitality" [durability], premised on the idea that he was the incarnation of divine wisdom), and the fact that all these expressions appeared quite shortly after his death. The persuasiveness of this congruence is also suggested by the secondary testimony based on the original "apostolic" statements as the declaration of faith of the first Christian generations. This robust church tradition must be measured against the original testimonies because it is not unambiguous, but at its core, which constitutes its identity, it itself bears the marks of testimony (witnesses are ready to make sacrifices, they agree despite differences in confession and so on). In this way Christian testimony acquires a peculiar character that we must never lose sight of: it is founding a community, it has a social function.[21]

Only in certain circumstances can we manage without a second independent witness — for example, when it is clear that a witness could not have had an interest in inventing what he or she claims. One record that fulfills this criterion is, for example, the information contained in the slanders against Jesus preserved in the texts of the gospels (e.g., Luke [Q] 7:33-34 and par.). This rule of possible substitution for a second witness had been developed in historical exegesis (see above, §4.4).

The third feature of authentic testimony, which we have already noted in §4.4.3, is *its objective congruence with other testimony about other aspects of the same cause.* This is not a question of information about the same event. For example, the tradition reporting Jesus as helping the sick, blessing children, defending foreigners (Samaritans) and having sympathy with the poor (Luke 6:20 and 7:22 [Q]) is congruent with his beatitudes of the poor. The thoughts on faith that set his words and actions in a broader context also have indirect value as testimony. In biblical texts this aspect of congruence is expressed by intertextuality (§3.7.1) and statements setting the testimony in an overall picture of the world (generalization). These are primarily the statements that develop the idea of his significance back into the past (involving preexistence [Phil. 2:6] or his being the mediator of creation [1 Cor. 8:6 and Col. 1:16]), and forward into the eschatological (furthest) future (Jesus as judge, as he who is owned at the end of history as the Son of Man — commissioned by God and intercessor at the judgment [Rom. 8:34]).

The fourth feature of authentic testimony is *the willingness of the witness to answer questions asked by the judge.* This function of feedback that testimony must concede if it is to be taken seriously is something that we have considered earlier in relation to historical criticism, in §3.7.2.

Even if testimony has the four features listed here, this still does not mean that it must be accepted as proof and that its recipient — that is, the judge, who is in this case anyone who encounters Christian testimony — is freed of his or her duty to decide. This is something that we must not forget. Not even testimony supported from various different sides frees any judge from the obligation to make up his or her own mind and give judgment. The authenticity of the testimony means only that it cannot be ignored and that reasons must be given if the judgment is against it. Naturally, many people

---

21. K. Berger, *Hermeneutik des Neuen Testaments* (Gütersloh: Gütersloher Verlagshaus, 1988), 164, cf. 51, 73, 104.

Interpretation

have no desire to accept the function of a judge. This is a possible decision, and such people cannot be forced to judge. If they refuse the challenge, however, they have alienated themselves from a serious dimension of human life and have impoverished their lives.

Does the testimony, according to which the Jesus story appears as a divine revelation, meet the criteria given? From the outset, the fundamental reliability of the testimony contained in the traditions from which a picture of Jesus may be derived has been threatened by a tendency to ideologize the various pictures with which individual expressions of Jesus' significance had associated in the various different groups of his followers. These were tendencies that the emergent church sought to counter by including in the canon of the Christian Bible various testimonies based on various concepts arising from broader experience. In contrast, the Christian church in the period from Constantine up to the modern age, an age when it had a direct influence on political power in many countries, often violated the first criterion of witness. If the Christian witness is not accepted by a large proportion of society today, it is not just because those who reject it are all alienated groups who avoid responsibility in confrontation with the testimony. To a major extent it is because the majority of people have not encountered authentic testimony and have found arguments against its inauthentic forms. Moreover, part of society has accepted Christian witness but recognizes only Jesus, not the church.

It is true that any testimony can be abused, but a return to its authenticity — a fifth criterion — makes it possible for a group that has accepted such testimony to continue to create a living and regenerating and open tradition in the midst of contemporary society, and above all to analyze its own failures and admit them (repentance). We encounter this kind of self-critical concept of history as early as what is known as the Deuteronomistic layer of the Jewish Bible (the Christian Old Testament: see above, §3.7.4)

The concept of revelation that has enabled us to define some momentous common features of the texts of the Jewish and Christian Scripture is, from the hermeneutical point of view, only an extreme, striking case, applicable to the whole of human experience. It is experience with an event in history that is chance and fleeting in its unrepeatability but still gives real meaning to the traditional structures within which we encounter it (see §3.7.5). The function of such an event becomes apparent retrospectively.

If in Christian theology the concept of revelation was adopted as the basic expression of the second (i.e., the Christological) article of Christian faith, this meant the discovery of the common denominator of all the expressions of the meaning of Jesus (his resurrection, ascension, death as sacrifice, etc.), which define his story as an event ("emplotment"), from the perspective of which the meaning of history as a whole may be retrospectively revealed (§3.7.5). Thus in John 1 we read that Jesus is the incarnation of God's Word — the plan (*logos sarx egeneto*, v. 14) of "interpreting" ("exegeting") God (*exēgēsato*, v. 18), who cannot be directly seen. Today systematic theology defines Jesus from the point of view of Christian faith as the "parable"[22] of God in history.[23]

There are many events of a lower order that appear to most people to be merely transient and minor episodes but later turn out to be stories that give unity to whole stages of the history of a certain society and in some aspects transcend the limits of these stages and mark out the character of future endeavors. If we look at such events in Czech history, as they appear to us in state festivals, commemorative days, and portraits on bank notes, we are confronted with a strange gallery of characters and their stories: the expulsion of the early missionaries Cyril and Methodius, the murdered Prince Wenceslas, Agnes of Bohemia living in her convent, Jan Hus burned at the stake, the exiled Comenius, the historian Jan Palacký from the Protestant minority, the reviled defender of the right to critical thought Tomáš G. Masaryk, the political prisoner Václav Havel — all these are people who struggled apparently vainly against the alienating pressure of history. It is a pressure that seemed at the time as irreversible as the death of our universe according to the Second Law of Thermodynamics (entropy). Even in the oldest surviving texts from the dawn of history, fears were expressed about the irreversible and early end of civilization as a result of the decline of morals, but if we retrospectively study the reasons why this imminent end failed to materialize, we can see that, apart from the tendency to destruction, there have been traditions in history woven from the strong warp and weave of events that can be called partial revelations. Usually these events do not look particularly important and crucial on the surface of history, which means that their witnesses have had to demonstrate and draw attention to their significance. We have noted that this reality was recognized in Hebraic thought long before the time of Christ, and now we have tried to suggest that it is a phenomenon applicable even to our historical tradition and the perspective arising from it. This surprising continuity of history, visible only where there is a will to listen to testimony pointing to the key character of certain events, is itself a proof of their inner per-

---

22. The expression "parable" is in this case itself employed metaphorically.

23. On the meaning of this Christological concept, see particularly E. Schweizer, *Jesus als Gleichnis Gottes* (Göttingen: Vandenhoeck & Ruprecht, 1995).

suasiveness. When we interpret the sayings of the Jesus tradition on the last judgment and the coming kingdom of heaven as an open future, from the perspective of which history and lives can be seen as a whole and positive meaning can be clearly distinguished from absurdity, ours is a view that will be inevitably suspected of being an illusion. It seems that the courage to see some deeper meaning in history and lives hangs on the thread of this trust (in Christian tradition: faith). Yet if we look back at history from this perspective, traditions begin to emerge that are at the very least just as surprising, have demonstrable historical traces and an influence right down to the present, and cannot be ignored. At the beginning of this chapter we spoke of the common horizon of the reader and the text, which is never entirely attainable; revelation may be understood as its prefiguration.

Theology is systematic reflection on the basic biblical tradition of witness. Its ideas can find support in this witness and can test the possibilities of the thought derived from it when addressing fundamental questions of human life and history. As we have shown (§3.7.2), biblical exegesis can be the feedback of this project.

With interpretation of the function of revelation, we have reached the very limit of philosophical hermeneutics, and in a certain sense we have already gone beyond it. We need to admit this and at the same time to remind ourselves why we resolved to do so: it is to make clear that, under certain circumstances, witness can and should be taken seriously; that biblical testimony relates to the absolute future; and that **any kind of search for meaning in history and any understanding of the self must take the possibility of eschatological transcendence seriously and come to terms with its best-known Hebraic-Christian historical expressions.** As we have already said, this is in any case the direct or indirect motivation of our work with the preserved texts of the past.

In the last subchapter we spoke of the fact that revelation is not something miraculous or alien, but that it can reveal the hidden axis of history. In this context Eberhard Jüngel comments that a statement concerning the recognition of wider connections that open up like a window on the world at a particular place and with a particular historical event also applies even when we do not name God[24] and do not speak about the revelation of the last things. Biblically conceived **revelation** as an extreme (eschatological) experience of this kind **can help reveal the hidden structure of various different areas of our own world.**

---

24. Jüngel, "Extra Christum nulla salus," 190.

Index of Authors

Aesop, 38
Aland, B., 159
Aletti, N., 145, 147
Amador, J. D. H., 138
Amherdt, F.-X., 60
Aristotle, 91, 99
Ast, F., 2
Auerbach, E., 119-20
Augustine, 25, 26, 129, 184

Barbour, R. S., 157
Barth, K., 61
Barthes, R., 54, 55, 138
Barton, J., 1, 92, 123, 149, 157
Bayer, O., 13, 44, 67, 131, 184
Becker, J., 170
Bengel, J. A., 132
Benjamin, W., 24
Berger, K., 171, 196
Bergson, H., 25
Blahoslav, J., 18
Bonnard, P., 67
Brinkmann, H., 124
Brooke, G. J., 139
Bultmann, R., 53, 60, 65, 89, 130, 153, 171, 173, 187, 188
Burridge, R., 116, 118
Buzetti, C., 13

Calloud, J., 139

Čapek, F., 85
Čapek, J., x, 72
Carson, D. A., 1
Cassidy, G. E., 62
Cassion, J., 130
Charlesworth, J. H., 28, 177
Chelčický, P., 69
Childs, B., 104
Chladenius, M., 2
Chomsky, N., 30, 32
Cimrman, J. (fictive author), 128
Comenius (Komenský), J. A., 128, 198
Conzelmann, H., 175
Corvez, M., 31
Croatto, J. S., 88
Crossan, J. D., 170
Cyril, St., 198

Daněk, S. C., 60
Davidson, D., 42, 50
Derrida, J., 13, 182
Deuteronomist, 46
Dibelius, M., 171, 173
Didymus the Blind, 129
Dihle, A., 68
Dilthey, W., 2, 15
Dostálová, R., 133
Drewermann, E., 55

Ebach, J., 24

Index of Authors

Egger, W., 67, 123, 152, 171
Eliade, M., 55
Ephraim of Syria, 128
Erasmus, 48-49

Ferrua, A., 163
Flacius Illyricus, M., 2, 132
Figal, G., 9, 69
Fink, E., 15
Firbas, J., 74
Fischl, V., 115
Fontain, J. de, 38
Freud, S., 29
Frey, J., 92
Frye, N., 1, 44, 56, 85, 191
Fuchs, E., 32, 33, 128, 153
Fučík, J., 158

Gadamer, H.-G., 13, 39, 49, 52, 80, 81, 91, 94, 118, 180, 182, 184
Gavrilov, A. K., 92
Gibran, K., 24, 25, 34
Goodman, N., 42, 50
Greenwood, D., 28, 139
Greimas, A., 31, 139
Griesch, J., 189
Grondin, J., 1, 3, 130
Gunkel, H., 171
Güttgemanns, E., 28, 30, 32

Hajičová, E., 30
Hatina, T. R., 84
Heckel, U., 159
Hegel, G. W. F., 98-99, 184
Heidegger, M., 69, 89, 91, 131, 154, 177, 186
Hejdánek, L., 80, 177, 184
Hess, R. S., 133
Hippolytus of Rome, 57
Hirsch, E. D., Jr., 140
Hübner, H., 104, 108
Husserl, E., 15, 16

Iersel, B. van, 80
Ingarden, R., 16, 67
Iser, W., 89, 92

Jack, A. M., 7, 13, 88
Jasper, D., 1
Jauss, H. R., 89, 92
Jeanrond, W. G., 1, 5
Jensen, A. S., 1
Johnson, M., 40, 49
Jüngel, E., 41, 153, 191, 192, 199

Kaestli, J. D., 139
Kaiser, O., 157
Kant, I., 39
Karfíková, L., 130
Käsemann, E., 169
Kennedy, G. A., 139, 141
Kilpatrick, G. D., 175
Kirwan, M., 5
Klaudy, K., 133
Klemm, D., x
Kliková, A., 2
Koch, D., 15
Kosak, H., 124
Kouba, P., 177, 184
Kremer, J., 165
Kristeva, J., 85
Krylov, I. A., 38
Kulka, T., 50

Lakoff, G., 49
Lategan, B. C., 102
Leenhardt, F. J., 138
Lessing, H.-U., 1
Lévi-Strauss, C., 32
Lubac, H. de, 124
Lucian of Antioch, 128
Luhmann, N., 31, 32
Lundin, R., 85, 186
Luther, M., 19, 131, 160-61

Machon of Alexandria, 173
Mack, B. L., 152
Macquarrie, J., 192, 193
Magness, J. L., 115
Mann, T., 83
Martin-Achard, R., 138
Marx, K., 98
Marxsen, W., 175

Index of Authors

Masaryk, T. G., 96, 98
Mathauser, Z., 15, 80, 177
Mathesius, V., 19
Maturana, H., 32
McGrath, A. E., 193
Meier, G. E., 2
Meletinskij, E., 55
Merleau-Ponty, M., 17, 28
Methodius, St., 198
Meynet, R., 139, 149
Moore, S., 88
Morgan, R., 1, 123, 149, 157
Mounin, G., 133
Mudge, L. S., x
Muilenburg, J., 139

Nabert, J., 189
Nida, E., 133, 135-36

Oeming, M., 1, 91, 101, 102, 176
Origen, 129-30
Orwell, G., 38

Palacký, F., 178
Palmer, R., 1
Patočka, J., 7
Patte, D., 28, 139
Pearson, B. W. R., 116
Pechar, J., x
Perrin, N., 40, 169
Plato, 38, 56, 70, 91, 141
Pliny the Younger, 110
Pokorný, P., 1, 104, 115, 133, 159, 169
Polybius, 110
Porter, S. E., 1, 116, 133, 141
Pöttner, M., 67
Propp, N. Y., 31
Protagoras, 30
Prudký, M., 161
Pseudo-Homeros, 38

Quintilian, 39
Quispel, G., 163

Ressequil, J. L., 1
Ricoeur, P., x, 1, 2, 9, 17, 22, 28-44 passim,
52, 60, 62, 67, 76, 81, 83, 85, 87, 88, 94,
98, 100, 118, 139, 177, 186, 189, 194
Robbins, V. K., 67, 84, 85, 123, 139, 152-53, 173
Rohde, J., 175
Roloff, J., 123
Roskovec, J., 1
Rouiller, G., 138
Russell, D. A., 124

Sallustius (philosopher), 55
Sandburg, C., 85
Sanders, J. A., 104, 108
Saudek, E. A., 69
Saussure, F. de, 7, 9, 19, 29, 32, 74
Schenk, W., 80
Schleiermacher, F. D. E., 2, 8, 27, 118, 186
Schmidt, K. L., 174
Schulte-Sasse, J., 12, 78
Schweizer, E., 198
Sládek, J. V., 69
Socrates, 71
Sokol, J., 57, 80
Soskice, J. M., 46
Souček, J. B., 60, 114
Soulen, R. K., 1
Soulen, R. N., 1
Stalin (Dzhugashvili), J. V., 72
Stamps, D. L., 141
Starobinski, J., 55, 138
Stendahl, K., 175
Stephanus (Estienne), R., 155
Stern, J., 37
Strecker, G., 123
Szondi, P., 2, 89, 90

Taber, C. R., 133, 136
Tate, W. R., 2, 123, 149
Teilhard de Chardin, P., 21
Theissen, G., 170
Theodore of Mopsuestia, 129
Theodoret of Cyrrhus, 134
Theon (rhetor), 173
Thiselton, A. C., 85, 89, 186
Tracy, D., 5, 92, 177, 183

Index of Authors

Voskovec, J., 83
Voster, W. S., 102, 116

Waldenfels, B., 9
Walhout, C., 85
Warren, A., 67, 75, 119
Weder, H., 2, 43
Wellek, R., 67, 75, 119
Werich, J., 83
Werner, R., 12, 78

Wierzbicka, A., 40
Wilcox, P., 11
Wilder, A. N., 119, 120, 139
Wilder, T., 120
Wischmeyer, O., 2

Xenophon, 7

Žák, J., 35
Zima, P., 108

Index of Biblical and Other Ancient References

BIBLICAL BOOKS		21:1-6	97	12:2-6	129
Genesis		**2 Samuel**		**Isaiah**	
1:1–2:4a	57, 164	24	113	9	128
1:1	51			11	128
2:4b-26	57, 164	**1 Kings**		42:2	96
11	133	3:11	161	51:17	157
17:7	120	5:5	46	66:1	46
37–47	83	8:27	46		
				Jonah	115
Exodus		**2 Kings**			
12:46	34	25	96	**Zechariah**	
16:3	63			9:9	127
20:11	98	**1 Chronicles**		9:10	127
		22:8	46		
Deuteronomy		22:10	46	**Matthew**	
5:15	97			1:22-23	126
26	190	**Job**		3:14-15	168
26:5b-10a	190	1:1	124	5	98
				5:17	97
Joshua		**Psalms**		6:9b-13	157
10:12-13	161	5:7	46	10:28	151
24:2-13	190	8:4	26	11:18-19	168
		90:7	141-42	12:31	168
Judges		90:12-14	142	12:32	168
9:7-5	129	105	190	14:8b	74
15:4-8	41	136	190	17:15	20
				17:24-27	107, 172
1 Samuel		**Ecclesiastes**		20:1-16	170
15	161	11:9b	74	28:19	20

Index of Biblical and Other Ancient References

Mark		Luke		10:9b	142
	115			10:10a	143
1:1	176	1:46-55	172	10:10b	143, 145
1:2-4	126	2:1	112, 125	10:11	22, 142-43
1:9-11	168	2:1-20	112	10:13	143
1:21-34	173	2:7	193	10:14	142-43
1:29-31	165	2:14	114, 193	10:15	144
1:35-37	110	3:1-2	125	10:16	144
1:35-45	173	3:23-38	113	10:17	142
2:1	75	6:20	43, 196	10:17a	144
2:1-12	173	6:21	48	10:17b	144
2:23-26	97	7:22	196	10:18	142
3:1-6	150-51	7:33-34	196	10:18a	144
3:4	97	7:33-35	168	10:18b	144
3:20-35	76	10:20	53	11	165
3:28-29	168	10:21-22	157, 193	12:27	157
4:1-34	173	10:25-37	169	19:33-34	34
4:30	43	12:10	168		
5:1-20	165	12:15-21	77	**Acts**	115
5:21-42	76	12:19	77	2	133
5:21-43	173	12:22	77	3:17	160
6:7-30	76	13:32	41	3:21a	193
6:25b	74	15:11-32	79, 169, 170	5:37	113
7:24	175	15:13	76	7	83
7:24-30	64	15:13-14	75	8:26-40	92
7:32-36	166	15:17-19	76	17:28b	125
8:22	175	17:21	175	26:8	192
8:22-26	166	17:33	63		
10:38-39	157	19:1-10	181	**Romans**	
10:45	151	22:43-44	160	3:21–4:25	59
11:12-24	76	23:34	160	4:13-24	126
13	173	24:13	138	4:17	192
14:1-11	76			5:14	128
14:22-24	60	**John**		6	79
14:22-25	173	1	198	6:1-11	65
14:26-72	76	1:1	33	7:7-25	145-50
14:32-42	156	1:1-16	62	7:10-11	148
14:34	157	1:4-5	163	7:17	148
14:36	87	1:14	33, 198	7:25	148
15:25	76	1:29	168	8:1-17	148
15:31	111	3:4b	48	8:15	87, 157
15:33	76	8:6	70	8:34	196
15:34	76	9:1-5	166	12:21	181
16:6	111, 151	10:7	22, 142-43	14:14a	48
16:6-7	176	10:7-18	142-45	14:17	48
16:8	111	10:8	143		
16:9-20	176	10:9	142-43		

206

Index of Biblical and Other Ancient References

1 Corinthians
1:23	87
2:10	193
4:1-13	87
8:6	62, 196
9:7	85
11:23-25	173
11:23-26	60
11:27-34	165
11:30	165
12:12-26	156
12:31a	156
12:31b	156
13	156
13:8-9	156
13:12	53
14:1	156
14:1b	156
15:3b	95
15:3b-5	127
15:12	192
15:12-56	97
15:35-50	192

2 Corinthians
1:9	97, 192
5:16-17	87
5:18–6:10	59
11:30	195

Galatians
3:6-14	126
3:16-19	127
4:1-5	126
4:6	157
4:21-31	128

Ephesians
1:21	49
1:21-26	165

Philippians
1:21-26	165
2:6	196
2:6-11	58
4:3	53

Colossians
1:16	196
2:20-22	48

2 Thessalonians
3:10	127

1 Timothy
6:6	18

Hebrews
1:1ff.	191
2:6	26
5:8-9	157
11:1	69

1 John
4:1-3	87

2 John
7	87

Jude
9	125

Revelation
3:5	53
3:7	64
3:8	64
12	58
12:1-2	58
12:4-5	58
18:2	109
21:3-4	109-10

INTERTESTAMENTAL WRITINGS

Assumption of Moses 125

Joseph and Aseneth 84

Psalms of Solomon
17:21-25	113

EARLY CHRISTIAN WRITINGS

Augustine
Confessions
11.17	25
11.27	26
11.28	26
11.29	26
11.32	27
13	129

Ignatius
Letter to the Magnesians
8.2	191

Infancy Gospel of Thomas
6:12	110

Irenaeus
Against Heresies
1.21.3	164
4.20.5	191

Nag Hammadi Codices
I/3: *Gospel of Truth*	57
II/2: *Gospel of Thomas*	
log. 2	91
II/3: *Gospel of Philip*	
74	164

Theodoret of Cyrrhus
PG 82.335	135

Valentinian Gnosis
tomb inscription	163

ANCIENT AND CLASSICAL TEXTS

Aratus
Phaenomena 125

Index of Biblical and Other Ancient References

Aristotle
Poetics
21 — 39
22:1457a-1459a — 39

Enuma Elish — 164

Homer
Iliad
6.474 — 181

Plato
Apology
22B-C — 141
Laws
318 — 56
379 — 56
Phaedrus
274e-275e — 69
Philebus
18bff. — 69

Quintilian
Institutio oratoria
11.2.18-22 — 25

Sallustius (Greek philosopher)
De diis et mundo
4 — 55

Virgil
Aeneid — 164

www.ingramcontent.com/pod-product-compliance
Lightning Source LLC
Chambersburg PA
CBHW021141230426
43667CB00005B/207